ADVANCED MANUFACTURING SYSTEMS

CMR332 - AS PER ANNA UNIVERSITY R2021

ANAND JAYAKUMAR ARUMUGHAM

Copyright © Anand Jayakumar Arumugham
All Rights Reserved.

This book has been self-published with all reasonable efforts taken to make the material error-free by the author. No part of this book shall be used, reproduced in any manner whatsoever without written permission from the author, except in the case of brief quotations embodied in critical articles and reviews.

The Author of this book is solely responsible and liable for its content including but not limited to the views, representations, descriptions, statements, information, opinions and references ["Content"]. The Content of this book shall not constitute or be construed or deemed to reflect the opinion or expression of the Publisher or Editor. Neither the Publisher nor Editor endorse or approve the Content of this book or guarantee the reliability, accuracy or completeness of the Content published herein and do not make any representations or warranties of any kind, express or implied, including but not limited to the implied warranties of merchantability, fitness for a particular purpose. The Publisher and Editor shall not be liable whatsoever for any errors, omissions, whether such errors or omissions result from negligence, accident, or any other cause or claims for loss or damages of any kind, including without limitation, indirect or consequential loss or damage arising out of use, inability to use, or about the reliability, accuracy or sufficiency of the information contained in this book.

Made with ♥ on the Notion Press Platform
www.notionpress.com

This book is dedicated to my mother Mrs Jeevalakshmy Arumugham

Contents

Preface   *vii*

Acknowledgements   *ix*

Prologue   *xi*

1. Overview Of Lean Manufacturing   1

2. Overview Of Agile Manufacturing   5

3. Overview Of Sustainable Manufacturing   10

4. Overview Of Intelligent Manufacturing   16

5. Overview Of Smart Manufacturing   21

6. Lean Manufacturing   26

7. Agile Manufacturing   73

8. Sustainable Manufacturing   84

9. Intelligent Manufacturing   99

10. Smart Manufacturing   118

11. Question Bank   154

Preface

The world of manufacturing is undergoing a transformative shift, driven by the increasing demands for efficiency, sustainability, and technological advancements. This book aims to provide a comprehensive guide to the latest methodologies in manufacturing, equipping students, researchers, and industry professionals with the necessary knowledge to navigate the complexities of modern production systems.

The content is structured into five key units, each addressing a crucial aspect of contemporary manufacturing:

Unit I: Introduction to Lean Manufacturing This unit introduces the foundational principles of Lean Manufacturing, highlighting its objectives and benefits over traditional manufacturing systems. Topics such as continuous improvement (Kaizen), worker involvement, 5S principles, Just-in-Time (JIT) systems, Kanban methodologies, and Lean Six Sigma are explored. The integration of Lean Manufacturing with Enterprise Resource Planning (ERP) and ISO 9001:2000 is also discussed to provide a holistic understanding.

Unit II: Agile Manufacturing In response to rapidly changing consumer demands and market conditions, Agile Manufacturing has emerged as a critical approach. This unit explores the distinctions between Agile and Mass Manufacturing, agile product development, technology adoption, cost considerations, and implementation strategies that enhance agility in production environments.

Unit III: Sustainable Manufacturing Sustainability is an essential component of modern manufacturing. This unit delves into the strategies that align manufacturing with environmental and economic sustainability. Topics include structured strategy formulation, competitive manufacturing strategies, sustainable system design, and new strategy realization to foster long-term success.

Unit IV: Intelligent Manufacturing As industries embrace digital transformation, Intelligent Manufacturing has become a focal point. This unit covers advanced strategies and decision-making frameworks driven by data analytics, artificial intelligence, and automation. It also explores how intelligent systems enhance productivity, adaptability, and efficiency in manufacturing.

Unit V: Smart Manufacturing The final unit introduces cutting-edge Smart Manufacturing techniques that leverage digital technologies such as blockchain, predictive maintenance, supply chain visibility, and plant digitization. The applications of automation, cost reduction strategies, and waste management solutions are also discussed to illustrate the potential of smart factories in modern industry.

This book serves as a valuable resource for those looking to understand and implement contemporary manufacturing methodologies. By bridging the gap between theory and practice, it aims to equip readers with the skills and knowledge required to drive innovation and excellence in the manufacturing sector.

We hope this book serves as an insightful and practical guide to the evolving world of manufacturing.

Author

Anand Jayakumar Arumugham

jay4upeople@gmail.com

Acknowledgements

The satisfaction and euphoria of successful completion of any task could be incomplete without mentioning the people who made it possible, whose constant guidance and encouragement crown my efforts with success.

I take this opportunity to express my sincere gratitude to the Chairman Shri.V.Lakshminarayanasamy MBA, Suguna College of Engineering, for providing me with a successful environment and his encouragement in the right path to develop a fine book.

I am thankful to the Secretary - Suguna Charitable Trust Dr. Srikanth Kannan, for his constant encouragement and support throughout the preparation of the book.

I am thankful to the Director Dr.R.Prakasm M.E, Ph.D., for his constant encouragment and support thoughout the preparation of the book.

I am also very much grateful and would like to express my sincere thanks to my Principal Dr.R.Maguteeswaran, M.E, Ph.D., who provided me with constant support and encouragement in preparing this book.

I am also very much grateful and would like to express my sincere thanks to my Head of Department Dr.R.Vasanth, M.E., Ph.D., and Assistant Head of Department Mr.N.Duraishankar, M.E., who provided me with constant support and encouragement in preparing this book.

I would like to extend my sincere thanks to all the faculty members and lab technicians for their constant support and coordination in bringing out this book.

Above all I thank my beloved mother and brother for their moral support, encouragment and their prayers during the preparation of this book.

Prologue

In today's rapidly evolving industrial landscape, manufacturing processes must continuously adapt to changing demands, technological advancements, and sustainability concerns. The evolution of manufacturing strategies has led to the emergence of Lean, Agile, Sustainable, Intelligent, and Smart Manufacturing, each contributing uniquely to operational efficiency and competitive advantage.

This syllabus is designed to provide students with a comprehensive understanding of modern manufacturing principles, covering foundational concepts and advanced techniques that drive efficiency, quality, and sustainability in production environments.

Unit I: Introduction to Lean Manufacturing This unit lays the groundwork for Lean Manufacturing by exploring its key principles and objectives. The transition from traditional manufacturing to lean methodologies is examined, emphasizing continuous improvement (Kaizen), worker involvement, Just-in-Time (JIT) systems, Kanban techniques, and 5S principles. Additionally, the integration of Lean Manufacturing with Six Sigma, ERP, and ISO 9001:2000 is explored to demonstrate its real-world applicability.

Unit II: Agile Manufacturing Agility in manufacturing is a key differentiator in highly dynamic markets. This unit contrasts Agile Manufacturing with traditional mass production and delves into its implementation for product development and new technology adoption. The significance of agility in decision-making, cost optimization, and supply chain adaptability is also discussed, providing students with insights into its practical application in industry.

Unit III: Sustainable Manufacturing Sustainability is no longer an option but a necessity in modern manufacturing. This unit introduces competitive and manufacturing strategies that align with sustainability objectives. Students will explore strategic improvement programs, structured strategy formulation, and sustainable manufacturing system designs, gaining an understanding of how businesses can integrate environmental responsibility with economic success.

Unit IV: Intelligent Manufacturing The manufacturing industry is embracing intelligence-driven decision-making through technologies such as AI, IoT, and big data analytics. This unit focuses on the principles of Intelligent Manufacturing, exploring competitive strategies, system design, and the realization of new manufacturing paradigms that enhance efficiency, automation, and adaptability in production environments.

Unit V: Smart Manufacturing The final unit presents the cutting-edge advancements in Smart Manufacturing, highlighting various techniques such as blockchain-based inventory management, supply chain digitization, predictive maintenance, automated systems, and waste reduction strategies. Students will develop an understanding of how these smart technologies revolutionize manufacturing and create interconnected, data-driven production environments.

By the end of this course, students will gain a holistic understanding of modern manufacturing strategies, equipping them with the knowledge to drive efficiency, sustainability, and innovation in industrial settings. This syllabus serves as a guide to mastering contemporary manufacturing methodologies and preparing for the future of industrial advancements.

CHAPTER ONE

Overview of Lean Manufacturing

Lean Manufacturing

1. What is Lean Manufacturing?

Lean manufacturing is a production philosophy that focuses on minimizing waste while maximizing productivity. It aims to create more value for customers with fewer resources by eliminating inefficiencies.

2. Why is Lean Manufacturing Important?

Reduces costs by eliminating waste

Improves efficiency and productivity

Enhances product quality

Increases customer satisfaction

Helps businesses stay competitive

3. Who Uses Lean Manufacturing?

Manufacturing industries (automobile, electronics, aerospace, etc.)

Service industries (healthcare, logistics, retail, etc.)

Companies of all sizes, from small businesses to large corporations

4. When Was Lean Manufacturing Developed?

The concept originated from the Toyota Production System (TPS) in the mid-20th century, particularly in the 1950s and 1960s, pioneered by Taiichi Ohno and Shigeo Shingo.

5. Where is Lean Manufacturing Applied?

Lean principles are applied in:

Factories and production lines

Warehousing and supply chain management

Offices and service industries

Healthcare and hospitals

Software development (Lean Software Development)

6. How Does Lean Manufacturing Work?

Lean manufacturing operates based on key principles:

Identify Value – Understand what customers truly value.

Map the Value Stream – Analyze processes and eliminate waste.

Create Flow – Ensure smooth workflow with minimal interruptions.

Establish Pull – Produce only what is needed, when it's needed.

Seek Perfection – Continuously improve processes through Kaizen.

Conclusion

Lean manufacturing helps businesses optimize operations, reduce costs, and improve efficiency. It is widely used across industries and continues to evolve with modern technology.

History of Lean Manufacturing

The history of Lean Manufacturing can be traced back to multiple influences over time. Here's a timeline of its evolution:

1. Early Influences (Pre-1900s)

The basic principles of efficiency and waste reduction were practiced informally in various industries.

Eli Whitney (1799): Introduced interchangeable parts in manufacturing, which allowed for mass production.

Frederick Winslow Taylor (1911): Developed Scientific Management, which emphasized productivity through standardization and time studies.

2. Ford's Assembly Line (1913)

Henry Ford introduced the moving assembly line at Ford Motor Company.

This method drastically reduced production time and costs, making automobiles affordable to the masses.

However, Ford's system lacked flexibility, producing only one model in a single color (Model T in black).

3. Toyota Production System (TPS) – 1940s to 1970s

Toyota engineers Taiichi Ohno and Shigeo Shingo developed the Toyota Production System (TPS) in response to post-war resource shortages in Japan.

They studied Ford's mass production system but improved it by adding flexibility, waste reduction, and continuous improvement (Kaizen).

Key elements of TPS:

Just-In-Time (JIT): Producing only what is needed, when it is needed.

Kanban: A visual scheduling system for inventory control.

Jidoka: Automation with a human touch (machines stop when an issue is detected).

Muda, Mura, Muri: Eliminating waste (Muda), unevenness (Mura), and overburden (Muri).

4. Western Adoption & Lean Emergence (1980s – 1990s)

In the 1980s, Western companies studied Toyota's success.

The MIT study (1980s), published in the book The Machine That Changed the World (1990) by Womack, Jones, and Roos, coined the term "Lean Manufacturing."

Companies like General Motors and Boeing started adopting Lean principles to compete globally.

5. Lean Beyond Manufacturing (2000s – Present)

Lean principles expanded into healthcare, software development (Lean Software Development), logistics, and service industries.

Concepts like Lean Six Sigma emerged, combining Lean's waste reduction with Six Sigma's quality control.

Industry 4.0 now integrates Lean with smart manufacturing, IoT, and AI for further optimization.

Conclusion

Lean Manufacturing has evolved over centuries, from Ford's assembly lines to Toyota's flexible production, and now to digital transformation. It continues to shape industries worldwide by focusing on efficiency, quality, and customer value.

Examples of Lean Manufacturing with Case Studies

Lean manufacturing has been successfully implemented in various industries. Here are some real-world case studies:

1. Toyota – The Pioneer of Lean Manufacturing

Background

Toyota developed the Toyota Production System (TPS), which became the foundation of Lean Manufacturing. The company faced limited resources in post-war Japan and needed a cost-effective production system.

Lean Principles Used

Just-In-Time (JIT): Producing only what is needed, reducing inventory costs.

Kaizen (Continuous Improvement): Employees contribute ideas for small improvements.

Kanban System: A visual signal system to control inventory and workflow.

Jidoka (Automation with a Human Touch): Machines stop when defects are detected.

Results

? Increased production efficiency while maintaining high quality.

? Reduced waste and optimized resources.

? Became a global leader in the automotive industry.

? Key Lesson: Lean reduces costs while improving quality and efficiency.

2. Boeing – Reducing Waste in Aircraft Production

Background

Boeing faced long production times and high costs in aircraft manufacturing. The company needed a more efficient production system.

Lean Principles Used

Value Stream Mapping (VSM): Analyzing processes to identify and eliminate waste.

Just-In-Time (JIT): Parts delivered exactly when needed, reducing inventory costs.

5S Methodology: Organizing workspaces for efficiency and safety.

Results

? Reduced airplane assembly time by 50%.

? Cut production costs by millions.

? Improved on-time delivery and customer satisfaction.

? Key Lesson: Streamlining processes reduces costs and increases productivity.

3. Nike – Lean Manufacturing in Footwear

Background

Nike faced sustainability challenges and inefficiencies in its global supply chain. The company implemented Lean to improve production while reducing environmental impact.

Lean Principles Used

Lean Supply Chain: Reducing overproduction and material waste.

Continuous Improvement (Kaizen): Encouraging workers to optimize processes.

Standardized Workflows: Improving consistency and reducing errors.

Results

? Increased production efficiency and reduced costs.

? 20% reduction in waste across production lines.

? Improved worker conditions and sustainability.

? Key Lesson: Lean can enhance both business efficiency and environmental sustainability.

4. Dell – Lean in Computer Manufacturing

Background

Dell revolutionized the PC industry with its build-to-order model, reducing inventory and costs.

Lean Principles Used

Pull System: Computers were built only after customer orders.

Just-In-Time (JIT): Components arrived just before assembly, reducing storage needs.

Supply Chain Optimization: Partnering with suppliers for efficient logistics.

Results

? Reduced lead time from weeks to days.

? Lowered costs by cutting unnecessary inventory.

? Improved customer satisfaction through customization.

? Key Lesson: Lean enables mass customization and efficient supply chain management.

5. Healthcare – Virginia Mason Medical Center (USA)

Background

Virginia Mason applied Lean to improve patient care and hospital efficiency.

Lean Principles Used

Value Stream Mapping (VSM): Identifying non-value-adding steps in patient care.

5S Methodology: Organizing medical tools and supplies.

Standardized Workflows: Reducing waiting times for patients.

Results

? Reduced patient wait times by 50%.

? Fewer medical errors and improved patient outcomes.

? Increased staff efficiency and job satisfaction.

? Key Lesson: Lean can be successfully applied in healthcare to enhance service quality.

Conclusion

Lean Manufacturing is not limited to cars—it is used in aviation, footwear, computers, and even healthcare! It helps businesses eliminate waste, improve quality, and increase efficiency.

The Story of Lean Manufacturing: The Tale of Factory X

Once upon a time, in the bustling city of Industropolis, there was a company called Factory X that made bicycles. Factory X was famous for its craftsmanship, but it had one big problem—production was slow, costs were high, and customers had to wait months for their orders.

The factory owner, Mr. Smith, was frustrated. He called a meeting with his team.

"Why are we struggling so much?" he asked.

The Problems:

Huge Inventory: There were piles of unused parts everywhere.

Long Waiting Times: Workers often had to wait for materials or approvals.

Defective Products: Some bikes had to be reworked because of poor quality.

Overproduction: They built more bikes than needed, leading to wasted storage.

One day, Mr. Smith's friend, Mr. Tanaka, visited from Japan. He had worked at Toyota and knew the secret of efficient production—Lean Manufacturing.

"You need to remove waste and focus only on what adds value!" Mr. Tanaka advised.

The Lean Transformation Begins

? Step 1: Just-In-Time (JIT) Production

Instead of storing unnecessary parts, Factory X ordered materials only when needed. This reduced clutter and saved money.

? Step 2: Value Stream Mapping (VSM)

The team mapped every step of their process and found unnecessary delays. By eliminating extra steps, they made production 30% faster.

? Step 3: 5S Methodology

Workers organized tools neatly so they could be found instantly. No more wasted time searching!

? Step 4: Kaizen (Continuous Improvement)

Employees were encouraged to suggest small daily improvements. A simple change—placing screws closer to the assembly line—saved 5 minutes per bike!

? Step 5: Kanban System

They introduced a Kanban board to track production flow. Everyone knew what to work on next, reducing confusion.

The Results

✔? Production time dropped by 40%

✔? Defects fell by 50%

✔? Customers got their bikes twice as fast

✔? Profits soared

Mr. Smith was thrilled. Factory X became the most efficient bicycle company in the city. Workers were happier, and customers got their bikes on time.

The Moral: By removing waste, organizing work better, and continuously improving, any company can become more efficient—just like Factory X! ?♂?

CHAPTER TWO

Overview of Agile Manufacturing

Agile Manufacturing Explained Using 5W & 1H

Agile Manufacturing is a modern approach that helps companies quickly adapt to changes in demand, technology, and market conditions. It focuses on flexibility, innovation, and customer responsiveness. Let's break it down using the 5W & 1H technique:

1. What is Agile Manufacturing?

Agile Manufacturing is a production strategy that emphasizes speed, flexibility, and efficiency in responding to customer needs and market changes. It integrates technology, automation, and lean principles to enhance productivity and competitiveness.

2. Why is Agile Manufacturing Important?

Customers today demand customized products with faster delivery.

Technology and market conditions change rapidly.

Traditional manufacturing methods are too rigid to adapt quickly.

It helps companies reduce waste, improve efficiency, and enhance customer satisfaction.

3. Who Uses Agile Manufacturing?

Automotive Industry: Tesla adapts production based on customer demands and new technology.

Electronics Industry: Companies like Apple and Samsung modify designs frequently.

Aerospace Industry: Boeing and Airbus adjust production schedules dynamically.

Custom Manufacturing: Small businesses and startups producing personalized goods.

4. When Did Agile Manufacturing Start?

The concept of agility emerged in the 1990s, inspired by Lean Manufacturing and advancements in digital technology.

It gained popularity with the rise of automation, IoT, AI, and cloud computing.

5. Where is Agile Manufacturing Applied?

Factories and production lines using smart manufacturing.

Supply chains optimizing logistics and material flow.

Product development teams responding to market trends.

Industries that need rapid customization, such as healthcare (medical devices) and fashion (fast fashion).

6. How Does Agile Manufacturing Work?

Agile Manufacturing relies on four key principles:

Modular Production: Factories are designed to quickly switch between different products.

Smart Technology & Automation: AI, robotics, and IoT help optimize production and reduce downtime.

Customer-Centric Approach: Companies produce what customers want, when they want it.

Collaborative Supply Chains: Suppliers, manufacturers, and distributors work together seamlessly.

Conclusion

Agile Manufacturing allows businesses to stay competitive in a fast-changing world. By leveraging technology, flexible processes, and real-time data, companies can produce high-quality products efficiently while responding to market needs.

History of Agile Manufacturing

Agile Manufacturing evolved as a response to rapid market changes, increasing customization demands, and advancements in technology. Below is a timeline of its historical development:

1. Early Foundations (Pre-1980s)

Before Agile Manufacturing, companies focused on mass production (Ford's assembly line, 1913) and later, Lean Manufacturing (Toyota Production System, 1950s).

Henry Ford (1913): Introduced the moving assembly line, focusing on efficiency but lacking flexibility.

Toyota Production System (1950s-1970s): Introduced Lean Manufacturing, emphasizing waste reduction and continuous improvement (Kaizen).

However, Lean Manufacturing was not enough in industries that required frequent design changes and customization.

2. The Birth of Agile Manufacturing (1980s - 1990s)

The idea of Agile Manufacturing emerged as technology advanced and customer demands shifted.

1980s: Companies started facing shorter product life cycles, requiring faster and more flexible production methods.

1991: The concept of Agile Manufacturing was first introduced in a U.S. government-funded study by the ICAM (Integrated Computer-Aided Manufacturing) program.

1995: The book Agile Competitors and Virtual Organizations by Goldman, Nagel, and Preiss formally defined Agile Manufacturing as a system that enables companies to rapidly respond to customer needs and market changes.

Key principles introduced:

? Customer responsiveness – Producing what customers need, when they need it.

? Rapid reconfiguration – Adapting production lines quickly.

? Technology-driven agility – Using automation, AI, and robotics.

3. Adoption of Agile Manufacturing (2000s - Present)

With the rise of digital transformation, Agile Manufacturing became more practical.

2000s: Companies started integrating automation, robotics, and real-time data analytics.

2010s: The Industry 4.0 revolution led to the adoption of IoT (Internet of Things), AI, and smart factories.

2020s: Agile Manufacturing is now a standard in industries like automotive (Tesla), electronics (Apple, Samsung), and aerospace (Boeing, SpaceX).

Key Technologies Driving Agile Manufacturing Today

? IoT & AI: Smart machines optimize production in real time.

? Automation & Robotics: Reduce errors and increase efficiency.

? Cloud Computing & Digital Twins: Simulating production before physical changes.

?? 3D Printing & Additive Manufacturing: Faster prototyping and small-batch production.

Conclusion

Agile Manufacturing evolved from mass production and lean principles to a highly flexible, technology-driven system. With automation, AI, and real-time data, manufacturers can adapt quickly to customer needs, making Agile Manufacturing the future of production.

Agile Manufacturing: Case Studies & Real-World Examples

Agile Manufacturing helps companies quickly adapt to market changes, customer demands, and technological advancements. Below are real-world case studies showcasing its success.

1. Tesla – Rapid Adaptation in Electric Vehicle (EV) Production

Background:

Tesla disrupted the automotive industry by introducing electric vehicles (EVs) with cutting-edge technology. Unlike traditional car manufacturers, Tesla operates on an Agile Manufacturing model.

Agile Principles Used:

? Flexible Production Lines: Tesla's factories can reconfigure assembly lines to introduce new models quickly.

? Over-the-Air (OTA) Updates: Instead of recalling cars, Tesla updates software remotely to fix issues or add features.

? Vertical Integration: Tesla controls battery production, software, and supply chain, reducing dependency on third parties.

? Rapid Prototyping: Tesla uses 3D printing and AI-driven simulations to speed up design changes.

Results:

✓? Model upgrades happen faster than competitors.

✓? Tesla adapts to market changes in real time.

✓? The company has cut costs and increased efficiency by reducing third-party dependencies.

? Key Lesson: Agile Manufacturing allows Tesla to innovate faster and respond to customer needs without long delays.

2. Dell – Customization and Build-to-Order Strategy

Background:

Dell revolutionized the computer industry with its direct-to-customer, build-to-order (BTO) model. Instead of mass-producing PCs, Dell allows customers to customize their computers before assembly.

Agile Principles Used:

? Build-to-Order System: Dell manufactures products only after a customer order, reducing inventory costs.

? Just-In-Time (JIT) Manufacturing: Components arrive exactly when needed, avoiding overstock.

? Flexible Supply Chain: Dell adjusts its supply chain based on demand fluctuations.

? Customer-Centric Approach: Buyers choose custom configurations (processor, RAM, storage, etc.), giving them control over their product.

Results:

✓? Reduced production lead time from weeks to days.

✓? Cut inventory costs by eliminating unnecessary stock.

✓? Increased customer satisfaction through personalization.

? Key Lesson: Agile Manufacturing helps businesses adapt quickly and reduce waste while offering customized products.

3. Boeing – Agile in Aerospace Manufacturing

Background:

Boeing faces unpredictable demand and complex production challenges in the aerospace industry. To stay competitive, it adopted Agile Manufacturing principles.

Agile Principles Used:

? Digital Twin Technology: Boeing uses virtual models to test designs before physical production, saving time and reducing defects.

? Additive Manufacturing (3D Printing): The company uses 3D printing for rapid prototyping and lightweight parts.

? Modular Assembly: Aircraft components are built in separate locations and assembled efficiently at final facilities.

? Supplier Collaboration: Boeing works closely with suppliers to ensure real-time production adjustments.

Results:

✓? Production times reduced by 30%.

✓? Less material waste due to precision manufacturing.

✓? Improved adaptability to new aircraft models and regulations.

? Key Lesson: Agile Manufacturing allows Boeing to reduce development time and improve operational flexibility.

4. Zara – Fast Fashion with Agile Manufacturing

Background:

Zara, a global fashion retailer, must constantly update its collections based on changing trends. Unlike traditional retailers that plan months ahead, Zara uses Agile Manufacturing to respond to fashion trends in real time.

Agile Principles Used:

? Short Production Cycles: Zara produces new designs in 2-3 weeks instead of months.

? Small-Batch Manufacturing: Instead of overproducing, Zara manufactures small batches, reducing unsold inventory.

? Real-Time Data Collection: Zara's stores track customer preferences and send data to production teams for quick design changes.

? Nearshore Manufacturing: Most production happens in Europe (closer to its main market), ensuring faster delivery.

Results:

✓? Reduced unsold inventory, cutting waste by 15%.

✓? Increased customer engagement with frequent new designs.

✓? Faster response to changing trends, boosting sales and profits.

? Key Lesson: Agile Manufacturing helps Zara stay ahead in the fast-moving fashion industry by responding instantly to customer preferences.

5. SpaceX – Agility in Aerospace Innovation

Background:

SpaceX, founded by Elon Musk, changed the space industry by introducing reusable rockets and rapid development cycles.

Agile Principles Used:

? Iterative Development: SpaceX tests and improves rocket designs quickly through rapid prototyping.

? In-House Production: Manufacturing most components in-house allows faster modifications and innovation.

? Reusable Rockets: Instead of building a new rocket for every mission, SpaceX reuses parts, reducing costs.

? Parallel Development: SpaceX works on multiple projects simultaneously, such as Starship and Falcon rockets.

Results:

✓? Reduced launch costs by over 50%.

✓? Developed the first reusable orbital rocket (Falcon 9).

✓? Completed missions faster than NASA's traditional approach.

? Key Lesson: Agile Manufacturing enables SpaceX to develop and launch rockets faster, cheaper, and more efficiently than traditional aerospace companies.

Conclusion

Agile Manufacturing is transforming industries from automobiles to aerospace and fashion. By embracing flexibility, smart technology, and rapid adaptation, companies can stay ahead of market changes.

The Story of Agile Manufacturing: The Rise of SwiftTech Electronics

In the bustling city of Innovatia, there was a company called SwiftTech Electronics. SwiftTech was known for producing smartphones and gadgets, but they faced a serious problem—their competitors were launching new models faster than they could keep up.

The company's owner, Mr. Adams, was worried. "We take a whole year to develop a new product, but customers want something new every six months! If we don't adapt, we'll be left behind."

The Problem

? Slow Production: New products took too long to develop.

? High Inventory Costs: They produced too many units that didn't sell.

? Outdated Designs: By the time a product launched, customer preferences had changed.

One day, Mr. Adams met Ms. Lee, an expert in Agile Manufacturing. She listened to his concerns and said,

"Your problem is that your manufacturing process is too rigid. You need to be agile—adapt to changes, reduce waste, and use technology wisely."

The Agile Transformation Begins

? Step 1: Modular Production

Instead of building entire phones from scratch, SwiftTech divided production into modular components—camera, battery, screen, and software updates were developed separately. This allowed faster upgrades without redesigning the whole phone.

? Step 2: Customer Feedback Integration

SwiftTech started using real-time customer feedback. They set up an AI-powered analytics system that collected data from customer reviews and market trends. This helped them adjust features before launching a product.

? Step 3: Just-In-Time (JIT) Manufacturing

Rather than producing thousands of units and hoping they would sell, SwiftTech started a small-batch production model. This reduced inventory waste and allowed them to respond to real demand.

? Step 4: 3D Printing for Rapid Prototyping

Instead of waiting months for new designs, SwiftTech used 3D printing to create prototypes in days. Engineers could test and improve models faster than ever.

? Step 5: Smart Supply Chain

They implemented an AI-driven supply chain that predicted demand and adjusted production schedules automatically. No more overproduction!

The Results

✓? Product development time reduced by 50%

✓? Inventory costs cut by 40%

✓? New models launched every 6 months instead of 12

✓? Customer satisfaction increased with frequent updates

Mr. Adams was amazed. "This is incredible! We are not just keeping up with competitors—we're leading the market!"

The Moral of the Story

Agile Manufacturing is about speed, flexibility, and customer focus. Companies that embrace change, use technology, and optimize production can thrive in a fast-moving world—just like SwiftTech Electronics!

CHAPTER THREE

Overview of Sustainable Manufacturing

Sustainable Manufacturing Explained Using 5W & 1H

Sustainable Manufacturing is a modern approach to production that focuses on minimizing environmental impact, conserving resources, and ensuring economic and social responsibility. Let's break it down using the 5W & 1H technique:

1. What is Sustainable Manufacturing?

Sustainable Manufacturing is the creation of products using processes that:

? Reduce waste and emissions

? Use renewable energy sources

? Optimize resource efficiency (water, materials, energy)

? Ensure worker safety and fair labor practices

? Support long-term economic growth

It balances profit, planet, and people to ensure manufacturing remains viable for future generations.

2. Why is Sustainable Manufacturing Important?

? Environmental Protection: Reduces pollution, carbon footprint, and waste.

? Cost Savings: Efficient resource use leads to lower operational costs.

? Competitive Advantage: Consumers prefer eco-friendly brands.

? Regulatory Compliance: Governments enforce stricter sustainability laws.

?? Long-Term Business Growth: Ensures continuous access to natural resources.

Without sustainability, industries risk environmental damage, increased costs, and legal penalties.

3. Who Uses Sustainable Manufacturing?

? Automobile Industry: Tesla, Toyota, and BMW use recyclable materials and energy-efficient production.

?? Fashion Industry: Brands like Patagonia and H&M use recycled fabrics and ethical labor.

? Electronics Industry: Apple and Dell use e-waste recycling programs.

? Construction Industry: Companies like Lafarge use low-carbon cement.

?? Food Industry: Nestlé and Unilever focus on water conservation and waste reduction.

Every industry can adopt sustainability to reduce its impact and enhance profitability.

4. When Did Sustainable Manufacturing Start?

1970s: The first environmental laws (Clean Air Act, Clean Water Act) pushed industries to reduce pollution.

1990s: Companies began eco-friendly practices due to consumer demand.

2000s: Adoption of renewable energy, circular economy, and green supply chains.

Present: Global movements like Net Zero 2050 and the Paris Agreement drive sustainable innovation.

Sustainability is now a global priority for businesses and governments alike.

5. Where is Sustainable Manufacturing Applied?

? Factories: Energy-efficient machinery, waste reduction, and water recycling.

? Supply Chains: Eco-friendly transportation and packaging.

? Renewable Energy Plants: Solar, wind, and hydro-powered manufacturing.

? Smart Buildings: Energy-efficient offices and green infrastructure.

Sustainability can be integrated at every stage of production.

6. How Does Sustainable Manufacturing Work?

? Eco-Friendly Materials: Use recycled or biodegradable resources.

? Energy Efficiency: Optimize power consumption with smart grids and renewable energy.

? Waste Reduction: Implement circular economy (reuse, recycle, remanufacture).

? Green Supply Chains: Work with ethical, sustainable suppliers.

? Carbon Offsetting: Invest in projects that reduce CO_2 emissions (e.g., tree planting).

By combining these practices, companies minimize waste, save money, and protect the planet.

Conclusion

Sustainable Manufacturing is the future of industry. It ensures companies can produce goods efficiently, ethically, and environmentally responsibly while remaining profitable.

The History of Sustainable Manufacturing

Sustainable Manufacturing has evolved over time as industries recognized the need to balance economic growth, environmental protection, and social responsibility. Below is a timeline of its key developments:

1. Early Industrial Revolution (1700s - 1800s): The Age of Mass Production & Pollution

? What Happened?

The Industrial Revolution (1760-1840) introduced coal-powered factories, mechanization, and large-scale manufacturing.

There was little concern for environmental damage, leading to air pollution, deforestation, and water contamination.

? Key Challenge:

? Uncontrolled waste, carbon emissions, and poor working conditions.

2. The Rise of Environmental Awareness (1900s - 1970s): The Beginning of Regulations

? What Happened?

After World War II, industrial growth led to high pollution levels.

Major environmental disasters (e.g., The Great Smog of London, 1952) raised concerns.

The 1960s environmental movement began pushing for cleaner industry practices.

? Key Milestones:

? 1962: Rachel Carson's book Silent Spring exposed the dangers of industrial pollution.

? 1970: The first Earth Day was celebrated, increasing environmental activism.

? 1970s: Governments introduced pollution control laws, including:

Clean Air Act (USA, 1970)

Clean Water Act (USA, 1972)

Environmental Protection Agency (EPA) formed in 1970

? Key Challenge:

? Industries resisted change due to high costs of cleaner technologies.

3. The Sustainable Development Era (1980s - 1990s): The Concept of Sustainability Emerges

? What Happened?

The 1987 Brundtland Report (by the UN) introduced the term "sustainable development"—economic growth without harming future generations.

The ISO 14000 Environmental Management Standards (1996) helped industries adopt eco-friendly practices.

? Key Milestones:

? 1987: UN defines Sustainable Development in the Brundtland Report.

? 1992: The Rio Earth Summit led to international agreements on sustainability.

? 1996: The ISO 14000 Series provided global guidelines for sustainable industry practices.

? Key Challenge:

? Limited technology for large-scale green manufacturing.

4. The Green Revolution in Manufacturing (2000s - 2010s): Adoption of Eco-Friendly Practices

? What Happened?

Companies began implementing energy efficiency, waste reduction, and renewable energy.

The rise of corporate social responsibility (CSR) made sustainability a competitive advantage.

? Key Milestones:

? 2005: Kyoto Protocol implemented to reduce global carbon emissions.

? 2010s: Green supply chains and circular economy concepts became mainstream.

? Companies like Tesla, Apple, and Unilever led the way in sustainable production.

? Key Challenge:

? Transitioning from fossil fuels to renewable energy remained expensive.

5. The Industry 4.0 & Net-Zero Era (2020s - Present): Digital & Sustainable Manufacturing

? What's Happening Now?

The Paris Agreement (2015) set a global target to limit global warming to below 2°C.

Industry 4.0 technologies (AI, IoT, automation) enable real-time energy optimization.

The Net-Zero Movement (2050 goal) pushes manufacturers to eliminate carbon emissions.

? Key Trends:

? Smart Factories: AI-powered production reduces waste.

? Circular Economy: Reuse and recycling of materials (e.g., Apple's recycling robots).

? Carbon Neutrality: Companies invest in renewable energy, carbon capture, and green logistics.

? Key Challenge:

? Scaling sustainable practices globally across all industries.

Conclusion

Sustainable Manufacturing has evolved from a polluting, wasteful system to a tech-driven, eco-friendly approach. The future will see industries fully adopting carbon-neutral, AI-powered, and circular production models to ensure long-term sustainability.

Sustainable Manufacturing: Case Studies of Leading Companies

Sustainable manufacturing focuses on reducing waste, minimizing carbon emissions, conserving resources, and promoting ethical production. Below are real-world case studies of companies successfully implementing sustainable practices.

1. Tesla: Sustainable Automotive Manufacturing

Background:

Tesla is a pioneer in electric vehicle (EV) production, aiming to reduce the world's dependence on fossil fuels.

Sustainable Manufacturing Practices:

? 100% Electric Vehicles: Tesla's cars produce zero emissions, unlike gasoline-powered vehicles.

? Gigafactories with Renewable Energy: Tesla's Gigafactories use solar panels and battery storage to reduce reliance on fossil fuels.

? Battery Recycling: Tesla has a closed-loop recycling system to recover materials from used batteries.

? Water Conservation: Tesla's factories use low-water processes to minimize industrial water waste.

Results:

✔? Tesla's Gigafactories run on 100% renewable energy, reducing CO_2 emissions.

✔? Battery recycling reduces the need for new raw materials like lithium and cobalt.

✔? Over 4 million Tesla vehicles have been sold, preventing millions of tons of CO_2 emissions.

? Key Lesson: Investing in electric and renewable energy-based manufacturing can significantly reduce carbon footprints.

2. Unilever: Sustainable FMCG (Fast-Moving Consumer Goods) Production

Background:

Unilever, a global leader in food, personal care, and household products, launched its Sustainable Living Plan to reduce waste and emissions.

Sustainable Manufacturing Practices:

? Eco-Friendly Packaging: Use of biodegradable and recycled plastic.

? Water & Energy Efficiency: Factories reduced CO_2 emissions by 65% and water use by 40% since 2008.

? Sustainable Sourcing: Palm oil, tea, and cocoa are 100% sustainably sourced.

? Zero Waste to Landfill: Unilever factories now send zero non-hazardous waste to landfills.

Results:

✔? Carbon footprint per product reduced by 50%.

✔? Unilever products like Dove and Hellmann's use 100% recycled plastic.

✔? Over 1.3 million small farmers trained in sustainable agriculture.

? Key Lesson: Sustainable sourcing and efficient resource management help create eco-friendly and ethical supply chains.

3. Apple: Green Electronics Manufacturing

Background:

Apple has committed to 100% carbon neutrality by 2030 across its supply chain and products.

Sustainable Manufacturing Practices:

? Renewable Energy Factories: All Apple production facilities run on 100% renewable energy.

? Recycling Robots (Daisy & Taz): These robots disassemble old iPhones, recovering precious metals for reuse.

? Carbon-Neutral Supply Chain: Apple is working with suppliers to achieve net-zero emissions.

? Low-Impact Materials: Devices use recycled aluminum, rare earth elements, and bio-based plastics.

Results:

✔? Reduced carbon footprint by over 45% since 2015.

✔? Every iPhone 15 is made using 99% recycled rare earth elements.

✔? Apple's suppliers cut over 23 million metric tons of CO_2 emissions.

? Key Lesson: Advanced recycling technology and renewable energy can make electronics production more sustainable.

4. Patagonia: Sustainable Fashion & Ethical Manufacturing

Background:

Patagonia, an outdoor apparel brand, is committed to environmentally responsible clothing production.

Sustainable Manufacturing Practices:

? Recycled Materials: Over 70% of Patagonia's products are made from recycled fabrics.

? Fair Trade & Ethical Labor: Patagonia ensures fair wages and safe working conditions for factory workers.

? Repair & Reuse Program: Customers are encouraged to repair their clothes instead of buying new ones.

? Carbon-Neutral Operations: By 2025, Patagonia aims to be 100% carbon neutral.

Results:

✔? Over 10 million plastic bottles recycled into clothing fabric annually.

✔? Fair Trade program supports 72,000+ workers worldwide.

✔? Patagonia donates 1% of sales to environmental organizations.

? Key Lesson: Sustainable fashion is possible by using recycled materials, ethical labor, and waste reduction.

5. IKEA: Green Supply Chain & Circular Economy

Background:

IKEA, the world's largest furniture retailer, is leading the way in sustainable manufacturing and retailing.

Sustainable Manufacturing Practices:

? Sustainable Wood Sourcing: 98% of wood is FSC-certified (from responsibly managed forests).

? Renewable Energy Factories: IKEA runs on 100% wind and solar energy.

? Recyclable & Flat-Pack Design: Products are designed for easy transport & minimal waste.

? Second-Hand Program: Customers can return used furniture for resale or recycling.

Results:

✓? IKEA aims for 100% circular products by 2030 (fully recyclable & reusable).

✓? Over 1 million solar panels installed at IKEA stores & factories.

✓? Reduced waste by 90% in manufacturing.

? Key Lesson: Circular economy principles (reuse, recycle, and repair) reduce waste and extend product life cycles.

Conclusion

These companies prove that sustainable manufacturing is not just possible—it's profitable and necessary for the future.

The Green Factory: A Story of Sustainable Manufacturing

In the bustling city of EcoVille, there was a company called GreenTech Industries. For decades, GreenTech had been a successful manufacturer of home appliances, but they faced a growing problem—rising energy costs, excessive waste, and environmental concerns.

One day, the CEO, Mr. Carter, received a letter from a customer that changed everything.

? "Dear GreenTech, I love your products, but I'm concerned about the waste and pollution caused by big manufacturers. I hope you can create eco-friendly products that help protect our planet. Sincerely, Emily (12 years old)."

Mr. Carter was deeply moved. "If a 12-year-old can see the problem, why can't we?" he thought. He called an emergency meeting with his team.

?? "We need to rethink our manufacturing. From now on, GreenTech will become the leader in Sustainable Manufacturing."

The Transformation Begins

1?? Reducing Waste & Recycling Materials

? Instead of using virgin plastics and metals, GreenTech started using recycled aluminum and biodegradable plastics for its appliances.

? They launched a Take-Back Program, where customers could return old appliances for recycling.

? Results:

✓? 50% reduction in waste production.

✓? Customers loved the idea of eco-friendly appliances!

2?? Switching to Renewable Energy

? GreenTech installed solar panels on their factory roofs.

? They partnered with a wind energy farm to power their production lines.

? Results:

✓? Reduced electricity bills by 40%.

✓? Became a carbon-neutral factory in just three years!

3?? Implementing Water Conservation

? The factory used rainwater harvesting to supply cooling systems.

? Wastewater was treated and recycled instead of being dumped into rivers.

? Results:

✓? Saved 2 million liters of water annually.

✓? Local environmental groups praised GreenTech for its efforts.

4?? Ethical & Sustainable Supply Chain

? GreenTech partnered with suppliers that followed fair labor practices.

? They ensured that all raw materials were sustainably sourced (FSC-certified wood, conflict-free metals).

? Results:

✓? Employee satisfaction increased by 30%.

✓? The company earned a global sustainability certification.

The Final Outcome: A Greener Future

After five years, GreenTech became a leading example of sustainable manufacturing.

? **Achievements:**

? 100% recyclable products.

? Zero waste sent to landfills.

? Customers trusted GreenTech more, leading to a 20% increase in sales.

One day, Mr. Carter received another letter. It was from Emily, now 17 years old.

? "Dear GreenTech, Thank you for listening to my letter. You have shown the world that companies can be successful and sustainable. I'm studying Environmental Science now and hope to work for you someday! Sincerely, Emily."

Mr. Carter smiled. Sustainability was not just a business decision—it was a promise for the future.

Moral of the Story

? Sustainable Manufacturing is not just good for the planet—it's good for business and people. Companies that innovate save costs, build customer trust, and create a better future.

CHAPTER FOUR

Overview of Intelligent Manufacturing

Intelligent Manufacturing Explained Using 5W & 1H Technique

Intelligent Manufacturing (IM) integrates Artificial Intelligence (AI), Internet of Things (IoT), robotics, and big data to optimize production, reduce costs, and improve quality. Let's break it down using the 5W & 1H technique.

1?? **What is Intelligent Manufacturing?**

Intelligent Manufacturing is an advanced production system that uses AI, machine learning, automation, and real-time data to enhance efficiency and flexibility.

? Example: A smart factory where machines predict failures, robots adjust operations autonomously, and AI optimizes production schedules.

2?? **Why is Intelligent Manufacturing Important?**

? Increases Productivity: Automates tasks, reducing errors and delays.

? Reduces Costs: Minimizes material waste and downtime.

? Improves Quality: AI ensures precision and consistency.

? Enhances Flexibility: Quickly adapts to market changes and custom orders.

? Sustainability: Optimizes energy usage and reduces environmental impact.

? Example: Tesla's AI-driven Gigafactories adjust production in real-time based on demand and material availability.

3?? **Who Uses Intelligent Manufacturing?**

? Automobile Industry (Tesla, BMW) – Smart robots assemble cars autonomously.

? Electronics Industry (Apple, Samsung) – AI-powered testing ensures quality.

? Pharmaceuticals (Pfizer, Moderna) – Automated labs speed up drug production.

? Aerospace (Boeing, Airbus) – AI designs lightweight, efficient aircraft parts.

? Food & Beverage (Coca-Cola, Nestlé) – Smart packaging systems reduce waste.

? Example: BMW uses AI-powered cameras to detect manufacturing defects instantly.

4?? **When is Intelligent Manufacturing Used?**

✓? Real-time monitoring: Sensors track production efficiency.

✓? Predictive maintenance: AI predicts machine failures before they happen.

✓? Automated decision-making: AI adjusts production speed based on demand.

✓? Supply chain optimization: IoT monitors raw material availability.

? Example: Amazon warehouses use AI-powered robots to sort, pack, and ship products with 99% accuracy.

5?? **Where is Intelligent Manufacturing Applied?**

? Smart Factories: Automated production with minimal human intervention.

?? Industrial IoT (IIoT): Machines communicate via the internet for optimization.

? Advanced Robotics: Robots perform precise, repetitive tasks 24/7.

? Cloud Computing: Real-time data access for global operations.

? Additive Manufacturing (3D Printing): AI designs complex structures efficiently.

? Example: GE Aviation uses 3D printing to manufacture jet engine parts, reducing weight and fuel consumption.

6?? **How Does Intelligent Manufacturing Work?**

? Step 1: Data Collection → IoT sensors monitor machines and processes.

? Step 2: Data Processing → AI analyzes patterns and predicts issues.

? Step 3: Decision Making → AI adjusts production in real time.

? Step 4: Automation & Robotics → Robots execute tasks efficiently.

? Step 5: Continuous Learning → Machine learning improves processes over time.

? Example: A smart textile factory uses AI to detect fabric defects before shipping.

Conclusion

? Intelligent Manufacturing is the future of industry—automating processes, reducing costs, improving quality, and making production more sustainable. Companies adopting IM gain a competitive edge in efficiency and innovation.

The History of Intelligent Manufacturing

Intelligent Manufacturing (IM) has evolved over centuries, driven by technological advancements such as automation, artificial intelligence (AI), and the Internet of Things (IoT). Here's a timeline of its development:

1?? **The First Industrial Revolution (18th - 19th Century) – Mechanization**

? Time Period: Late 1700s - early 1800s

? Key Innovations: Steam engines, mechanized textile production, and early assembly lines.

? Impact: Transition from handcraft to machine-based manufacturing.

? Example: The invention of the steam engine by James Watt enabled mass production in factories.

2?? **The Second Industrial Revolution (Late 19th - Early 20th Century) – Mass Production**

? Time Period: Late 1800s - early 1900s

? Key Innovations: Electricity, conveyor belts, and mass production techniques.

? Impact: The rise of large-scale factory automation and increased production speeds.

? Example: Henry Ford's Assembly Line (1913) revolutionized automobile manufacturing by standardizing production and reducing costs.

3?? **The Third Industrial Revolution (1950s - 2000s) – Automation & Computers**

? Time Period: Mid 20th century - early 21st century

? Key Innovations:

? Computers & CNC Machines: Allowed precise, programmable manufacturing.

? Robotics: Automated repetitive tasks, improving efficiency.

? Flexible Manufacturing Systems (FMS): Machines adjusted production without manual intervention.

? Example: Toyota's Lean Manufacturing (1950s-60s) introduced automation with human intelligence (Jidoka) and Just-in-Time (JIT) production to reduce waste.

4?? **The Fourth Industrial Revolution (2000s - Present) – Intelligent Manufacturing**

? Time Period: 21st century

? Key Innovations:

? Artificial Intelligence (AI): Machines learn and make decisions.

? Industrial IoT (IIoT): Sensors collect and analyze real-time data.

? Big Data & Cloud Computing: Factories optimize production based on insights.

? 3D Printing (Additive Manufacturing): AI-designed, lightweight, customizable parts.

? Digital Twins: Virtual models of manufacturing processes for real-time monitoring.

? Example: Tesla's Smart Factories use AI-powered robots, predictive maintenance, and real-time data analytics to optimize production.

5?? **The Future: Industry 5.0 – Human-AI Collaboration**

? Emerging Trends:

? Human-Robot Collaboration: AI and humans work together.

? Sustainable & Smart Factories: Focus on eco-friendly, energy-efficient production.

? Quantum Computing: Solves complex manufacturing challenges.

? Hyper-Automation: AI-driven, fully autonomous production lines.

? Example: BMW's AI-powered manufacturing plants use machine learning to predict quality issues before they occur, ensuring near-zero defects.

Conclusion

? Intelligent Manufacturing evolved from mechanization to AI-driven smart factories. Today, companies use AI, IoT, robotics, and real-time data to enhance efficiency, reduce costs, and enable flexible production.

Case Studies on Intelligent Manufacturing

Intelligent Manufacturing (IM) leverages AI, IoT, robotics, and big data to optimize production, reduce waste, and enhance flexibility. Here are real-world case studies showcasing how companies have successfully implemented IM.

1. Tesla: AI-Driven Smart Manufacturing

Background:

Tesla's Gigafactories produce electric vehicles (EVs) and batteries at an unprecedented scale. The company faced challenges with production delays and quality control due to high demand.

Intelligent Manufacturing Strategies:

? AI-Powered Robotics: Tesla deployed AI-driven robots to automate assembly lines.

? Predictive Maintenance: Sensors detect machine faults before failures occur.

? Real-Time Data Analytics: AI monitors production in real-time, making instant adjustments.

? Automated Quality Control: Computer vision systems identify defects on production lines.

Results:

✓? Increased production efficiency by 30%.

✓? Reduced downtime by 50% due to predictive maintenance.

✓? Improved defect detection, ensuring high product quality.

? Key Lesson: AI and automation can accelerate production while maintaining high-quality standards.

2. Siemens: Industry 4.0 Smart Factory

Background:

Siemens wanted to create a fully digitalized factory to improve efficiency and flexibility.

Intelligent Manufacturing Strategies:

? Digital Twin Technology: Created virtual models of production lines for real-time monitoring.

? Industrial IoT (IIoT): Sensors collected data on machines to optimize performance.

? Autonomous Robots: Robots adjusted operations dynamically without human intervention.

? Cloud-Based Manufacturing Execution System (MES): Integrated cloud computing for remote monitoring.

Results:

✓? Production output increased by 25%.

✓? Energy consumption reduced by 15%.

✓? Lead time shortened due to real-time optimization.

? Key Lesson: Digital twins and IoT integration improve efficiency, reduce costs, and enhance production flexibility.

3. General Electric (GE): AI-Enabled Jet Engine Manufacturing

Background:

GE Aviation manufactures jet engines, requiring high precision and reliability.

Intelligent Manufacturing Strategies:

? 3D Printing (Additive Manufacturing): AI-optimized designs for lighter, more efficient engine parts.

? AI-Driven Quality Inspection: Machine learning detects micro-defects in engine components.

? Predictive Analytics: AI predicts component wear and tear, preventing failures.

Results:

✓? Jet engine weight reduced by 20%, improving fuel efficiency.

✓? Manufacturing time reduced by 30% due to optimized production.

✓? Defect rates decreased by 40%.

? Key Lesson: AI-powered 3D printing and predictive maintenance revolutionize high-precision industries.

4. Foxconn: Smart Automation in Electronics Manufacturing

Background:

Foxconn, the world's largest electronics manufacturer (Apple, Dell, HP), needed to improve efficiency in its high-speed, high-volume production environment.

Intelligent Manufacturing Strategies:

? Smart Robots ("Foxbots") replaced manual labor for repetitive tasks.

? AI-Based Supply Chain Optimization reduced component shortages.

? Edge Computing & IoT Sensors enabled real-time factory monitoring.

? AI-Powered Defect Detection improved quality assurance.

Results:

✓? Labor costs reduced by 30%.

✓? Productivity increased by 25% due to automation.

✓? Error rates decreased by 40%, improving product quality.

? Key Lesson: AI-driven automation and supply chain analytics help large-scale manufacturers stay competitive.

5. Haier: Customization with AI & IoT

Background:

Haier, a global leader in home appliances, needed to shift from mass production to mass customization while maintaining efficiency.

Intelligent Manufacturing Strategies:

? AI-Powered Customization: Customers design products online, and AI adjusts production accordingly.

? Flexible Manufacturing Lines: Machines adapt to different product configurations instantly.

? IoT-Enabled Smart Factories: Real-time data improves supply chain efficiency.

Results:

✓? Orders fulfilled 70% faster.

✓? Inventory waste reduced by 35%.

✓? Customer satisfaction improved due to personalized products.

? Key Lesson: AI and flexible manufacturing enable mass customization without increasing costs.

Conclusion

These case studies show that Intelligent Manufacturing improves efficiency, reduces costs, and enhances quality. By leveraging AI, robotics, IoT, and big data, companies across industries are transforming their operations for the future.

The Smart Factory Revolution: A Story of Intelligent Manufacturing

In the city of Techville, there was a company called FutureWorks that had been manufacturing automobile parts for decades. While once a leader in the industry, FutureWorks was now struggling. Machines broke down frequently, production was slow, and customer complaints about defects were rising.

One evening, the CEO, Mr. Anderson, received an urgent call from his biggest client:

? "Anderson, your parts are arriving late, and their quality is inconsistent. If this continues, we'll have to switch suppliers."

Mr. Anderson knew that if he didn't find a solution, the company would collapse.

The Turning Point

The next day, he gathered his team and asked:

?? "What if our machines could think, predict failures, and optimize production on their own?"

The room fell silent—until the chief engineer, Sarah, spoke up.

? "We can make this happen using Intelligent Manufacturing. AI, IoT, and automation can transform our factory into a Smart Factory."

Excited, they formed a plan to integrate AI-driven systems, IoT sensors, and cloud computing.

The Intelligent Transformation

1?? AI-Powered Predictive Maintenance

? Problem: Machines frequently broke down, causing delays.

? Solution: They installed IoT sensors on machines to monitor temperature, vibration, and wear. AI analyzed the data and predicted failures before they happened.

? Result:

✓? Machine breakdowns dropped by 60%.

✓? Production never stopped unexpectedly.

2?? Smart Robots for Automation

? Problem: Workers spent too much time on repetitive, manual tasks.

? Solution: They introduced AI-powered robotic arms that adjusted their movements based on product type.

? Result:

✓? Production speed increased by 40%.

✓? Human workers focused on design & innovation, rather than repetitive tasks.

3?? AI-Driven Quality Control

? Problem: Defective parts reached customers, leading to returns and complaints.

? Solution: Computer vision AI inspected every part in real-time, detecting even the smallest defects.

? Result:

✓? Defect rate dropped from 5% to 0.5%.

✓? Customers were happier than ever!

4?? Smart Supply Chain with IoT & Cloud

? Problem: Raw materials arrived late, slowing production.

? Solution: The factory connected to suppliers using IoT, so AI could predict when materials would be needed and reorder them automatically.

? Result:

✓? Zero material shortages.

✓? Delivery times improved by 35%.

The Final Success

Six months later, Mr. Anderson received another call from his client. But this time, it was different.

? "Anderson, your parts are arriving early, and the quality is top-notch. We want to sign a long-term contract with you!"

Mr. Anderson smiled—Intelligent Manufacturing had saved his company.

Moral of the Story

? AI, IoT, and automation can turn struggling factories into industry leaders.

? Predictive maintenance, smart robotics, and real-time analytics enhance efficiency and quality.

? Businesses that embrace Intelligent Manufacturing stay ahead of the competition.

CHAPTER FIVE

Overview of Smart Manufacturing

Smart Manufacturing Explained Using 5W & 1H Technique

Smart Manufacturing (SM) uses automation, data analytics, IoT (Internet of Things), AI, and robotics to enhance production efficiency, quality, and flexibility. Let's break it down using 5W & 1H:

1?? What is Smart Manufacturing?

Smart Manufacturing is a modern approach to production that integrates real-time data, AI-driven automation, and IoT sensors to create highly efficient, adaptable, and optimized manufacturing processes.

? Example: A smart factory where machines automatically adjust operations based on demand and detect issues before they cause downtime.

2?? Why is Smart Manufacturing Important?

? Boosts Efficiency: Reduces waste and maximizes productivity.

? Reduces Costs: Minimizes downtime and resource consumption.

? Improves Quality: AI detects defects in real time.

? Enhances Flexibility: Quickly adapts to custom orders and demand changes.

? Supports Sustainability: Optimizes energy and material use to reduce environmental impact.

? Example: Siemens' digital factories use AI-powered predictive maintenance to prevent breakdowns, saving millions in downtime.

3?? Who Uses Smart Manufacturing?

? Automobile Industry (Tesla, BMW) – AI-driven robots assemble cars.

? Electronics Industry (Apple, Foxconn) – Automated production lines optimize efficiency.

? Pharmaceuticals (Pfizer, Moderna) – AI-enhanced labs speed up drug production.

? Aerospace (Boeing, Airbus) – AI-powered 3D printing creates lightweight components.

? Food & Beverage (Nestlé, Coca-Cola) – Smart packaging systems reduce waste.

? Example: BMW's AI-powered quality control system scans vehicles to detect defects before they leave the factory.

4?? When is Smart Manufacturing Used?

✓? Real-Time Monitoring: IoT sensors track machine performance.

✓? Predictive Maintenance: AI predicts machine failures before they happen.

✓? Automated Decision-Making: AI optimizes production schedules based on demand.

✓? Supply Chain Optimization: AI manages raw material logistics to prevent shortages.

? Example: Amazon's smart warehouses use AI-powered robots to sort, pack, and ship products efficiently.

5?? Where is Smart Manufacturing Applied?

? Smart Factories: Automated production with minimal human intervention.

?? Industrial IoT (IIoT): Machines communicate via the internet for optimization.

? Advanced Robotics: AI-powered robots perform precise, repetitive tasks 24/7.

? Cloud Computing: Real-time data access enables remote monitoring.

? 3D Printing (Additive Manufacturing): AI optimizes complex part designs.

? Example: GE Aviation's 3D-printed jet engine parts improve fuel efficiency while reducing production time.

6?? How Does Smart Manufacturing Work?

? Step 1: Data Collection → IoT sensors gather data from machines and processes.

? Step 2: Data Processing → AI analyzes patterns and predicts issues.

? Step 3: Decision Making → AI adjusts production speed and quality controls.

? Step 4: Automation & Robotics → Smart machines execute tasks with precision.

? Step 5: Continuous Improvement → AI learns from past data to improve efficiency.

? Example: Tesla's Gigafactories use AI-powered robots that adjust production in real time based on supply chain conditions and demand.

Conclusion

? Smart Manufacturing is the future of industry—it optimizes production, reduces costs, and improves quality using AI, IoT, and automation. Companies that embrace Smart Manufacturing gain a competitive edge in efficiency and innovation.

The History of Smart Manufacturing

Smart Manufacturing (SM) has evolved over centuries, driven by technological advancements like automation, artificial intelligence (AI), robotics, and the Internet of Things (IoT). Below is a timeline of its history:

1?? First Industrial Revolution (1760 - 1840) – Mechanization

? Key Innovations: Steam engines, mechanized textile production, and early factories.

? Impact: Shift from handcrafting to machine-based production.

? Example: The steam-powered spinning jenny allowed mass textile production.

2?? Second Industrial Revolution (1870 - 1914) – Mass Production & Electricity

? Key Innovations: Electricity, assembly lines, and mass production techniques.

? Impact: Factories became more efficient, and goods were produced at a larger scale.

? Example: Henry Ford's Assembly Line (1913) revolutionized car manufacturing with standardization and automation.

3?? Third Industrial Revolution (1950s - 2000s) – Automation & Computers

? Key Innovations:

? Computers & CNC Machines: Allowed precise, programmable manufacturing.

? Industrial Robotics: Automated repetitive tasks (e.g., robotic arms in car factories).

? Flexible Manufacturing Systems (FMS): Machines adapted to different product designs.

? Example: Toyota's Lean Manufacturing (1950s-60s) optimized production with automation and Just-in-Time (JIT) manufacturing.

4?? Fourth Industrial Revolution (2000s - Present) – Smart Manufacturing & Industry 4.0

? Key Innovations:

? AI & Machine Learning: Machines make real-time decisions.

? Industrial IoT (IIoT): Sensors collect and analyze real-time data.

? Cloud Computing: Remote monitoring and data storage.

? Digital Twins: Virtual models of production systems.

? 3D Printing: AI-driven additive manufacturing.

? Example: Tesla's Gigafactories use AI-powered robots, predictive maintenance, and real-time analytics for optimized production.

5?? The Future: Industry 5.0 – Human-AI Collaboration & Sustainability

? Emerging Trends:

? Human-Robot Collaboration: AI and humans work together.

? Sustainable & Smart Factories: Focus on eco-friendly, energy-efficient production.

? Quantum Computing: Solves complex manufacturing problems.

? Hyper-Automation: AI-driven, self-optimizing production lines.

? Example: BMW's AI-powered smart factories integrate machine learning and real-time data analytics for defect-free, efficient production.

Conclusion

? Smart Manufacturing evolved from mechanization to AI-driven factories. Today, companies use AI, IoT, robotics, and big data to improve efficiency, reduce costs, and enhance flexibility.

Smart Manufacturing Case Studies

Smart Manufacturing integrates AI, IoT, robotics, and real-time data analytics to optimize production. Here are three real-world case studies showing how companies have successfully implemented Smart Manufacturing.

1?? Tesla: AI-Powered Smart Factories

Problem:

Tesla needed to scale production of electric vehicles (EVs) while maintaining high quality and low costs. Traditional manufacturing methods were too slow and inefficient.

Smart Manufacturing Solution:

? AI & Automation: Tesla's Gigafactories use AI-powered robotic arms for assembling cars.

? IoT & Real-Time Data: Sensors track every stage of production to prevent defects.

? Predictive Maintenance: AI analyzes data to predict and prevent machine failures before they happen.

Results:

✔? Production increased 3X while maintaining precision.

✔? Manufacturing defects dropped significantly due to AI-powered quality control.

✔? Tesla reduced downtime and improved supply chain efficiency.

? Lesson Learned: AI-driven automation and predictive analytics can boost efficiency and reduce waste in large-scale production.

2?? Siemens: Digital Twin Technology for Smart Factories

Problem:

Siemens wanted to test and optimize factory operations before implementing changes to avoid costly errors.

Smart Manufacturing Solution:

? Digital Twin Technology: They created a virtual simulation of their entire factory to test different scenarios before making real-world changes.

? IoT & Cloud Computing: Real-time data from IoT sensors was used to continuously update the digital twin.

? AI-Based Decision Making: AI analyzed production bottlenecks and suggested optimizations.

Results:

✔? 30% reduction in production costs by preventing inefficiencies.

✔? Near-zero defects due to AI-driven quality checks in simulations.

✔? Faster design-to-production cycle for new products.

? Lesson Learned: Digital Twin technology enables manufacturers to test and optimize operations before real-world implementation, reducing costs and defects.

3?? General Electric (GE): Industrial IoT for Smart Manufacturing

Problem:

GE faced challenges in machine breakdowns and inefficiencies across its manufacturing plants, causing delays and high maintenance costs.

Smart Manufacturing Solution:

? Industrial IoT (IIoT): Sensors were placed on machines to monitor performance and detect wear and tear.

? AI-Powered Predictive Maintenance: AI analyzed sensor data to predict failures before they occurred.

? Cloud-Based Analytics: All data was sent to a centralized cloud platform for real-time decision-making.

Results:

✔? Downtime reduced by 20%, improving productivity.

✔? Maintenance costs dropped by 25% due to predictive analytics.

✔? Increased energy efficiency, reducing operational costs.

? Lesson Learned: IIoT and AI-driven predictive maintenance help manufacturers minimize downtime and optimize machine efficiency.

Conclusion

These case studies show that Smart Manufacturing can:

? Increase production efficiency (Tesla)

? Improve quality control with AI & Digital Twins (Siemens)

? Reduce downtime and costs through IoT & AI (GE)

The Smart Factory Transformation: A Story of Smart Manufacturing

In the city of Techville, there was an old factory named Precision Motors that had been manufacturing automobile parts for over 50 years. Once a leader in the industry, the company was now struggling.

? **Challenges they faced:**

? High defect rates – 5% of parts had quality issues.

?? Machine breakdowns – leading to production delays.

? Supply chain disruptions – causing frequent material shortages.

? Rising costs – making them less competitive.

One day, the CEO, Mr. Carter, received an alarming call from their biggest client:

? "Mr. Carter, your parts are arriving late, and quality is inconsistent. If this continues, we will switch to another supplier."

This was a wake-up call. Something had to change.

The Smart Manufacturing Revolution

Determined to save the company, Mr. Carter called a meeting with his team.

?? "We need to transform our factory into a Smart Factory using the latest technology."

His chief engineer, Sophia, introduced Smart Manufacturing, explaining how AI, IoT, and automation could solve their problems.

Step 1: AI-Powered Quality Control

? Problem: Many defective parts were reaching customers.

? Solution: They installed AI-powered cameras and sensors to inspect every part in real time.

? Result:

✓? Defect rate dropped from 5% to 0.5%.

✓? Customer complaints reduced by 80%.

Step 2: IoT for Predictive Maintenance

? Problem: Machines often broke down unexpectedly.

? Solution: IoT sensors were added to machines, monitoring temperature, vibrations, and wear. AI analyzed the data to predict failures before they happened.

? Result:

✓? Machine downtime decreased by 40%.

✓? Maintenance costs dropped by 25%.

Step 3: Smart Supply Chain Management

? Problem: Production delays due to material shortages.

? Solution: AI-driven software monitored inventory and automatically reordered materials before they ran out.

? Result:

✓? No more supply chain disruptions.

✓? Production became 30% more efficient.

The Final Success

Six months later, Mr. Carter received another call from the same client.

? "Mr. Carter, your parts are now arriving early, and quality is outstanding. We want to sign a long-term contract with you!"

The factory had transformed into a fully automated, AI-driven Smart Factory. Employees were happier, costs were lower, and Precision Motors was once again an industry leader.

Moral of the Story

? AI and IoT improve quality, reduce defects, and cut costs.

? Predictive maintenance prevents breakdowns and increases efficiency.

? Smart supply chains eliminate delays and boost production.

? Companies that embrace Smart Manufacturing stay competitive and thrive.

CHAPTER SIX

Lean Manufacturing

The objectives of Lean Manufacturing are focused on maximizing value while minimizing waste. The key goals include:

Reduce Waste (Muda) – Eliminate unnecessary activities, materials, and processes that do not add value, such as overproduction, waiting time, and excess inventory.

Improve Efficiency – Streamline production by optimizing workflows and reducing downtime.

Enhance Quality – Implement continuous improvement strategies to ensure defect-free products and reduce rework.

Increase Productivity – Improve employee performance, machine utilization, and overall operational efficiency.

Reduce Costs – Lower production expenses by optimizing resource use, reducing waste, and improving process efficiency.

Enhance Flexibility – Adapt quickly to customer demands and market changes through a responsive and agile production system.

Improve Customer Satisfaction – Deliver high-quality products on time while meeting or exceeding customer expectations.

Empower Employees – Engage workers in problem-solving and decision-making to drive continuous improvement.

Streamline Supply Chain – Ensure smooth material flow and reduce delays by improving coordination with suppliers and logistics.

Achieve Continuous Improvement (Kaizen) – Foster a culture of ongoing enhancements in processes, products, and services.

These objectives align with Lean principles like Just-in-Time (JIT), 5S, Value Stream Mapping (VSM), and Standardized Work to create a more efficient and cost-effective production system.

Key Principles of Lean Manufacturing

Lean Manufacturing is built on several core principles that guide organizations in optimizing their processes while minimizing waste. These principles include:

Identify Value – Understand what customers value and focus on delivering it efficiently.

Map the Value Stream – Analyze the entire production process to identify and eliminate waste.

Create Flow – Ensure a smooth and continuous production process with minimal interruptions.

Establish Pull Systems – Use a demand-driven (Just-in-Time) approach to produce only what is needed, reducing inventory and overproduction.

Pursue Perfection (Continuous Improvement) – Encourage ongoing process improvements (Kaizen) to achieve maximum efficiency and quality.

Implications of Lean Manufacturing

Implementing Lean Manufacturing has significant implications across various aspects of production and management:

1. Operational Efficiency

Reduces cycle times and increases throughput.

Improves machine utilization and reduces downtime.

Leads to smoother workflows with fewer bottlenecks.

2. Cost Reduction

Eliminates waste, lowering production costs.

Reduces excess inventory and storage expenses.

Minimizes rework and defect-related costs.

3. Quality Improvement

Enhances product quality through error-proofing techniques.

Encourages early defect detection and resolution.

Promotes a culture of continuous improvement.

4. Workforce Engagement

Empowers employees to contribute to problem-solving.

Encourages teamwork and cross-functional collaboration.

Requires training and upskilling to adapt to lean processes.

5. Supply Chain Optimization

Encourages better supplier relationships and Just-in-Time deliveries.

Reduces lead times and improves responsiveness to market demands.

Minimizes excess inventory and associated costs.

6. Customer Satisfaction

Ensures faster delivery times with improved reliability.

Provides high-quality products at competitive prices.

Enhances overall customer trust and brand reputation.

By integrating these principles, Lean Manufacturing helps organizations achieve higher productivity, lower costs, and a more agile and competitive production system.

The 8 Types of Waste in Lean Manufacturing (TIMWOODS)

Lean Manufacturing identifies eight types of waste (also called Muda) that do not add value to the final product. These wastes are commonly remembered using the acronym TIMWOODS:

T – Transportation ?

Unnecessary movement of materials, products, or information between processes.

Example: Moving parts between distant workstations without adding value.

I – Inventory ?

Excess raw materials, work-in-progress (WIP), or finished goods that tie up capital and storage space.

Example: Overstocking components due to inaccurate demand forecasting.

M – Motion ?♂?

Unnecessary movement by workers or machines that does not add value.

Example: Workers walking long distances to fetch tools or materials.

W – Waiting ?

Idle time when workers, machines, or processes are waiting for materials, approvals, or information.

Example: A production line stops due to delayed supply deliveries.

O – Overproduction ?

Producing more than needed or before it is required, leading to excess inventory.

Example: Manufacturing large batches before customer demand exists.

O – Overprocessing ??

Performing extra work that does not add value, such as excessive polishing or redundant inspections.

Example: Using higher-quality materials or complex machining when not required.

D – Defects ?

Errors or faulty products that require rework or scrap, increasing costs.

Example: A misaligned assembly process leads to defective parts.

S – Skills (Underutilization of Talent) ?

Not fully utilizing employees' skills, creativity, and problem-solving abilities.

Example: Assigning highly skilled workers to repetitive manual tasks instead of innovation or improvements.

How to Eliminate Waste?

Implement 5S methodology (Sort, Set in Order, Shine, Standardize, Sustain).

Use Just-in-Time (JIT) to reduce inventory waste.

Apply Kaizen (Continuous Improvement) to involve employees in eliminating waste.

Optimize layouts and workflows to reduce motion and transportation waste.

Use Poka-Yoke (Error Proofing) to prevent defects.

Kaizen: Continuous Improvement with Case Studies

Kaizen (Japanese for "change for better") is a continuous improvement philosophy used in Lean Manufacturing to enhance productivity, quality, and efficiency. It focuses on small, incremental changes that lead to significant long-term benefits.

Key Principles of Kaizen

Small, Ongoing Improvements – Rather than major overhauls, Kaizen emphasizes gradual changes.

Involves Everyone – From top management to shop-floor workers, everyone participates.

Eliminates Waste – Focuses on reducing inefficiencies, defects, and unnecessary processes.

Standardization & Documentation – Once an improvement is made, it becomes the new standard.

PDCA Cycle (Plan-Do-Check-Act) – A structured approach to implementing Kaizen.

Case Studies on Kaizen Implementation

Case Study 1: Toyota – Kaizen in Automotive Manufacturing ?

? Challenge:

Toyota needed to improve efficiency, reduce waste, and enhance quality in its production process.

? Kaizen Implementation:

Just-in-Time (JIT): Toyota adopted a "pull" production system, producing only what was needed, reducing overproduction.

5S Methodology: Organized the workspace to eliminate wasteful movement and improve efficiency.

Employee Involvement: Workers were encouraged to suggest daily improvements, leading to faster assembly times.

? Results:

50% reduction in defects and improved vehicle quality.

Reduction in inventory costs due to better supply chain management.

Faster production times, improving overall efficiency.

Case Study 2: Ford – Kaizen for Productivity & Quality ?

? Challenge:

Ford faced high production costs and quality issues in its manufacturing plants.

? Kaizen Implementation:

Used Value Stream Mapping (VSM) to identify process inefficiencies.

Implemented Poka-Yoke (Error Proofing) to reduce assembly defects.

Adopted Gemba Walks, where managers regularly observed processes on the factory floor.

? Results:

20% reduction in production time.

Defects per vehicle decreased by 30%.

Higher employee engagement due to problem-solving involvement.

Case Study 3: Nestlé – Kaizen in Food Processing ?

? Challenge:

Nestlé wanted to improve productivity in its packaging and processing lines to meet increasing customer demand.

? Kaizen Implementation:

Introduced lean layouts to reduce unnecessary worker movement.

Used SMED (Single-Minute Exchange of Dies) to cut down machine changeover time.

Encouraged cross-functional teams to analyze and optimize workflows.

? Results:

40% reduction in machine downtime.

Higher production output with the same workforce.

Cost savings of millions per year due to efficiency improvements.

Case Study 4: Amazon – Kaizen in Warehouse Operations ?

? Challenge:

Amazon needed to reduce order processing time and improve warehouse efficiency to meet customer expectations.

? Kaizen Implementation:

Optimized warehouse layouts to minimize employee walking distance.

Introduced automation and robotics for faster picking and packaging.

Implemented real-time tracking to reduce lost or misplaced inventory.

? Results:

Cut order processing time by 50%.

Reduced errors in shipments, improving customer satisfaction.

Improved warehouse efficiency while handling higher order volumes.

Conclusion: Why Kaizen Works?

Kaizen empowers employees, reduces waste, and continuously improves processes, leading to long-term success. Companies like Toyota, Ford, Nestlé, and Amazon have successfully applied Kaizen to achieve higher productivity, lower costs, and better quality.

The Kaizen Journey: A Factory's Transformation

In the heart of a bustling industrial town, there stood Horizon Manufacturing, a factory that had once thrived but was now struggling. Orders were delayed, products had defects, and employees felt frustrated by inefficient processes. The company's owner, Mr. Tanaka, knew something had to change.

One day, a Lean consultant, Ms. Sato, visited the factory. She introduced a philosophy called Kaizen – continuous improvement. "It's not about making huge changes overnight," she explained. "It's about small, daily improvements that lead to extraordinary results."

Day 1: The Wake-Up Call

Ms. Sato gathered the workers for a Gemba Walk—a tour of the shop floor. She asked, "Where do you see waste?"

Rahul, a machine operator, pointed at piles of unfinished parts waiting for assembly. "We overproduce because we fear running out of stock."

Maria, from packaging, complained about walking long distances to fetch materials. "I waste half my shift just moving around!"

David, a technician, noted, "Our machines take too long to changeover. That's why we have so many delays."

Ms. Sato smiled. "You've just identified the first step of Kaizen—recognizing problems."

Week 1: Small Changes, Big Impact

The team started with 5S—a workplace organization system.

Sort: They removed unnecessary tools and materials, freeing up space.

Set in Order: They rearranged workstations so everything was within easy reach.

Shine: They deep-cleaned machines, making maintenance easier.

Standardize: Labels and visual guides were placed to ensure consistency.

Sustain: Each worker took ownership of maintaining their station.

By the end of the week, employees noticed fewer delays and less time wasted searching for tools.

Month 1: The Power of Continuous Improvement

Next, the team tackled machine changeover times using SMED (Single-Minute Exchange of Die).

Before Kaizen: Changing a mold on the stamping machine took 2 hours.

After small improvements: They reduced it to 30 minutes by preparing tools in advance and using quick-release fasteners.

Meanwhile, Maria's walking distance was reduced by bringing materials closer to her workstation. Her efficiency improved by 20%!

Month 3: A New Culture

With Kaizen in full swing, something remarkable happened—employees started suggesting their own improvements!

Rahul proposed a Kanban system to produce only what was needed, eliminating overproduction.

Maria recommended a color-coded bin system for easier inventory management.

David set up a daily five-minute team meeting to discuss small fixes.

The factory transformed. Defects dropped by 35%, lead times reduced, and customer satisfaction soared.

One Year Later: The New Horizon Manufacturing

Mr. Tanaka walked through his factory, amazed. Kaizen had not just improved processes—it had changed the mindset of his people. Workers felt empowered, waste was minimized, and the factory thrived again.

As he thanked Ms. Sato, she simply replied, "Kaizen is not a one-time project—it's a journey of never-ending improvement."

And so, Horizon Manufacturing continued its journey—one small step at a time.

Moral of the Story:

Kaizen isn't about drastic changes but about continuous, daily improvements. When employees are engaged and empowered, even small changes lead to big results! ?

Case Studies on Worker Involvement in Lean Manufacturing

1. Toyota – Empowering Workers with Kaizen (Automobile Industry) ?

? Challenge:

Toyota wanted to reduce production defects and improve efficiency in their assembly lines.

? Worker Involvement:

Employees were trained in Kaizen and encouraged to suggest daily improvements.

The Andon Cord System was introduced, allowing any worker to stop the assembly line if they spotted a problem.

Workers participated in Gemba Walks with supervisors to analyze real-time challenges.

? Results:

? 50% reduction in defects in some production areas.

? Higher worker engagement, leading to an increase in morale and productivity.

? Faster problem resolution, reducing downtime.

2. Boeing – Lean Employee Training for Waste Reduction (Aerospace Industry) ✈?

? Challenge:

Boeing struggled with high production costs and waste in aircraft assembly.

? Worker Involvement:

Employees were trained in Lean principles like 5S (Sort, Set in Order, Shine, Standardize, Sustain).

Teams mapped the value stream to identify inefficiencies.

Boeing introduced Worker-Led Process Improvements, giving teams the freedom to redesign workflows.

? Results:

? Eliminated 50,000 labor hours per aircraft.

? Reduced defects in aircraft components by 30%.

? Saved millions in material costs by reducing unnecessary inventory.

3. Starbucks – Employee-Led Efficiency in Service (Retail & Food Industry) ?

? Challenge:

Starbucks faced slow service times and inconsistent customer experience across locations.

? Worker Involvement:

Frontline baristas and managers suggested improvements through Kaizen meetings.

The company adopted Lean workflow changes, including optimized coffee preparation and standardized drink-making stations.

Employee-led training ensured consistent service quality.

? Results:

? Service time reduced by 20%.

? Higher employee engagement and lower turnover rates.

? Improved customer satisfaction and order accuracy.

4. Intel – Worker-Led Lean Implementation (Electronics Manufacturing) ??

? Challenge:

Intel faced inefficiencies in its semiconductor production, leading to long lead times.

? Worker Involvement:

Employees at every level were trained in Lean problem-solving techniques.

Factory workers used Kaizen events to reduce machine downtime.

Teams redesigned workstation layouts to reduce motion waste.

? Results:

? Reduced production time by 60%.

? Increased factory output without adding extra shifts.

? Boosted employee ownership and innovation.

Conclusion: Why Worker Involvement is Essential in Lean?

Workers are closest to the process → They identify inefficiencies faster.

Higher engagement leads to continuous improvement → Employees take pride in fixing problems.

Companies benefit from reduced costs, higher quality, and increased productivity.

? Takeaway: Companies that empower their workers achieve better Lean results than those that rely solely on top-down decision-making.

The Power of Worker Involvement: A Lean Manufacturing Story

In the heart of an industrial city, Titan Auto Parts was a manufacturing plant struggling with delays, defects, and low worker morale. Orders piled up, customers complained, and machines frequently broke down. Mr. Kumar, the plant manager, knew they needed a change.

One day, the company hired Ms. Aisha, a Lean consultant. She gathered the employees and said, "You are the experts. You work here every day. Let's find the solutions together."

Day 1: The Workers Speak Up

Ms. Aisha started with a Gemba Walk, observing the shop floor with workers.

Rahul, a machine operator, said, "I waste time searching for tools. If everything had a proper place, I'd work faster."

Meera, from the assembly line, complained, "We keep making the same defects, but no one fixes the root cause."

John, a logistics worker, pointed out, "We stock too many parts. Finding the right ones takes forever."

Ms. Aisha smiled. "You've just identified three types of waste—motion, defects, and inventory. Let's start fixing them."

Week 1: Small Changes, Big Impact

The team implemented 5S (Sort, Set in Order, Shine, Standardize, Sustain):

? Sorted tools and labeled storage spaces to reduce time wasted searching.

? Created a defect tracking system, where workers could report issues and suggest fixes.

? Reduced excess inventory using a Kanban system, ensuring only needed parts were stocked.

By the end of the week, assembly errors dropped by 20%, and workers felt more in control of their tasks.

Month 1: Workers Take the Lead

Seeing the improvements, the workers became more involved.

Rahul suggested a quick-changeover system to reduce machine downtime.

Meera proposed Poka-Yoke (Error Proofing) by adding guides to prevent assembly mistakes.

John optimized the warehouse layout, cutting down retrieval time by 30%.

For the first time, employees felt valued and heard. Productivity increased, and defects continued to drop.

Six Months Later: A Transformed Factory

Titan Auto Parts had transformed. Lead times reduced by 40%, and customers noticed better quality. Workers were happier and more engaged, offering new ideas weekly.

As Mr. Kumar watched his team take ownership of improvements, he realized something: Lean Manufacturing wasn't just about efficiency—it was about empowering people.

? Titan Auto Parts had become a Lean powerhouse—not because of top management, but because of its workers.

Moral of the Story:

When workers are involved in Lean Manufacturing, they become the driving force of change. Small improvements lead to big success.

5S in Lean Manufacturing

5S is a workplace organization system in Lean Manufacturing designed to improve efficiency, reduce waste, and create a safe, productive work environment. It consists of five Japanese principles, all starting with the letter "S."

1?? Seiri (Sort) – Eliminate What's Not Needed ?

? Action: Remove unused tools, equipment, and materials.

? Goal: Reduce clutter, free up space, and improve efficiency.

? Example: A factory removes outdated spare parts to free up storage space.

2?? Seiton (Set in Order) – Organize for Efficiency ?

? Action: Arrange tools and materials logically, labeling everything.

? Goal: Reduce time spent searching for items and improve workflow.

? Example: In an automotive plant, wrenches and screwdrivers are stored near the assembly area for quick access.

3?? Seiso (Shine) – Keep It Clean ?

? Action: Regularly clean the workplace and equipment.

? Goal: Identify potential defects, prevent breakdowns, and ensure safety.

? Example: In a food processing plant, daily cleaning reduces contamination risks.

4?? Seiketsu (Standardize) – Maintain Consistency ?

? Action: Develop guidelines, schedules, and checklists.

? Goal: Ensure that best practices are followed by all employees.

? Example: A hospital uses standardized color codes for medical tools to avoid misplacement.

5?? Shitsuke (Sustain) – Make It a Habit ?

? Action: Train employees, perform regular audits, and encourage continuous improvement.

? Goal: Create a culture where 5S is part of daily work habits.

? Example: A manufacturing plant holds monthly 5S audits and rewards teams for maintaining standards.

Benefits of 5S in Lean Manufacturing

? Increases productivity by reducing time wasted searching for tools.

? Enhances safety by keeping the workspace clean and organized.

? Reduces waste by eliminating unnecessary items and inefficiencies.

? Improves quality by ensuring proper maintenance of tools and equipment.

? Boosts employee morale by creating a structured, efficient workplace.

5S Implementation at ABC Auto Parts

1?? Seiri (Sort) – Removing Unnecessary Items

? Before: Old tools, unused equipment, and expired materials cluttered the factory.

? Action Taken:

? Employees sorted essential vs. non-essential items.

? Unused tools were disposed of or stored properly.

? Inventory levels were optimized to prevent excess stock.

? Result: 50% reduction in unnecessary clutter, creating more workspace.

2?? Seiton (Set in Order) – Organizing Tools & Equipment

? Before: Workers spent up to 30 minutes per shift searching for tools.

? Action Taken:

? Created shadow boards for tool placement.

? Labeled storage areas for quick identification.

? Redesigned workstations for better workflow.

? Result: Time wasted searching for tools dropped by 40%, improving efficiency.

3?? Seiso (Shine) – Cleaning & Maintaining Equipment

? Before: Dust and oil buildup caused frequent machine breakdowns.

? Action Taken:

? Introduced daily cleaning schedules.

? Operators performed regular machine inspections.

? Workers were trained in preventive maintenance techniques.

? Result: Machine breakdowns reduced by 60%, leading to fewer production delays.

4?? Seiketsu (Standardize) – Creating Work Standards

? Before: Workers followed different procedures, leading to inconsistent product quality.

? Action Taken:

? Developed Standard Operating Procedures (SOPs).

? Created visual guides for work processes.

? Implemented checklists for daily tasks.

? Result: Defect rates reduced by 30% due to consistent quality control.

5?? Shitsuke (Sustain) – Maintaining the 5S Culture

? Before: Improvements didn't last because there was no system to sustain them.

? Action Taken:

? Conducted monthly 5S audits.

? Rewarded teams with "Best 5S Area" incentives.

? Held regular 5S training sessions.

? Result: Sustained improvements with increased employee involvement.

? Final Results After 6 Months of 5S Implementation

? Productivity increased by 35%.

? Time wasted searching for tools dropped by 40%.

? Machine downtime reduced by 60%.

? Defect rates decreased by 30%.

? Employee morale improved, as workers felt empowered.

? Key Takeaways from This Case Study

✓? 5S is not just about cleaning; it's about efficiency and organization.

✓? Worker involvement is essential for 5S to succeed.

✓? Continuous improvement is key to sustaining 5S benefits.

✓? Small changes lead to big results!

5S Implementation at FreshMart Superstore

1?? Seiri (Sort) – Removing Unnecessary Items

? Before: Old promotional materials, outdated stock, and unnecessary paperwork cluttered the backroom and aisles.

? Action Taken:

? Removed expired and slow-moving products.

? Cleared old promotional displays that blocked customer pathways.

? Digitized paperwork to reduce physical clutter.

? Result: 20% more storage space and cleaner aisles.

2?? Seiton (Set in Order) – Organizing for Efficiency

? Before: Employees took too long to restock shelves because items were stored randomly in the backroom.

? Action Taken:

? Created clearly labeled storage sections for easy stock retrieval.

? Implemented a FIFO (First In, First Out) system to rotate inventory efficiently.

? Reorganized the checkout area to keep commonly used supplies within easy reach.

? Result: Restocking time reduced by 30%, and expired product waste dropped.

3?? Seiso (Shine) – Keeping the Store Clean & Presentable

? Before: Aisles were often messy, and customers complained about dirty floors and unorganized shelves.

? Action Taken:

? Introduced daily cleaning schedules for employees.

? Employees were trained to check and fix shelf organization during each shift.

? Created a "clean-as-you-go" policy for spills and misplaced items.

? Result: Customer complaints about store cleanliness dropped by 50%.

4?? Seiketsu (Standardize) – Creating Work Standards

? Before: Each shift had different ways of stocking, cleaning, and managing customers, leading to inconsistencies.

? Action Taken:

? Created Standard Operating Procedures (SOPs) for restocking, cleaning, and checkout processes.

? Introduced visual guides in storage areas to help employees find items quickly.

? Implemented a shift checklist to ensure every task was completed properly.

? Result: Employees became 40% more efficient due to clear guidelines.

5?? Shitsuke (Sustain) – Maintaining the 5S Culture

? Before: Previous improvements would fade over time due to lack of follow-through.

? Action Taken:

? Conducted weekly 5S audits with employee participation.

? Recognized "Employee of the Month" for best 5S compliance.

? Provided ongoing training to reinforce good habits.

? Result: Sustained efficiency improvements and better employee engagement.

? Final Results After 6 Months of 5S Implementation

? Checkout times reduced by 25%.

? Restocking efficiency improved by 30%.

? Expired stock waste dropped by 40%.

? Customer satisfaction scores improved by 35%.

? Store cleanliness ratings increased significantly.

? Key Takeaways from This Case Study

✓? 5S improves both customer experience and employee efficiency.

✓? FIFO (First In, First Out) reduces expired stock and waste.

✓? A clean, organized store leads to higher customer satisfaction.

✓? Employee involvement is crucial for long-term success.

Case Study: 5S Implementation in a Healthcare Facility

Organization: BrightCare Hospital (Multi-Specialty Healthcare Center)

? Location: Chicago, USA

? Industry: Healthcare & Patient Services

? Challenge: Disorganized workstations, long patient wait times, difficulty locating medical supplies, and hygiene issues.

? Problem Statement

BrightCare Hospital struggled with inefficiencies in patient care and operational workflows. The key issues included:

? Medical staff wasting time searching for supplies.

? Crowded storage rooms with expired and redundant medical equipment.

? Delayed response times in emergency situations.

? Unhygienic conditions in some areas due to clutter and improper waste disposal.

To address these challenges, hospital management implemented the 5S methodology to streamline operations and improve patient care.

? 5S Implementation at BrightCare Hospital

1?? Seiri (Sort) – Eliminating Unnecessary Items

? Before: Storage areas were cluttered with outdated medical equipment, unnecessary paperwork, and expired medicines.

? Action Taken:

? Removed expired medicines and supplies to prevent accidental use.

? Digitized patient records to reduce paperwork clutter.

? Created essential vs. non-essential stock categories to prioritize storage.

? Result: Storage space increased by 30%, and the risk of using expired medication was eliminated.

2?? Seiton (Set in Order) – Organizing Medical Supplies for Quick Access

? Before: Doctors and nurses spent excessive time searching for medical tools during emergencies.

? Action Taken:

? Labeled and color-coded medical supplies for different departments.

? Implemented a "Grab & Go" emergency kit system with pre-packed essentials.

? Created dedicated storage zones for different categories (e.g., emergency, surgical, general use).

? Result: Response time in emergencies improved by 40%, reducing delays in critical care.

3?? Seiso (Shine) – Maintaining Hygiene & Cleanliness

? Before: Some hospital areas had poor sanitation due to misplaced medical waste and cluttered spaces.

? Action Taken:

? Introduced daily deep-cleaning protocols in all patient-care areas.

? Placed biomedical waste disposal bins in all necessary locations.

? Trained staff on proper sanitation and equipment maintenance.

? Result: Hospital-acquired infections reduced by 35%, improving overall patient safety.

4?? Seiketsu (Standardize) – Creating Hospital-Wide Best Practices

? Before: Different shifts followed inconsistent procedures, leading to inefficiencies.

? Action Taken:

? Developed Standard Operating Procedures (SOPs) for medical supply management, sanitation, and patient care.

? Conducted cross-departmental training sessions for all hospital staff.

? Installed visual guides and checklists for daily and weekly tasks.

? Result: Standardized workflows reduced errors by 25% and improved coordination between departments.

5?? Shitsuke (Sustain) – Ensuring Long-Term Success

? Before: Initial improvements would fade over time due to lack of follow-through.

? Action Taken:

? Conducted monthly 5S audits with staff participation.

? Rewarded departments with best 5S implementation for motivation.

? Provided continuous training and refresher courses for hospital teams.

? Result: Sustained improvements in efficiency, hygiene, and patient satisfaction.

? Final Results After 6 Months of 5S Implementation

? Emergency response times improved by 40%.

? Medical supply retrieval time reduced by 50%.

? Hospital-acquired infections decreased by 35%.

? Expired medication waste dropped by 45%.

? Patient satisfaction scores increased by 30%.

? Key Takeaways from This Case Study

✓? 5S enhances patient safety and healthcare efficiency.

✓? Organized workspaces save valuable time in emergencies.

✓? Proper waste management reduces infection risks.

✓? Standardized procedures improve coordination between medical teams.

Case Study: 5S Implementation in an Educational Institution

Institution: Greenfield High School (Public School)

? Location: California, USA

? Industry: Education & School Management

? Challenge: Cluttered classrooms, disorganized learning materials, inefficient administrative processes, and low student engagement.

? Problem Statement

Greenfield High School faced inefficiencies in classroom management and school operations. The key issues included:

? Overcrowded classrooms with unnecessary materials and outdated books.

? Teachers wasting time searching for lesson materials.

? Administrative delays due to paperwork clutter.

? Unhygienic school environment, affecting student health and focus.

To improve organization, efficiency, and learning experiences, the school implemented the 5S methodology.

? 5S Implementation at Greenfield High School

1?? Seiri (Sort) – Removing Unnecessary Items

? Before: Classrooms and storage rooms were filled with outdated textbooks, broken furniture, and unused teaching materials.

? Action Taken:

? Disposed of damaged furniture and old, irrelevant books.

? Introduced digital storage for lesson plans to minimize paperwork.

? Created a centralized resource area for frequently used materials.

? Result: Classroom clutter reduced by 50%, creating a more open and comfortable learning space.

2?? Seiton (Set in Order) – Organizing Learning & Administrative Materials

? Before: Teachers struggled to find teaching materials, and students had trouble accessing school resources.

? Action Taken:

? Labeled storage areas for books, supplies, and teaching aids.

? Created designated shelves for student projects and homework submissions.

? Organized administrative files in digital folders, reducing paperwork.

? Result: Teachers saved 30% of preparation time, and students could find materials more easily.

3?? Seiso (Shine) – Keeping the School Clean & Safe

? Before: Classrooms, hallways, and common areas were often dirty and disorganized.

? Action Taken:

? Implemented daily classroom cleaning routines led by students and staff.

? Installed waste bins and recycling stations in every classroom.

? Created a "Clean & Green" campaign to encourage students to maintain a tidy environment.

? Result: School cleanliness improved by 60%, reducing distractions and health risks.

4?? Seiketsu (Standardize) – Creating Consistent School-Wide Practices

? Before: Each teacher followed different classroom organization methods, leading to inconsistencies.

? Action Taken:

? Developed standard classroom layouts for easy access to materials.

? Introduced color-coded labels for subjects and grade levels.

? Implemented weekly classroom inspections for organization and hygiene.

? Result: Classroom organization and learning material access improved school-wide.

5?? Shitsuke (Sustain) – Maintaining the 5S Culture

? Before: Previous organization efforts would fade over time due to lack of follow-through.

? Action Taken:

? Conducted monthly 5S audits with teacher and student participation.

? Introduced classroom rewards for best 5S compliance.

? Integrated 5S principles into student leadership programs.

? Result: Sustained improvements in organization, efficiency, and student engagement.

? Final Results After 6 Months of 5S Implementation

? Classroom clutter reduced by 50%.

? Teaching preparation time improved by 30%.

? School cleanliness increased by 60%.

? Administrative delays dropped by 40%.

? Student engagement in maintaining the school improved.

? Key Takeaways from This Case Study

✓? 5S enhances classroom organization and efficiency.

✓? A clean, structured environment improves student focus and learning.

✓? Organized learning materials save time for teachers and students.

✓? Sustained involvement from students and staff ensures long-term success.

? 5S Implementation at SwiftLogistics Inc.

1?? Seiri (Sort) – Removing Unnecessary Items

? Before: The warehouse contained unused equipment, outdated labels, and excessive stock.

? Action Taken:

? Removed obsolete inventory and relocated slow-moving stock to secondary storage.

? Cleared damaged pallets and unnecessary equipment to free up space.

? Optimized inventory levels to avoid overstocking and understocking.

? Result: 20% more floor space and reduced congestion in aisles.

2?? Seiton (Set in Order) – Organizing for Efficiency

? Before: Workers wasted time locating items, slowing down order fulfillment.

? Action Taken:

? Implemented barcode scanning and digital inventory tracking.

? Reorganized storage using ABC classification (A = fast-moving, B = medium-moving, C = slow-moving).

? Created designated storage zones for frequently used tools and packaging materials.

? Result: Order picking time reduced by 35%, and accuracy improved.

3?? Seiso (Shine) – Maintaining Cleanliness & Safety

? Before: The warehouse had dirty, slippery floors, blocked emergency exits, and excessive dust.

? Action Taken:

? Introduced daily cleaning schedules and assigned cleaning responsibilities.

? Installed safety markings and clear paths for forklifts and workers.

? Implemented a "clean as you go" policy to prevent mess buildup.

? Result: Workplace safety improved, and accident rates decreased by 40%.

4?? Seiketsu (Standardize) – Creating Warehouse Best Practices

? Before: Different shifts used inconsistent picking and storage methods, leading to confusion.

? Action Taken:

? Developed Standard Operating Procedures (SOPs) for inventory management and shipping.

? Installed visual guides and signs for storage and workflow areas.

? Conducted training sessions for all employees on best warehouse practices.

? Result: Picking errors dropped by 50%, and employee efficiency increased.

5?? Shitsuke (Sustain) – Ensuring Long-Term Success

? Before: Warehouse improvements would fade over time due to lack of enforcement.

? Action Taken:

? Introduced weekly 5S audits to track compliance.

? Rewarded teams with best 5S area awards to motivate employees.

? Provided ongoing refresher training to reinforce 5S habits.

? Result: Sustained efficiency, fewer errors, and better workplace discipline.

? Final Results After 6 Months of 5S Implementation

? Order fulfillment time reduced by 35%.

? Picking errors dropped by 50%.

? Warehouse safety improved, reducing accidents by 40%.

? Storage space optimized, creating 20% more usable area.

? Employee morale and efficiency increased significantly.

? Key Takeaways from This Case Study

✓? 5S reduces order fulfillment time and improves accuracy.

✓? Organized inventory storage increases efficiency.

✓? A clean and safe warehouse reduces accidents and improves productivity.

✓? Standardized procedures ensure consistency across shifts.

Just-in-Time (JIT) Concept in Manufacturing & Business

? What is Just-in-Time (JIT)?

Just-in-Time (JIT) is a lean manufacturing philosophy aimed at reducing waste by producing goods only when they are needed, in the right quantity, and at the right time. The goal is to minimize inventory costs, improve efficiency, and ensure smooth production without excess stock or delays.

? Developed by: Toyota (as part of the Toyota Production System - TPS)

? Key Idea: "Make only what is needed, when it is needed, and in the amount needed."

?? Key Principles of Just-in-Time (JIT)

1?? Demand-Driven Production: Items are produced only based on actual customer demand, reducing overproduction.

2?? Minimal Inventory: Keeping only the necessary amount of raw materials, work-in-progress (WIP), and finished goods.

3?? Continuous Workflow: Ensuring a smooth and uninterrupted production process to eliminate bottlenecks.

4?? Elimination of Waste: Reducing waste in time, materials, and effort (aligned with lean manufacturing principles).

5?? Supplier Integration: Establishing strong relationships with suppliers for timely deliveries.

6?? Quality Focus: Ensuring high-quality production to minimize defects and rework.

7?? Employee Involvement: Encouraging workers to participate in problem-solving and process improvements.

? Benefits of JIT Implementation

? Reduced Inventory Costs: Less need for warehousing and storage.

? Lower Waste: Avoids overproduction, obsolete stock, and defects.

? Faster Production Cycles: Increases responsiveness to customer demand.

? Better Cash Flow: Money isn't tied up in excess inventory.

? Higher Product Quality: Problems are detected early, preventing large-scale defects.

? Increased Efficiency: Streamlined production processes reduce downtime.

?? Challenges & Risks of JIT

? Supply Chain Disruptions: Any delay from suppliers can halt production.

? Requires Strong Supplier Relationships: Needs reliable suppliers for timely deliveries.

? No Buffer Stock: Any unexpected demand surge can lead to stockouts.

? High Initial Implementation Effort: Requires a well-organized system and training.

? Real-World Example: Toyota's Just-in-Time System

? Toyota pioneered JIT in the 1970s as part of its Toyota Production System (TPS).

? Instead of maintaining large inventories, Toyota only orders and produces parts when needed.

? Key Features of Toyota's JIT:

Close collaboration with suppliers.

Small batch production.

Continuous improvement (Kaizen).

? Result: Toyota achieved faster production cycles, reduced costs, and high product quality.

? JIT in Other Industries

? Retail: Walmart & Amazon use JIT for stock replenishment based on demand trends.

? Healthcare: Hospitals use JIT for medication and medical supply inventory management.

? Restaurants: Fast food chains like McDonald's prepare food only when ordered, reducing waste.

? Tech & Electronics: Apple and Dell use JIT to reduce electronic component stockpiling.

? Key Takeaways

✓? JIT minimizes waste and improves efficiency by producing only what is needed.

✓? It requires strong supplier coordination to avoid disruptions.

✓? It enhances product quality through early defect detection.

✓? It is widely used in various industries, from manufacturing to healthcare.

? JIT Implementation at Toyota

1?? Demand-Driven Production

? Before: Toyota produced cars in large batches, leading to overproduction and storage issues.

? Action Taken:

? Switched to make-to-order (MTO) instead of mass production.

? Implemented a pull system where parts are produced only when needed.

? Result: Reduced overproduction, leading to lower storage costs and waste.

2?? Inventory Reduction

? Before: Toyota kept large stocks of raw materials and spare parts, increasing warehousing costs.

? Action Taken:

? Established close ties with suppliers for frequent, small deliveries instead of bulk stockpiling.

? Used the Kanban system (visual signaling) to request materials only when necessary.

? Result: Inventory holding costs decreased by 50%, improving cash flow.

3?? Streamlined Production Process

? Before: Long production cycles due to inefficient workflows and frequent rework.

? Action Taken:

? Implemented cellular manufacturing, organizing workstations in U-shaped layouts.

? Adopted single-minute exchange of dies (SMED) to reduce machine changeover time.

? Result: Lead time reduced by 40%, enabling faster production and deliveries.

4?? Supplier Integration & Just-in-Time Deliveries

? Before: Unreliable supplier deliveries led to production halts or excessive stock.

? Action Taken:

? Developed a tiered supplier system, ensuring timely delivery of quality parts.

? Trained suppliers in JIT principles to maintain efficiency in the supply chain.

? Result: Production continuity improved, reducing supply chain disruptions.

? Final Results After JIT Implementation

? Inventory costs reduced by 50%.

? Production lead time improved by 40%.

? Defect rates dropped by 30%, improving product quality.

? Storage space optimized, allowing better factory utilization.

? Toyota became the world's most efficient automobile manufacturer.

? Key Takeaways from This Case Study

✓? JIT reduces inventory costs by producing only what is needed.

✓? Strong supplier relationships ensure smooth, on-time deliveries.

✓? Lean manufacturing techniques improve efficiency and quality.

✓? A pull-based system prevents overproduction and waste.

Other Companies Using JIT:

? Dell: Produces laptops only when orders are received, reducing component storage.

? McDonald's: Prepares food only when customers order, reducing food waste.

? Zara: Uses JIT to manufacture fashion trends quickly, minimizing unsold stock.

? JIT Implementation at Walmart

1?? Demand-Driven Restocking

? Before: Walmart overstocked products based on forecasts, leading to waste.

? Action Taken:

? Adopted real-time sales tracking to restock based on actual demand.

? Used point-of-sale (POS) data to monitor sales trends and adjust inventory.

? Result: Reduced overstocking, minimizing waste and markdown losses.

2?? Vendor-Managed Inventory (VMI)

? Before: Suppliers had no visibility into store-level inventory, causing late deliveries.

? Action Taken:

? Allowed suppliers to monitor inventory levels in real-time via Walmart's Retail Link system.

? Suppliers were responsible for timely restocking using JIT principles.

? Result: Faster replenishment and fewer stockouts, improving customer satisfaction.

3?? Cross-Docking for Faster Supply Chain Movement

? Before: Goods were stored in warehouses before being distributed, increasing handling costs.

? Action Taken:

? Introduced cross-docking, where products move directly from supplier trucks to store trucks without storage.

? Reduced warehouse reliance, ensuring fast deliveries and lower storage costs.

? Result: Reduced distribution center costs by 25% and improved delivery speed.

4?? Automated Supply Chain & Logistics

? Before: Inventory tracking was manual and inefficient.

? Action Taken:

? Invested in RFID (Radio Frequency Identification) to track inventory in real time.

? Used automated restocking alerts to prevent stockouts.

? Result: Reduced inventory errors by 30%, improving store efficiency.

? Final Results After JIT Implementation

? Inventory carrying costs reduced by 40%.

? Stock shortages decreased by 35%, improving customer experience.

? Warehouse storage costs cut by 25% due to cross-docking.

? Faster restocking, ensuring high-demand products were always available.

? Higher profitability and competitive advantage in retail.

? Key Takeaways from This Case Study

✓? JIT minimizes excess stock, reducing storage and operational costs.

✓? Real-time inventory tracking ensures efficient restocking.

✓? Vendor-managed inventory improves supplier coordination and speed.

✓? Cross-docking accelerates distribution, making products available faster.

Other Retail Companies Using JIT:

? Amazon: Uses JIT for demand-driven warehousing and fast order fulfillment.

? Zara: Manufactures fashion items based on real-time sales data to reduce unsold stock.

? McDonald's: Uses JIT to prepare food only when customers order, reducing waste.

? JIT Implementation at McDonald's

1?? Made-to-Order Cooking (Instead of Pre-Cooked Burgers)

? Before: McDonald's used a batch cooking system, preparing food in advance and keeping it under heat lamps, which led to waste if not sold.

? Action Taken:

? Shifted to a "Made-for-You" system, where food is cooked only after an order is placed.

? Installed automated kitchen screens to direct staff on real-time orders.

? Result: Food waste reduced by 30%, and fresher meals improved customer satisfaction.

2?? Real-Time Ingredient Inventory Management

? Before: Stores overstocked ingredients, leading to spoilage.

? Action Taken:

? Implemented demand forecasting to adjust ingredient stock levels.

? Used supplier integration to ensure daily deliveries of fresh ingredients (e.g., vegetables, buns, meat).

? Result: Inventory costs reduced, and fresher ingredients improved food quality.

3?? Fast Supplier Deliveries & Cold Chain Management

? Before: Delayed deliveries led to ingredient shortages or spoilage.

? Action Taken:

? Partnered with logistics providers for daily JIT deliveries based on store sales data.

? Invested in temperature-controlled supply chains to maintain freshness.

? Result: Fewer ingredient shortages and reduced reliance on large storage facilities.

4?? Kitchen Layout & Automation for Efficiency

? Before: Staff moved inefficiently, causing slow service.

? Action Taken:

? Redesigned kitchen workflow for minimal movement and faster order processing.

? Installed automated fryers, toasters, and drink dispensers to speed up production.

? Result: Average order preparation time reduced by 50%.

? Final Results After JIT Implementation

? Food waste reduced by 30%, lowering costs.

? Inventory costs decreased by 25% due to better ingredient management.

? Customer wait times dropped by 50%, improving service speed.

? Freshness improved, leading to higher customer satisfaction and repeat visits.

? Faster supplier deliveries ensured stores always had fresh ingredients.

? Key Takeaways from This Case Study

✓? JIT ensures fresh food by preparing meals only when ordered.

✓? Supplier coordination is crucial for timely ingredient deliveries.

✓? Automated kitchen systems improve speed and reduce human errors.

✓? Optimized inventory prevents spoilage and excess storage costs.

Other Food Companies Using JIT:

? Domino's Pizza: Uses JIT to prepare fresh pizzas only after an order is placed.

? Starbucks: Manages real-time ingredient replenishment based on customer demand.

? Subway: Prepares sandwiches in front of customers, reducing pre-made waste.

Case Study: Just-in-Time (JIT) Implementation in the Electronics Industry – Dell

? Company: Dell Technologies

? Location: Global (Headquarters: USA)

? Industry: Computer & Electronics Manufacturing

? Challenge: High inventory costs, rapid technology obsolescence, and supply chain inefficiencies.

? Problem Statement

Before implementing JIT, Dell faced several key challenges:

? Excess inventory of computer components, leading to high storage costs.

? Technology obsolescence, as unsold parts quickly became outdated.

? Long production and delivery times, causing delays in fulfilling customer orders.

? Supply chain inefficiencies, leading to higher operational costs.

To address these challenges, Dell adopted a Just-in-Time (JIT) manufacturing and supply chain strategy, allowing them to produce and ship computers only when ordered by customers.

? JIT Implementation at Dell

1?? Build-to-Order (BTO) Model Instead of Mass Production

? Before: Dell manufactured computers in bulk, storing finished goods until sold.

? Action Taken:

? Shifted to a Build-to-Order (BTO) system, where computers were assembled only after a customer placed an order.

? Customers could customize specifications (RAM, storage, graphics card, etc.), ensuring demand-driven production.

? Result: Reduced unsold inventory and eliminated outdated stock.

2?? Supplier Integration for Just-in-Time Component Deliveries

? Before: Dell stocked large quantities of microprocessors, hard drives, and memory chips, increasing storage costs.

? Action Taken:

? Partnered with suppliers like Intel, Microsoft, and Seagate for real-time component deliveries.

? Implemented a Vendor-Managed Inventory (VMI) system, where suppliers monitored Dell's inventory levels and delivered components as needed.

? Result: Reduced component storage costs by 50% and improved supply chain efficiency.

3?? Lean Warehousing with Just-in-Time Logistics

? Before: Warehouses were filled with unsold pre-built computers.

? Action Taken:

? Used regional assembly plants, where computers were built and shipped within hours of receiving an order.

? Partnered with logistics providers (FedEx, UPS) to enable quick delivery directly to customers.

? Result: Shipping times reduced by 30%, leading to faster customer deliveries.

4?? Real-Time Demand Forecasting

? Before: Production was based on estimated demand, leading to overproduction or shortages.

? Action Taken:

? Implemented data-driven demand forecasting using AI and machine learning.

? Adjusted production based on real-time customer orders and sales trends.

? Result: Optimized production planning, reducing stockouts and excess inventory.

? Final Results After JIT Implementation

? Inventory costs reduced by 50%, increasing profitability.

? Production lead time decreased by 40%, enabling faster order fulfillment.

? Obsolete stock reduced by 60%, preventing outdated components from accumulating.

? Dell's market competitiveness improved due to faster customization and delivery.

? Key Takeaways from This Case Study

✓? JIT minimizes inventory costs by producing only what customers order.

✓? Strong supplier relationships ensure real-time component deliveries.

✓? A build-to-order system eliminates obsolete stock and improves efficiency.

✓? Just-in-time logistics reduce warehousing and speed up customer delivery.

Other Electronics Companies Using JIT:

? Apple: Uses JIT for iPhones, assembling them just before global product launches to avoid stockpiling.

? Sony: Implements JIT for PlayStation consoles, reducing unsold stock and increasing efficiency.

? Tesla: Uses JIT for electric car components, reducing storage costs and improving production speed.

Case Study: Just-in-Time (JIT) Implementation in Healthcare – Mayo Clinic

? Organization: Mayo Clinic

? Location: USA (Multiple Locations)

? Industry: Healthcare & Hospital Management

? Challenge: High medical supply costs, expired inventory, and delays in patient care.

? Problem Statement

Before implementing JIT, Mayo Clinic faced several operational challenges:

? Excess medical supplies in storage, leading to high inventory costs.

? Expired medications and equipment, resulting in wastage.

? Delays in getting critical supplies, affecting patient care.

? Inefficient supply chain, causing stockouts during emergencies.

To improve efficiency, Mayo Clinic implemented a Just-in-Time (JIT) system, ensuring medical supplies and medications were stocked and replenished only when needed.

? JIT Implementation at Mayo Clinic

1?? Demand-Driven Medical Supply Management

? Before: Mayo Clinic stocked large quantities of medical supplies, leading to waste.

? Action Taken:

? Shifted to a demand-based replenishment system, where supplies were ordered based on real-time usage.

? Used automated inventory tracking to monitor stock levels at each department.

? Result: Medical waste reduced by 35%, and costs lowered significantly.

2?? Supplier Integration for Just-in-Time Deliveries

? Before: Hospitals bulk-ordered medications and equipment, leading to expiration and excess storage.

? Action Taken:

? Partnered with medical suppliers for frequent, small deliveries instead of large stockpiles.

? Implemented a Vendor-Managed Inventory (VMI) system, where suppliers monitored Mayo Clinic's stock levels in real-time and delivered supplies as needed.

? Result: Eliminated expired medications and ensured continuous availability of critical supplies.

3?? JIT in Operating Rooms (ORs) & Emergency Departments (ERs)

? Before: ORs and ERs stored large amounts of surgical tools, medications, and equipment, many of which were rarely used.

? Action Taken:

? Implemented case cart systems, where surgical instruments and supplies were stocked based on the specific needs of scheduled procedures.

? Standardized supply kits for common procedures, reducing unnecessary storage.

? Result: Faster preparation for surgeries, reduced clutter, and optimized equipment usage.

4?? Real-Time Tracking of Hospital Beds & Equipment

? Before: Lack of real-time data led to delays in patient room availability and misplaced medical equipment.

? Action Taken:

? Installed RFID (Radio Frequency Identification) tracking to monitor hospital beds and medical devices.

? Used data analytics to predict bed occupancy trends and adjust resources accordingly.

? Result: Reduced patient wait times and improved overall hospital efficiency.

? Final Results After JIT Implementation

? Medical supply costs reduced by 30% due to precise demand-based ordering.

? Expired inventory decreased by 40%, preventing unnecessary waste.

? Surgical preparation time reduced by 25%, improving operating room efficiency.

? Patient wait times dropped by 20% due to better resource allocation.

? Faster response to emergencies, ensuring critical supplies were always available.

? Key Takeaways from This Case Study

✓? JIT reduces waste by ensuring medical supplies are used before expiry.

✓? Strong supplier relationships allow for timely replenishment of critical items.

✓? Automated tracking improves hospital efficiency and resource allocation.

✓? Demand-based ordering ensures supplies match actual patient needs.

Other Healthcare Institutions Using JIT:

? Cleveland Clinic: Uses JIT for medication management and surgical tool preparation.

? Johns Hopkins Hospital: Uses JIT for hospital bed allocation and patient flow optimization.

? Kaiser Permanente: Uses JIT for efficient vaccine distribution and pharmacy stock management.

Case Study: Just-in-Time (JIT) Implementation in Education – Arizona State University (ASU)

? Institution: Arizona State University (ASU)

? Location: USA

? Industry: Higher Education & Online Learning

? Challenge: High textbook costs, excess classroom materials, and inefficient resource management.

? Problem Statement

Before implementing JIT, ASU faced several challenges:

? Excess textbook inventory, leading to storage issues and financial losses.

? Outdated course materials, making learning resources obsolete.

? Inefficient classroom resource allocation, causing shortages or overstocking.

? Student demand fluctuations, making it hard to predict material needs.

To address these issues, ASU implemented a Just-in-Time (JIT) system, optimizing textbook distribution, digital learning resources, and classroom resource management.

? JIT Implementation at ASU

1?? Just-in-Time Textbook Distribution

? Before: ASU bookstores stocked large quantities of textbooks based on estimated demand.

? Action Taken:

? Shifted to a JIT textbook model, where books were ordered and printed only when students needed them.

? Introduced print-on-demand services for customized course materials.

? Result: Reduced textbook overstock by 40% and saved costs for both students and the university.

2?? Digital Learning & On-Demand Course Materials

? Before: Students had to purchase physical books, many of which became outdated quickly.

? Action Taken:

? Implemented e-books and digital subscriptions, allowing students to access materials instantly.

? Partnered with publishers for on-demand licensing, providing updated content when needed.

? Result: Saved students 50% on textbook costs and ensured up-to-date course materials.

3?? JIT Classroom & Lab Resource Management

? Before: Classrooms and science labs stocked supplies in advance, leading to waste.

? Action Taken:

? Used real-time inventory tracking to order only the required amount of lab supplies and teaching materials.

? Partnered with vendors for on-demand delivery of classroom resources.

? Result: Reduced classroom supply waste by 30% and improved budget efficiency.

4?? Just-in-Time Faculty & Course Scheduling

? Before: Courses were scheduled without considering real-time student demand, leading to overstaffed or understaffed classes.

? Action Taken:

? Used AI-driven enrollment forecasting to adjust faculty assignments dynamically based on actual student registrations.

? Implemented on-demand adjunct hiring, bringing in instructors only when a course exceeded expected enrollments.

? Result: Optimized faculty workload and reduced unnecessary teaching costs.

? Final Results After JIT Implementation

? Textbook costs reduced by 50% due to on-demand printing and digital materials.

? Storage costs cut by 40% due to optimized supply chain management.

? Course material updates improved by 60%, ensuring students had the latest information.

? Classroom and lab resource waste reduced by 30%, saving institutional costs.

? Faculty scheduling became more efficient, reducing unnecessary staffing expenses.

? Key Takeaways from This Case Study

✓? JIT reduces textbook waste and costs through digital and print-on-demand solutions.

✓? Just-in-time classroom supply management prevents overstocking and shortages.

✓? Real-time faculty scheduling ensures optimized resource allocation.

✓? Digital learning adoption enhances flexibility and cost efficiency.

Other Educational Institutions Using JIT:

? Harvard University: Uses JIT for digital course materials and adaptive learning platforms.

? MIT OpenCourseWare: Provides on-demand educational content, eliminating printed material waste.

? Khan Academy: Uses JIT for personalized learning, offering real-time content updates based on student needs.

Case Study: Just-in-Time (JIT) Implementation in Logistics – Amazon

? Company: Amazon

? Location: Global (Headquarters: USA)

? Industry: E-Commerce & Logistics

? Challenge: High warehousing costs, inefficient inventory management, and slow delivery times.

? Problem Statement

Before implementing JIT, Amazon faced several key challenges:

? Excess inventory in warehouses, leading to high storage costs.

? Delays in product delivery, affecting customer satisfaction.

? Inefficient order fulfillment, causing stock shortages or overstocking.

? High transportation costs, due to inefficient supply chain operations.

To address these issues, Amazon adopted Just-in-Time (JIT) logistics, ensuring inventory was stocked and shipped only when needed.

? JIT Implementation at Amazon

1?? Demand-Driven Inventory Management

? Before: Amazon stocked products based on sales forecasts, leading to overstocking or shortages.

? Action Taken:

? Implemented AI-powered demand forecasting to stock items only when required.

? Used automated systems to track real-time demand and adjust inventory levels.

? Result: Reduced warehousing costs by 30% and minimized excess stock.

2?? Just-in-Time Fulfillment with Regional Warehouses

? Before: Amazon shipped products from central warehouses, increasing delivery times.

? Action Taken:

? Opened regional fulfillment centers to store frequently ordered items closer to customers.

? Implemented a dynamic stock allocation system, where inventory was moved based on local demand.

? Result: Reduced delivery times from days to hours, improving customer satisfaction.

3?? Automated Warehouse & Robotics Integration

? Before: Human workers manually picked, packed, and sorted products, causing delays.

? Action Taken:

? Deployed Kiva robots in warehouses to transport inventory efficiently.

? Used automated conveyor belts and AI-based sorting systems to speed up order fulfillment.

? Result: Increased warehouse efficiency by 40%, reducing processing times.

4?? Just-in-Time Delivery with Amazon Prime & Same-Day Shipping

? Before: Customers had to wait several days for deliveries.

? Action Taken:

? Launched Amazon Prime's One-Day and Same-Day Delivery by using JIT logistics.

? Partnered with third-party couriers and local delivery networks to speed up shipping.

? Result: Faster deliveries, increasing customer loyalty and sales growth.

? Final Results After JIT Implementation

? Warehousing costs reduced by 30% due to optimized inventory levels.

? Order fulfillment speed increased by 50%, enabling same-day delivery.

? Delivery times reduced from 2–5 days to 1–2 days for Prime customers.

? Customer satisfaction improved, leading to a 20% increase in repeat purchases.

? Transportation costs optimized by 25% through regional fulfillment centers.

? Key Takeaways from This Case Study

✓? JIT minimizes inventory storage costs by stocking only what's needed.

✓? Regional fulfillment centers reduce delivery times and improve efficiency.

✓? Automation and robotics streamline warehouse operations.

✓? Real-time demand forecasting prevents overstocking and shortages.

Other Logistics Companies Using JIT:

? Walmart: Uses JIT for on-demand inventory replenishment in stores.

? UPS: Uses JIT for real-time package tracking and delivery optimization.

? FedEx: Implements JIT in overnight shipping logistics to minimize delays.

Case Study: Just-in-Time (JIT) Implementation in Construction – Toyota Home Japan

?? Company: Toyota Home

? Location: Japan

? Industry: Construction & Prefabricated Housing

? Challenge: High material waste, inefficient labor scheduling, and long construction timelines.

? Problem Statement

Before implementing JIT, Toyota Home faced several key challenges:

? Excess building material inventory, leading to high storage costs and waste.

? Delays in construction projects, due to inefficient scheduling and supply chain issues.

? Increased labor costs, because workers were idle while waiting for materials.

? Quality control issues, caused by inconsistent material deliveries and handling.

To solve these problems, Toyota Home implemented a Just-in-Time (JIT) construction system, focusing on prefabrication, lean supply chain management, and precise scheduling.

? JIT Implementation at Toyota Home

1?? Prefabrication of Housing Components

? Before: Materials were brought to the construction site and assembled, causing delays and excess inventory.

? Action Taken:

? Shifted to a prefabrication model, where walls, floors, and roof panels were pre-built in a factory.

? Delivered preassembled components to the site only when needed for installation.

? Result: Reduced on-site material waste by 50% and cut construction time by 40%.

2?? Just-in-Time Material Delivery

? Before: Large quantities of raw materials (cement, steel, lumber) were stored on-site, causing clutter and potential damage.

? Action Taken:

? Partnered with suppliers for real-time deliveries, ensuring materials arrived exactly when needed.

? Used RFID and AI tracking to monitor inventory and automatically trigger orders.

? Result: Lowered material storage costs and reduced excess inventory by 60%.

3?? Lean Workforce Scheduling

? Before: Workers often waited for materials to arrive, leading to inefficient labor use.

? Action Taken:

? Implemented real-time scheduling software to coordinate labor with material arrivals.

? Assigned workers just in time for their specific tasks, reducing downtime.

? Result: Labor productivity increased by 30%, reducing overall project costs.

4?? Waste Reduction & Sustainability

? Before: Excess materials were discarded, increasing construction waste.

? Action Taken:

? Used precision cutting machines to reduce material scrap.

? Recycled and reused materials in future projects.

? Result: Construction waste reduced by 50%, making projects more sustainable.

? Final Results After JIT Implementation

? Construction time reduced by 40% due to prefabrication and JIT material delivery.

? Material waste decreased by 50%, improving sustainability.

? Labor efficiency improved by 30%, reducing idle time.

? Project costs lowered by 25%, making homes more affordable.

? Customer satisfaction increased due to faster project completion and higher quality.

? Key Takeaways from This Case Study

✓? JIT reduces material waste by delivering resources only when needed.

✓? Prefabrication speeds up construction and minimizes delays.

✓? Real-time tracking and scheduling optimize labor efficiency.

✓? Lean supply chain management reduces costs and enhances sustainability.

Other Construction Companies Using JIT:

? Daiwa House (Japan): Uses JIT for modular housing projects, reducing build time by 50%.

? Turner Construction (USA): Implements JIT in commercial construction, improving project efficiency.

? Skanska (Europe): Uses JIT for green building projects, reducing waste and emissions.

Uniform Production Rate in Lean Manufacturing

? Definition

A uniform production rate in lean manufacturing refers to the process of producing goods at a steady, predictable pace to match customer demand. It eliminates fluctuations in production, reduces waste, and optimizes efficiency. This concept is closely tied to Heijunka (Production Leveling) in the Toyota Production System (TPS).

? Key Principles of Uniform Production Rate

1?? Production Smoothing (Heijunka)

? Instead of manufacturing in large batches, production is evenly spread over time.

? Helps balance workload and reduce bottlenecks.

2?? Demand-Based Scheduling

? Production aligns with actual customer demand (Pull System).

? Prevents overproduction and minimizes inventory.

3?? Small, Frequent Batches

? Producing in small, consistent batches reduces variation.

? Ensures continuous flow without interruptions.

4?? Standardized Workflows

? Operators follow standardized processes to maintain steady output.

? Leads to predictable cycle times and quality consistency.

5?? Load Balancing

? Work is evenly distributed across machines and workers.

? Prevents overburdening (Muri) and uneven work (Mura).

? Benefits of Uniform Production Rate

? Reduced Inventory – Avoids excess raw materials and finished goods.

? Lower Lead Time – Ensures faster and more reliable deliveries.

? Better Resource Utilization – Machines and workers operate efficiently.

? Improved Quality – Fewer defects due to stable processes.

? Higher Flexibility – Quickly adapts to changes in demand.

? Case Study: Toyota's Heijunka System

? Before: Toyota faced uneven production, causing inventory buildup and worker fatigue.

? Solution: Implemented Heijunka, where cars were produced in a steady sequence instead of large batches.

? Results:

? Reduced inventory by 40%

? Improved on-time delivery to 98%

? Lowered defect rates by 30%

?? How to Implement Uniform Production Rate?

1?? Analyze Demand: Use historical data to predict customer needs.

2?? Level the Workload: Distribute tasks evenly across shifts and workstations.

3?? Standardize Production Cycles: Maintain consistent cycle times.

4?? Use Kanban & JIT: Produce only what's needed, when it's needed.

5?? Monitor & Improve: Continuously track performance and adjust production rates.

? Final Thoughts

A uniform production rate is a fundamental principle of lean manufacturing that leads to efficiency, cost savings, and high-quality production. Companies like Toyota, Ford, and Amazon have successfully used this approach to streamline operations and maximize value.

Case Study: Uniform Production Rate in Retail – Walmart's Inventory & Supply Chain Management

? Company: Walmart

? Location: Global (Headquarters: USA)

? Industry: Retail & Supply Chain

? Challenge: Demand fluctuations, stock shortages, and overstocking in stores.

? Problem Statement

Before implementing a uniform production rate and lean supply chain, Walmart faced several issues:

? Uneven stock levels, causing shortages in high-demand products and overstock in others.

? Inconsistent supplier deliveries, leading to inefficiencies in store replenishment.

? High inventory holding costs, due to excess unsold stock in warehouses.

? Customer dissatisfaction, because of frequent stockouts and delayed restocking.

To address these challenges, Walmart adopted lean manufacturing principles, including a uniform production rate, Just-in-Time (JIT) restocking, and demand-based supply chain optimization.

? Uniform Production Rate Implementation at Walmart

1?? Demand-Based Inventory Forecasting

? Before: Walmart stocked products based on seasonal trends, leading to stock imbalances.

? Action Taken:

? Integrated AI-driven demand forecasting to predict customer buying patterns.

? Adjusted supply orders in real-time to match actual sales.

? Result: Reduced stockouts by 35% and eliminated overstocking issues.

2?? Just-in-Time Restocking & Distribution

? Before: Products were delivered in bulk, leading to inefficiencies in storage and sales.

? Action Taken:

? Implemented JIT restocking, where stores received products only as needed.

? Built regional distribution centers (RDCs) to enable faster restocking.

? Result: Cut inventory holding costs by 40% and improved shelf availability.

3?? Supplier Coordination for Steady Production Rates

? Before: Suppliers produced in large batches, leading to unpredictable store deliveries.

? Action Taken:

? Partnered with suppliers for steady, small-batch production instead of bulk orders.

? Used Vendor-Managed Inventory (VMI) to allow suppliers to replenish stock in real time.

? Result: Smoothed supply chain flow and reduced delivery delays by 30%.

4?? Lean Store Layout & Stock Rotation

? Before: Overstocked products took up space, while fast-moving goods ran out quickly.

? Action Taken:

? Optimized store layouts for better product flow and faster replenishment.

? Used FIFO (First-In-First-Out) stocking to maintain freshness and avoid expired items.

? Result: Sales increased by 20% due to better product availability and rotation.

? Final Results After Implementing Uniform Production Rate

? Stockouts reduced by 35%, ensuring products were always available.

? Inventory holding costs lowered by 40%, increasing profitability.

? Supply chain efficiency improved, reducing delivery delays by 30%.

? Customer satisfaction increased, boosting sales by 20%.

? Retail waste minimized, making Walmart's supply chain more sustainable.

? Key Takeaways from This Case Study

✔? Uniform production rate smooths out supply chain fluctuations and reduces waste.

✔? JIT restocking keeps store shelves stocked without excess inventory.

✔? AI-driven demand forecasting improves stock accuracy.

✔? Supplier coordination ensures steady product flow.

Other Retailers Using Uniform Production Rate & Lean Supply Chains:

? Amazon: Uses automated JIT restocking and AI demand forecasting.

? Target: Implements lean distribution centers for real-time inventory flow.

? Zara: Uses fast-fashion JIT production to reduce stock waste.

Case Study: Uniform Production Rate in Food Industry – McDonald's Made-for-You System

? Company: McDonald's

? Location: Global (Headquarters: USA)

?? Industry: Fast Food & Quick Service Restaurants (QSR)

? Challenge: Food waste, inconsistent customer service speed, and inefficient kitchen operations.

? Problem Statement

Before implementing a uniform production rate, McDonald's faced key issues:

? Overproduction of food, leading to excessive waste and financial loss.

? Uneven demand, where some periods had too much food ready while others had shortages.

? Longer customer wait times, as food had to be prepared fresh during rush hours.

? Quality inconsistencies, due to batch cooking and food sitting for too long.

To solve these challenges, McDonald's introduced the "Made-for-You" System, a lean-inspired process that focused on Just-in-Time (JIT) food preparation and a steady production flow.

? Uniform Production Rate Implementation at McDonald's

1?? Just-in-Time Cooking (JIT for Fast Food)

? Before: McDonald's cooked large batches of burgers and fries ahead of time, leading to waste.
? Action Taken:
? Switched to on-demand cooking, where food was made only when an order was placed.
? Used heated holding units to keep ingredients fresh for immediate assembly.
? Result: Food waste reduced by 50% and customers received fresher meals.

2?? Standardized Cooking Times for a Consistent Flow

? Before: Food preparation times varied, leading to bottlenecks in service.
? Action Taken:
? Set exact cooking times for each item (e.g., 42 seconds for fries, 90 seconds for burgers).
? Used automated timers and grill presses to ensure precision.
? Result: Increased kitchen efficiency and reduced order waiting time by 30%.

3?? Demand Forecasting for Steady Inventory Management

? Before: Restaurants stocked ingredients based on estimates, leading to shortages or excess.
? Action Taken:
? Integrated real-time sales tracking to predict demand more accurately.
? Adjusted ingredient orders based on daily/hourly demand trends.
? Result: Lowered ingredient waste by 40% and optimized stock levels.

4?? Balanced Workforce Scheduling for Uniform Production Rate

? Before: Too many employees during slow hours, too few during rush hours.
? Action Taken:
? Used AI-driven labor scheduling to match staffing levels with demand.
? Trained employees for multi-tasking, ensuring continuous workflow.
? Result: Labor costs reduced by 25% while maintaining service speed.

? Final Results After Implementing Uniform Production Rate

? Food waste reduced by 50%, cutting costs and improving sustainability.
? Customer wait time decreased by 30%, leading to better service.
? Ingredient stockouts reduced by 40%, ensuring consistent availability.
? Labor efficiency improved, reducing costs by 25%.
? Higher customer satisfaction due to fresher, made-to-order meals.

? Key Takeaways from This Case Study

✓? JIT food preparation ensures freshness and reduces waste.

✓? Standardized cooking times improve consistency and efficiency.

✓? Demand-based ingredient ordering optimizes stock levels.

✓? Balanced workforce scheduling maintains a steady service flow.

Other Food Chains Using Uniform Production Rate & Lean Principles:

? Starbucks: Uses JIT coffee brewing and inventory tracking to reduce waste.
? Subway: Prepares fresh ingredients in small batches to minimize leftovers.
? Domino's Pizza: Uses real-time demand forecasting for efficient pizza-making.

Uniform Production Rate Implementation at VMMC

1?? Standardized Patient Scheduling for Even Workload Distribution

? Before: Appointments were scheduled inconsistently, leading to rush hours and empty periods.
? Action Taken:
? Implemented Heijunka (Production Leveling) to balance patient flow throughout the day.
? Adjusted appointment slots to reduce peaks and valleys in demand.
? Result: Patient wait times decreased by 60%, improving satisfaction.

2?? Just-in-Time (JIT) Medical Supply Management

? Before: Hospitals stocked excessive inventory, leading to waste and storage issues.
? Action Taken:

? Used JIT inventory management, ensuring medical supplies arrived exactly when needed.

? Implemented real-time tracking of medication and equipment usage.

? Result: Inventory costs reduced by 50%, with zero stockouts of critical supplies.

3?? Load Balancing for Doctors & Nurses

? Before: Some doctors were overwhelmed while others had gaps in their schedules.

? Action Taken:

? Shifted to balanced patient distribution, ensuring even workload for staff.

? Created multi-skilled nurse teams to assist across departments as needed.

? Result: Staff burnout reduced by 40% and patient care consistency improved.

4?? Lean Operating Room (OR) Scheduling

? Before: Surgical teams faced delays due to unpredictable scheduling and resource shortages.

? Action Taken:

? Implemented real-time OR scheduling with lean principles.

? Ensured surgeries started and ended on time, avoiding delays.

? Result: Operating room efficiency increased by 35%, reducing patient backlog.

? Final Results After Implementing Uniform Production Rate

? Patient wait times reduced by 60%, improving hospital throughput.

? Inventory holding costs lowered by 50%, preventing waste.

? Staff workload balanced, reducing burnout by 40%.

? Operating room efficiency improved by 35%, allowing more surgeries per day.

? Overall patient satisfaction increased due to faster, more reliable care.

? Key Takeaways from This Case Study

✓? Heijunka scheduling smooths patient flow and reduces waiting times.

✓? JIT inventory prevents excess stock and ensures medical supplies are available.

✓? Balanced staffing optimizes resource utilization and improves morale.

✓? Efficient operating room scheduling increases hospital efficiency.

Other Healthcare Systems Using Uniform Production Rate & Lean Methods:

? Mayo Clinic (USA): Uses predictive patient flow analysis to level workload.

? Cleveland Clinic (USA): Implements JIT pharmacy management to reduce medication waste.

? NHS (UK): Uses lean scheduling for surgeries, improving efficiency.

Kanban System in Lean Manufacturing

? What is the Kanban System?

The Kanban system is a visual workflow management method used in lean manufacturing to control production and inventory levels. It is based on the pull system, meaning that work is only started when there is demand.

Kanban helps:

? Reduce overproduction and waste

? Improve efficiency and workflow

? Maintain optimal inventory levels

? Ensure Just-in-Time (JIT) production

? Key Principles of the Kanban System

1?? Visual Signals for Workflow Management

? Kanban uses cards, boards, or digital tools to track work progress.

? Employees can see what tasks are in progress, completed, or waiting to be started.

2?? Pull System (Demand-Based Production)

? Work begins only when there is a demand, reducing overproduction.

? No unnecessary inventory is stored, improving cash flow and efficiency.

3?? Work-in-Progress (WIP) Limits

? Limits are set on how many tasks/products can be in progress at one time.

? Prevents bottlenecks and ensures smooth production flow.

4?? Continuous Improvement (Kaizen)

? Teams analyze bottlenecks and adjust workflows to improve efficiency.

? Encourages problem-solving and waste reduction.

?? How the Kanban System Works in Manufacturing

1?? Customer Order Received → Triggers a signal (Kanban card) to start production.

2?? Raw Materials Pulled → Components are ordered only as needed.

3?? Production Process Begins → Workers complete tasks step by step, ensuring smooth flow.

4?? Finished Goods Moved → Completed products are sent to the next station or to the customer.

5?? Replenishment Signal Sent → When inventory is low, another Kanban card is triggered.

? Case Study: Toyota's Kanban System

? Company: Toyota

? Industry: Automotive Manufacturing

? Challenge: High inventory costs and production inefficiencies

? Problem:

Before Kanban, Toyota faced overproduction, excessive inventory storage, and long lead times.

? Solution:

? Implemented Kanban cards to signal demand and prevent overproduction.

? Adopted Just-in-Time (JIT) manufacturing to order parts only when needed.

? Used visual boards to track workflow and eliminate bottlenecks.

? Results:

✓? Inventory costs reduced by 50%

✓? Production efficiency improved by 30%

✓? Lead times shortened, increasing customer satisfaction

? Benefits of Using Kanban in Manufacturing

? Eliminates Overproduction – Produces only what is needed.

? Reduces Waste – Minimizes excess raw materials and finished goods.

? Optimizes Inventory Levels – Keeps materials and products flowing efficiently.

? Improves Flexibility – Quickly adapts to demand changes.

? Enhances Productivity – Clear workflow reduces delays and confusion.

?? Other Industries Using Kanban

? Retail (Walmart, Amazon): Kanban-based inventory tracking prevents stockouts.

? Healthcare (Hospitals, Pharmacies): Manages medical supply restocking efficiently.

? Food Industry (McDonald's, Starbucks): Uses JIT and Kanban for fresh food preparation.

? Electronics (Dell, Apple): Tracks components and assembly line processes.

Case Study: Kanban System in Retail – Walmart's Inventory Management

? Company: Walmart

? Location: Global (Headquarters: USA)

?? Industry: Retail & Supply Chain

? Challenge: Overstocking, stockouts, and inefficient inventory replenishment

? Problem Statement

Before implementing the Kanban system, Walmart faced several retail inventory challenges:

? Overstocking – Excess products filled warehouses, increasing storage costs.

? Stockouts – High-demand items were often unavailable, frustrating customers.

? Slow Replenishment – Store shelves were not refilled efficiently, leading to lost sales.

? Manual Tracking Issues – Traditional inventory checks were slow and inaccurate.

To solve these issues, Walmart introduced a Kanban-based inventory management system to optimize stock levels, reduce waste, and improve supply chain efficiency.

? Kanban System Implementation at Walmart

1?? Just-in-Time (JIT) Inventory Replenishment

? Before: Walmart restocked stores based on estimated demand, leading to inefficiencies.

? Action Taken:

? Implemented RFID (Radio Frequency Identification) Kanban tags on products.

? Automated restocking based on real-time sales data.

? Result: Stockouts reduced by 30% and overstocking minimized.

2?? Kanban Cards for Shelf Replenishment

? Before: Employees manually checked shelves, often leading to delays.

? Action Taken:

? Introduced digital Kanban cards to signal low-stock levels instantly.

? Store associates received automated alerts for restocking.

? Result: Shelf replenishment became 40% faster, improving customer experience.

3?? Vendor-Managed Inventory (VMI) with Kanban

? Before: Suppliers delivered stock in bulk, causing storage issues.

? Action Taken:

? Used Kanban signals to notify suppliers when restocking was needed.

? Allowed vendors to manage inventory levels directly using real-time demand data.

? Result: Reduced excess inventory by 25% and improved supplier coordination.

4?? Lean Warehouse Operations

? Before: Warehouses were overcrowded with unsold products.

? Action Taken:

? Implemented Kanban-driven automated ordering based on store sales trends.

? Shifted to small, frequent deliveries instead of large bulk shipments.

? Result: Warehouse storage costs lowered by 35%, and distribution efficiency improved.

? Final Results After Implementing Kanban in Retail

? Stockouts reduced by 30%, ensuring better product availability.

? Shelf replenishment became 40% faster, enhancing customer satisfaction.

? Excess inventory cut by 25%, reducing waste and storage costs.

? Warehouse efficiency improved by 35%, lowering operational costs.

? Supplier coordination improved, leading to a smoother supply chain.

? Key Takeaways from This Case Study

✔? Kanban enables real-time stock tracking and prevents shortages.

✔? Automated replenishment reduces manual errors and inefficiencies.

✔? Vendor-Managed Inventory (VMI) improves supply chain collaboration.

✔? Lean warehouse operations lower storage costs and optimize distribution.

Other Retailers Using Kanban Systems

? Amazon: Uses AI-driven Kanban for real-time inventory tracking.

? Zara: Implements Just-in-Time fashion production using Kanban.

? Target: Uses automated Kanban alerts for store shelf restocking.

Case Study: Kanban System in Healthcare – Virginia Mason Medical Center

? Organization: Virginia Mason Medical Center (VMMC)

? Location: Seattle, USA

?? Industry: Healthcare & Hospital Management

? Challenge: Inefficient inventory management, medical supply shortages, and high operational costs.

? Problem Statement

Before implementing the Kanban system, Virginia Mason Medical Center (VMMC) faced critical challenges:
? Frequent medical supply shortages, delaying patient treatments.
? Overstocking of unused supplies, leading to waste and high storage costs.
? Time-consuming manual inventory tracking, causing inefficiencies.
? Delayed surgeries and procedures due to missing essential items.

To address these challenges, VMMC adopted the Kanban system, inspired by Toyota's lean manufacturing, to streamline medical supply management and improve patient care.

? Kanban System Implementation in Healthcare

1?? Two-Bin Kanban System for Medical Supplies

? Before: Nurses manually checked supply levels, leading to errors and delays.
? Action Taken:
? Introduced a two-bin Kanban system where each medical supply had two bins.
? When the first bin emptied, it triggered an automated reorder signal.
? The second bin ensured there was enough stock until replenishment arrived.
? Result: Medical supply shortages reduced by 60%, ensuring continuous availability.

2?? Just-in-Time (JIT) Restocking for Pharmacy Inventory

? Before: Excess medication was stocked, leading to waste and expiration.
? Action Taken:
? Implemented Kanban-based JIT inventory to order medicines only as needed.
? Used RFID and barcode tracking to monitor medicine usage in real time.
? Result: Pharmacy waste reduced by 50%, cutting costs and improving efficiency.

3?? Kanban for Operating Room (OR) Equipment

? Before: Surgeons faced delays due to missing surgical tools.
? Action Taken:
? Introduced Kanban cards to track surgical instruments and tools.
? Ensured real-time restocking of critical OR supplies before each procedure.
? Result: Surgery delays reduced by 35%, improving patient outcomes.

4?? Digital Kanban Boards for Patient Flow Management

? Before: Patients experienced long wait times due to scheduling inefficiencies.
? Action Taken:
? Used electronic Kanban boards to track patient progress through each department.
? Implemented real-time alerts for staff to prepare for incoming patients.
? Result: Patient wait times decreased by 40%, leading to faster treatment.

? Final Results After Implementing Kanban in Healthcare

? Medical supply shortages reduced by 60%, ensuring continuous availability.
? Pharmacy waste decreased by 50%, cutting costs.
? Surgery delays reduced by 35%, improving operating room efficiency.
? Patient wait times lowered by 40%, enhancing service quality.
? Nurse workload optimized, allowing more focus on patient care.

? Key Takeaways from This Case Study

✓? The two-bin Kanban system ensures uninterrupted medical supply availability.
✓? JIT inventory prevents overstocking and reduces medicine waste.
✓? Kanban cards streamline operating room procedures and minimize delays.
✓? Digital Kanban boards improve patient flow management and reduce wait times.

Other Healthcare Systems Using Kanban

? Mayo Clinic (USA): Uses Kanban for real-time patient flow tracking.
? Cleveland Clinic (USA): Implements JIT Kanban for pharmacy restocking.
? National Health Service (NHS, UK): Uses Kanban to manage medical equipment efficiently.

Case Study: Kanban System in Electronics – Dell's Just-in-Time Manufacturing

? Company: Dell Technologies

? Location: Global (Headquarters: USA)

? Industry: Electronics & Computer Manufacturing

? Challenge: High inventory costs, long production lead times, and inefficient supply chain management.

? Problem Statement

Before implementing the Kanban system, Dell faced several major issues in its electronics manufacturing process:

? Overstocked raw materials, increasing storage costs.

? Production delays due to inefficient component supply.

? Slow response to customer demand, leading to lost sales.

? Waste of obsolete electronic parts, impacting profitability.

To solve these challenges, Dell adopted the Kanban system with Just-in-Time (JIT) production, ensuring on-demand manufacturing and efficient inventory control.

? Kanban System Implementation in Dell's Electronics Manufacturing

1?? Kanban-Based Just-in-Time (JIT) Component Supply

? Before: Dell stored large quantities of electronic components in warehouses.

? Action Taken:

? Implemented Kanban cards to signal when new components were needed.

? Suppliers delivered parts only when an order was placed (JIT model).

? Result: Raw material inventory reduced by 50%, lowering storage costs.

2?? Kanban-Driven Production Scheduling

? Before: Production lines operated on forecasted demand, leading to excess products.

? Action Taken:

? Used digital Kanban boards to track real-time customer orders.

? Shifted to build-to-order manufacturing, where products were assembled only after an order was received.

? Result: Production lead times reduced by 40%, improving order fulfillment speed.

3?? Automated Inventory Replenishment Using RFID & IoT

? Before: Manual tracking of components led to errors and stockouts.

? Action Taken:

? Installed RFID and IoT sensors on component bins.

? When stock reached a minimum level, Kanban signals automatically reordered parts.

? Result: Stockouts decreased by 30%, preventing production stoppages.

4?? Kanban for Supplier Coordination

? Before: Dell's suppliers delivered components in bulk, causing inefficiencies.

? Action Taken:

? Implemented a Vendor-Managed Inventory (VMI) Kanban system.

? Suppliers could access Dell's real-time inventory data and ship parts only when needed.

? Result: Supply chain efficiency improved by 35%, reducing waste.

? Final Results After Implementing Kanban in Electronics

? Raw material inventory reduced by 50%, lowering storage costs.

? Production lead times shortened by 40%, increasing responsiveness to orders.

? Stockouts reduced by 30%, ensuring uninterrupted production.

? Supply chain efficiency improved by 35%, optimizing vendor coordination.

? Customer order fulfillment improved, boosting satisfaction and sales.

? Key Takeaways from This Case Study

✓? Kanban enables JIT production, reducing excess inventory and storage costs.

✓? Digital Kanban boards improve real-time production scheduling.

✓? RFID and IoT automation streamline component restocking.

✓? Supplier Kanban integration enhances supply chain coordination.

Other Electronics Companies Using Kanban

? Apple: Uses Kanban-based JIT manufacturing for iPhone production.

? Samsung: Implements Kanban-driven semiconductor supply chain management.

? Sony: Uses Kanban to track and optimize gaming console production.

The Kanban Transformation: A Small Business Success Story

In the bustling city of Seattle, a small electronics repair shop named "TechFix" was struggling to keep up with customer demands. Despite having skilled technicians and a steady flow of customers, the business often faced delays, misplaced orders, and inefficiencies in handling spare parts. This led to frustrated customers, increased costs, and lost opportunities.

One day, the shop's owner, Emily Carter, attended a workshop on lean manufacturing and was introduced to the Kanban system. Intrigued, she decided to implement Kanban in her store to streamline operations and reduce delays.

Step 1: Visualizing the Workflow

The first thing Emily did was set up a Kanban board on the shop's wall. She divided it into three sections: To-Do, In Progress, and Completed. Each customer repair request was written on a sticky note and moved across the board as it progressed. This simple system provided immediate visibility into ongoing repairs and eliminated confusion about which tasks needed priority.

Step 2: Managing Spare Parts Efficiently

One of TechFix's biggest problems was running out of essential spare parts or overstocking unnecessary ones. To fix this, Emily introduced a two-bin Kanban system for inventory management. Each part had two bins—when the first bin emptied, a Kanban card was sent to reorder the item before the second bin ran out. This ensured that necessary components were always available, without excessive stock taking up space.

Step 3: Limiting Work in Progress (WIP)

Before Kanban, technicians often worked on multiple devices at once, leading to unfinished repairs piling up. Emily set a WIP limit, allowing each technician to handle only two repairs at a time. This forced them to complete one task before moving to the next, increasing efficiency and reducing turnaround time.

Step 4: Continuous Improvement (Kaizen)

With Kanban in place, Emily encouraged her team to suggest improvements. Over time, they refined processes further—implementing a digital Kanban board, setting up automatic reorder triggers for critical spare parts, and tracking repair time metrics to identify bottlenecks.

The Outcome

Within six months, TechFix transformed its operations. ✓ Repair turnaround time reduced by 40% ✓ Customer satisfaction increased by 30% ✓ Inventory costs dropped by 25% ✓ Employee productivity improved significantly

What was once a chaotic repair shop became a smooth-running, customer-friendly business. Thanks to the power of Kanban, TechFix not only survived in a competitive market but also thrived.

Moral of the Story: A simple, structured approach like Kanban can bring clarity, efficiency, and growth to any business—big or small!

Lean Implementation: A Step-by-Step Guide

Lean implementation is the process of applying Lean principles to improve efficiency, reduce waste, and enhance value delivery in any organization. It is widely used in manufacturing, healthcare, logistics, construction, retail, and other industries to create a culture of continuous improvement.

? Key Steps for Implementing Lean

1?? Identify Value (Customer Needs First)

✓? Understand what customers value the most (e.g., speed, quality, affordability).

✓? Focus only on processes that add value and remove unnecessary steps.

? Example: In a car manufacturing plant, customers value fast delivery and durable cars—so Lean focuses on streamlining production while maintaining quality.

2?? Map the Value Stream (Find Waste)

✔? Create a Value Stream Map (VSM) to visualize the entire workflow.

✔? Identify all steps in a process and highlight wasteful activities (delays, excess inventory, overproduction).

? Example: A hospital maps the patient journey from check-in to discharge and finds that 50% of waiting time is due to slow documentation. Lean suggests digitizing records to reduce delays.

3?? Create Flow (Eliminate Bottlenecks)

✔? Ensure that work moves smoothly and continuously without interruptions.

✔? Reduce batch processing, excessive waiting, or unnecessary movement.

? Example: In an electronics factory, instead of waiting for 100 units to be assembled before testing, Lean suggests testing after every 10 units to detect defects early.

4?? Implement Pull System (Just-in-Time Production)

✔? Use a Kanban system to produce only what is needed, when it's needed.

✔? Prevent overproduction and reduce excess inventory.

? Example: A retail store uses RFID tags to track inventory and reorder products only when shelves reach a minimum level.

5?? Pursue Continuous Improvement (Kaizen)

✔? Engage employees at all levels to identify and solve problems daily.

✔? Implement small, incremental improvements instead of major changes.

? Example: A logistics company holds weekly Kaizen meetings, where drivers suggest ways to optimize delivery routes, saving fuel and time.

? Challenges in Lean Implementation

? Resistance to Change – Employees may be hesitant to adopt new methods.

? Lack of Leadership Support – Without management commitment, Lean fails.

? Poor Training – Employees need education on Lean tools and principles.

? Short-Term Focus – Lean is a long-term strategy, not a quick fix.

? Benefits of Lean Implementation

✔? Faster Processes – Reduced delays, optimized workflows.

✔? Lower Costs – Less waste, fewer defects, optimized inventory.

✔? Higher Quality – Continuous improvement leads to better products.

✔? Employee Engagement – Workers contribute to process improvements.

✔? Customer Satisfaction – Faster and better service delivery.

Industries Using Lean Implementation

? Manufacturing – Toyota, Ford, Boeing

? Healthcare – Mayo Clinic, NHS, Cleveland Clinic

? Retail – Walmart, Amazon, Zara

? Logistics – FedEx, UPS, DHL

? Construction – Lean-built hospitals, skyscrapers, and homes

The Lean Transformation: A Factory's Journey to Efficiency

In the industrial town of Greenville, "SwiftTech Manufacturing" was known for producing high-quality auto parts. However, over the years, inefficiencies crept into the factory's operations. Production delays, excessive inventory, and quality defects led to unhappy customers and rising costs. The company's CEO, Mark Reynolds, knew they needed a change. That's when he decided to implement Lean Manufacturing.

Step 1: Identifying Waste

Mark and his team conducted a Value Stream Mapping (VSM) exercise to analyze the production process. They identified seven key wastes: ✔ Overproduction – Parts were produced in excess, leading to storage issues. ✔ Waiting Time – Machines sat idle while workers waited for materials. ✔ Defects – Reworking faulty parts increased costs and delays. ✓ Unnecessary Motion – Workers walked long distances for tools and materials. ✓ Inventory Excess – Overstocking led to cash flow problems. ✓ Transportation Delays – Moving materials between departments wasted time. ✓ Underutilized Talent – Workers' improvement ideas were ignored.

Step 2: Implementing Lean Principles

With a clear understanding of the problem areas, SwiftTech introduced Lean tools: ✓ 5S Methodology – Workstations were cleaned, organized, and labeled to improve efficiency. ✓ Kanban System – A pull-based production system ensured parts were produced only when needed. ✓ Just-in-Time (JIT) Production – Inventory was minimized by synchronizing production with demand. ✓ Kaizen (Continuous Improvement) – Employees were encouraged to suggest small, incremental improvements. ✓ Standardized Work – Clear instructions and visual guides reduced errors and defects.

Step 3: Overcoming Resistance

Initially, some employees were resistant to change. To address this, Mark: ✓ Held training sessions to educate workers on Lean principles. ✓ Implemented an Employee Feedback System, making workers feel valued. ✓ Created a Lean Task Force consisting of frontline workers to monitor improvements.

Step 4: Measuring Results

Within six months, SwiftTech saw remarkable improvements: ✓ Production time reduced by 35% – Faster manufacturing cycles. ✓ Defect rate dropped by 50% – Better quality products. ✓ Inventory costs reduced by 40% – Less waste and improved cash flow. ✓ Employee morale improved – Workers felt engaged in decision-making. ✓ Customer satisfaction increased – Faster delivery and fewer complaints.

The Transformation

SwiftTech, once struggling with inefficiencies, became a model of Lean success. By eliminating waste, improving workflows, and engaging employees, the company not only survived but thrived in the competitive market.

Moral of the Story: Lean is not just about cutting costs; it's about maximizing value, efficiency, and continuous improvement!

Reconciling Lean with Other Systems

Lean manufacturing focuses on reducing waste, improving efficiency, and delivering value to customers. However, many organizations use other management systems alongside Lean, such as Six Sigma, Agile, Total Quality Management (TQM), and Industry 4.0. Reconciling Lean with these systems ensures seamless integration without conflict.

? How Lean Aligns with Other Systems

1?? Lean & Six Sigma (Lean Six Sigma)

✓ Lean eliminates waste and improves flow.

✓ Six Sigma reduces process variation and defects.

? Reconciliation: Lean Six Sigma (LSS) combines both approaches—Lean streamlines operations, and Six Sigma ensures high-quality results.

? Example: In automobile manufacturing, Lean eliminates unnecessary movement, while Six Sigma reduces defects in engine assembly.

2?? Lean & Agile

✓ Lean focuses on efficiency and waste reduction.

✓ Agile emphasizes flexibility and rapid iterations.

? Reconciliation: Lean improves processes, while Agile adapts to customer needs quickly. Together, they create Lean-Agile workflows in industries like software development and manufacturing.

? Example: In software development, Agile ensures fast delivery, while Lean removes redundant tasks in coding and testing.

3?? Lean & Total Quality Management (TQM)

✔ Lean improves workflow and efficiency.

✔ TQM focuses on overall quality across the organization.

? Reconciliation: Lean reduces process inefficiencies, while TQM ensures quality control throughout production.

? Example: In healthcare, Lean reduces patient waiting times, while TQM ensures quality treatment protocols.

4?? Lean & Industry 4.0 (Smart Manufacturing)

✔ Lean simplifies processes and minimizes waste.

✔ Industry 4.0 introduces automation, AI, IoT, and robotics for digital transformation.

? Reconciliation: Lean prevents complexity and inefficiencies in Industry 4.0, ensuring technology enhances value instead of creating new waste.

? Example: In electronics manufacturing, Lean reduces manual handling, while Industry 4.0 introduces AI-driven predictive maintenance for machines.

? Challenges in Reconciling Lean with Other Systems

? Conflicting Priorities – Some systems prioritize quality over speed.

? Resistance to Change – Employees may struggle with multiple methodologies.

? Complexity – Integrating too many systems can lead to inefficiencies.

? Best Practices for Integration

✔ Align Goals – Ensure Lean and other systems work toward a common objective.

✔ Train Employees – Educate teams on how methodologies complement each other.

✔ Use Data & Metrics – Measure improvements across all systems.

? Final Takeaway

Lean doesn't replace other systems—it enhances them. Organizations should combine Lean with Six Sigma, Agile, TQM, and Industry 4.0 based on their unique needs to maximize efficiency, quality, and customer satisfaction.

Lean Six Sigma: A Powerful Combination

Lean Six Sigma (LSS) is a hybrid methodology that combines Lean Manufacturing and Six Sigma to improve efficiency, reduce waste, and ensure high-quality outcomes. It is widely used in manufacturing, healthcare, logistics, finance, IT, and other industries.

? The Combination of Lean & Six Sigma

1?? Lean (Eliminating Waste)

✔? Focuses on removing waste (non-value-added activities) from processes.

✔? Aims to improve speed, efficiency, and resource utilization.

✔? Uses tools like 5S, Kanban, Value Stream Mapping (VSM), and Just-in-Time (JIT).

2?? Six Sigma (Reducing Variation)

✔? Focuses on minimizing defects and process variation.

✔? Uses data-driven decision-making to improve quality.

✔? Uses tools like DMAIC (Define, Measure, Analyze, Improve, Control) and statistical analysis.

? Reconciliation: Lean streamlines processes, while Six Sigma ensures consistent, high-quality outputs. Together, they create a fast, efficient, and defect-free system.

?? Lean Six Sigma Methodology

1?? **Define** – Identify the problem and customer needs.

2?? **Measure** – Collect data on the current process performance.

3?? **Analyze** – Find the root causes of waste and defects.

4?? **Improve** – Implement Lean and Six Sigma techniques to optimize processes.

5?? **Control** – Maintain improvements and prevent regression.

? Example: A hospital using Lean Six Sigma reduced patient wait times by 40% by eliminating redundant paperwork (Lean) and standardizing procedures (Six Sigma).

? Key Benefits of Lean Six Sigma

✓ Faster Processes – Eliminates delays and bottlenecks.

✓ Higher Quality – Reduces defects and improves consistency.

✓ Lower Costs – Minimizes waste and rework.

✓ Better Customer Satisfaction – Faster service and high-quality results.

✓ Employee Engagement – Encourages workers to identify improvements.

? Lean Six Sigma in Different Industries

? Manufacturing – Reducing defects in automotive production.

? Healthcare – Improving patient flow and reducing medical errors.

? Retail – Optimizing inventory management and checkout efficiency.

? Finance – Reducing loan processing time and fraud detection.

? IT & Software – Enhancing software development and bug resolution.

Case Study: Lean Six Sigma in the Automotive Industry

Toyota's Journey to Quality and Efficiency

Company: Toyota Motor Corporation

Challenge: Reduce manufacturing defects and optimize production time.

Methodology Used: Lean Six Sigma (LSS)

? The Problem: High Defect Rates & Inefficiencies

Toyota, a pioneer of Lean Manufacturing, faced defects in vehicle assembly, particularly in welding and painting processes. These defects led to:

? Increased rework costs.

? Production delays due to quality checks.

? Customer dissatisfaction due to product inconsistencies.

To address this, Toyota implemented Lean Six Sigma to improve quality and efficiency.

? Lean Six Sigma Implementation

1?? Define (Identify the Problem)

Toyota's Quality Control team identified high defect rates in car door assembly and welding, affecting overall production.

2?? Measure (Data Collection & Analysis)

✓ Measured defect rates per 1,000 units.

✓ Collected data on cycle times and production errors.

✓ Identified bottlenecks in the welding and painting process.

3?? Analyze (Finding Root Causes of Waste & Defects)

Using DMAIC & Value Stream Mapping, Toyota found that:

✓ 20% of defects were due to inconsistent welding temperatures.

✓ 15% of delays came from unnecessary movement of materials.

✓ 10% of quality issues were due to variation in supplier materials.

4?? Improve (Lean Six Sigma Solutions)

Toyota applied the following improvements:

✓ Lean: Used 5S (Sort, Set in Order, Shine, Standardize, Sustain) to organize workstations.

✓ Kanban System: Implemented a Just-in-Time (JIT) strategy to reduce material waste.

✓ Six Sigma: Standardized welding temperature controls to reduce variation.

✓ Automation: Introduced robotic welding for higher precision.

5?? Control (Sustaining the Improvements)

✓ Created visual dashboards to track defects and process efficiency.

✓ Implemented daily Kaizen meetings for continuous improvement.

✓ Trained employees in Lean Six Sigma tools to maintain improvements.

? Results & Impact

? Defect rates dropped by 55%.

? Production time reduced by 30% per vehicle.

? Customer complaints decreased by 40% due to better quality.

? Cost savings of $10 million annually by reducing waste and rework.

? Conclusion: A Model for the Automotive Industry

Toyota's Lean Six Sigma approach helped it achieve higher efficiency, better quality, and cost savings, reinforcing its reputation for manufacturing excellence. Today, Toyota continues to use Lean Six Sigma principles to drive innovation and maintain its competitive edge.

Case Study: Lean Six Sigma in the Food Industry

McDonald's Journey to Speed & Quality

Company: McDonald's Corporation

Challenge: Reduce service time and food waste while maintaining quality.

Methodology Used: Lean Six Sigma (LSS)

? The Problem: Long Wait Times & Food Waste

McDonald's, a global fast-food giant, faced the following challenges:

? Long customer wait times at peak hours.

? Excess food waste from unsold or incorrectly prepared meals.

? Inconsistent food quality due to variation in preparation processes.

To enhance customer satisfaction, reduce waste, and optimize service speed, McDonald's adopted Lean Six Sigma principles.

? Lean Six Sigma Implementation

1?? Define (Identifying the Issue)

The company conducted a Value Stream Mapping (VSM) to analyze order fulfillment times and food waste across multiple locations.

2?? Measure (Data Collection & Analysis)

✔ Tracked average order fulfillment time per store.

✔ Monitored food waste levels due to overproduction.

✔ Analyzed customer complaints related to speed and order accuracy.

3?? Analyze (Finding Root Causes of Waste & Delays)

Using DMAIC & Cause-and-Effect Analysis, McDonald's found that:

✔ 25% of delays were caused by inefficient kitchen workflows.

✔ 18% of food waste resulted from preparing meals in advance that were not ordered.

✔ 12% of customer complaints were due to incorrect orders caused by miscommunication.

4?? Improve (Lean Six Sigma Solutions)

✔ Lean: Implemented a "Made-for-You" kitchen system, switching from pre-prepared to on-demand food preparation to reduce waste.

✔ Kanban System: Used real-time order tracking to ensure ingredients were restocked efficiently.

✔ Six Sigma: Standardized food preparation steps to reduce variation in cooking times.

✔ Automation: Introduced self-order kiosks to reduce human errors and speed up orders.

5?? Control (Sustaining the Improvements)

✔ Introduced real-time performance tracking dashboards to monitor service speed.

✔ Conducted Lean Six Sigma training for kitchen staff to ensure consistency.

✔ Implemented Kaizen (Continuous Improvement) meetings to gather employee feedback on further optimizations.

? Results & Impact

? Order fulfillment time reduced by 40% (from 3 minutes to 1.8 minutes).

? Food waste decreased by 50%, saving millions annually.

? Customer satisfaction improved by 30% due to fresher food and faster service.

? Operational efficiency increased, allowing stores to serve more customers per hour.

? Conclusion: A Model for Fast-Food Efficiency

McDonald's Lean Six Sigma approach transformed its operations by balancing speed, quality, and waste reduction. The Made-for-You kitchen system, process standardization, and automation helped the company set industry benchmarks for efficiency.

Case Study: Lean Six Sigma in the Education Industry

Improving Student Enrollment & Administrative Efficiency at a University

Institution: University of Texas (Example)

Challenge: Reduce enrollment processing time, improve student satisfaction, and minimize administrative errors.

Methodology Used: Lean Six Sigma (LSS)

? The Problem: Slow Enrollment & Administrative Bottlenecks

The university faced several issues in its enrollment and administrative processes:

? Long processing times for student applications (4-6 weeks).

? High error rates in student records due to manual data entry.

? Low student satisfaction due to delays and inefficiencies.

To enhance efficiency, reduce errors, and improve student experience, the university adopted Lean Six Sigma principles.

? Lean Six Sigma Implementation

1?? Define (Identifying the Issue)

✓ Analyzed student complaints and process inefficiencies.

✓ Conducted Value Stream Mapping (VSM) to map the entire enrollment journey.

2?? Measure (Data Collection & Analysis)

✓ Measured the average time taken for application processing.

✓ Tracked the number of errors in student records.

✓ Analyzed dropout rates due to enrollment delays.

3?? Analyze (Finding Root Causes of Waste & Delays)

Using DMAIC & Cause-and-Effect Analysis, the university found that:

✓ 30% of delays were caused by manual document verification.

✓ 20% of errors resulted from miscommunication between departments.

✓ 15% of application rejections were due to incomplete or incorrect submissions.

4?? Improve (Lean Six Sigma Solutions)

✓ Lean: Digitized the enrollment process with online document submission & automated verification.

✓ Kanban System: Implemented real-time tracking for student applications.

✓ Six Sigma: Standardized application guidelines to reduce submission errors.

✓ Automation: Introduced AI chatbots & automated email responses for FAQs to reduce staff workload.

5?? Control (Sustaining the Improvements)

✓ Developed automated dashboards for tracking applications in real time.

✓ Provided Lean Six Sigma training to administrative staff.

✓ Introduced Kaizen (Continuous Improvement) feedback loops from students and faculty.

? Results & Impact

? Enrollment processing time reduced by 50% (from 6 weeks to 3 weeks).

? Data entry errors decreased by 60%, improving record accuracy.

? Student satisfaction improved by 35% due to faster response times.

? Administrative workload reduced, allowing staff to focus on student engagement.

? Conclusion: A Model for Educational Efficiency

The university's Lean Six Sigma approach improved efficiency in enrollment, student satisfaction, and administrative accuracy. Digital transformation, automation, and process standardization set a benchmark for modern universities.

Case Study: Lean Six Sigma in the Construction Industry

Reducing Project Delays & Material Waste in a High-Rise Building Project

Company: Turner Construction (Example)

Challenge: Reduce project delays, minimize material waste, and improve efficiency in high-rise construction.

Methodology Used: Lean Six Sigma (LSS)

?? The Problem: Delays & Waste in Construction

Turner Construction was facing significant project delays and material waste while constructing a 50-story commercial building. The key challenges were:

? Frequent delays due to inefficient scheduling and coordination.

? High material waste from over-ordering and poor handling.

? Cost overruns due to rework and unexpected expenses.

To enhance efficiency, reduce costs, and complete the project on time, the company adopted Lean Six Sigma.

? Lean Six Sigma Implementation

1?? Define (Identifying the Issue)

✓ Conducted a root cause analysis of delays and waste.

✓ Used Value Stream Mapping (VSM) to map out the construction workflow.

2?? Measure (Data Collection & Analysis)

✓ Measured the average delay time per project phase.

✓ Tracked material waste percentages per construction activity.

✓ Monitored rework instances and associated costs.

3?? Analyze (Finding Root Causes of Waste & Delays)

Using DMAIC & Cause-and-Effect Analysis, the company found that:

✓ 35% of delays were due to poor subcontractor scheduling.

✓ 20% of material waste was caused by over-ordering and damage on-site.

✓ 15% of rework resulted from miscommunication in design changes.

4?? Improve (Lean Six Sigma Solutions)

✓ Lean: Introduced Just-in-Time (JIT) material delivery to reduce inventory waste.

✓ Kanban System: Implemented real-time project tracking for better scheduling of subcontractors.

✓ Six Sigma: Standardized quality control procedures to minimize defects and rework.

✓ Automation: Adopted Building Information Modeling (BIM) for better design coordination and fewer errors.

5?? Control (Sustaining the Improvements)

✓ Implemented a digital dashboard for monitoring construction progress.

✓ Provided Lean Six Sigma training for project managers and subcontractors.

✓ Conducted Kaizen (Continuous Improvement) reviews to refine processes.

? Results & Impact

? Project completion time reduced by 25%, saving 6 months.

? Material waste decreased by 40%, lowering costs.

? Rework instances reduced by 30%, improving efficiency.

? Total project cost savings of $5 million through optimized resource use.

? Conclusion: A Model for Efficient Construction

By applying Lean Six Sigma, Turner Construction improved scheduling, material management, and quality control, ensuring faster project completion and reduced costs.

Case Study: Lean Six Sigma in the Electronics Industry

Reducing Defects & Improving Production Efficiency in Smartphone Manufacturing

Company: Samsung Electronics (Example)

Challenge: Reduce production defects and optimize assembly line efficiency.

Methodology Used: Lean Six Sigma (LSS)

? The Problem: High Defect Rates & Inefficiencies

Samsung's smartphone production facility was facing issues with high defect rates and assembly line inefficiencies, leading to:

? Increased rework & scrap costs due to faulty components.

? Production bottlenecks slowing down output.

? Customer complaints regarding device quality.

To enhance production speed, reduce waste, and improve product quality, Samsung implemented Lean Six Sigma.

? Lean Six Sigma Implementation

1?? Define (Identifying the Issue)

✓ Collected customer feedback & defect reports.

✓ Used Value Stream Mapping (VSM) to analyze assembly line inefficiencies.

2?? Measure (Data Collection & Analysis)

✓ Measured the defect rate per 1,000 units.

✓ Tracked cycle time per production stage.

✓ Monitored downtime due to machine breakdowns.

3?? Analyze (Finding Root Causes of Defects & Delays)

Using DMAIC & Cause-and-Effect Analysis, the company found that:

✓ 40% of defects were caused by improper soldering of circuit boards.

✓ 25% of production delays were due to unplanned machine maintenance.

✓ 15% of customer complaints resulted from battery overheating issues.

4?? Improve (Lean Six Sigma Solutions)

✓ Lean: Implemented automated robotic soldering to improve precision.

✓ Kanban System: Introduced real-time tracking of components to prevent shortages.

✓ Six Sigma: Standardized battery testing procedures to eliminate overheating defects.

✓ Automation: Upgraded predictive maintenance systems to reduce machine breakdowns.

5?? Control (Sustaining the Improvements)

✓ Implemented AI-powered defect detection for quality assurance.

✓ Trained employees in Lean Six Sigma principles for continuous monitoring.

✓ Conducted Kaizen (Continuous Improvement) workshops to refine processes.

? Results & Impact

? Defect rates reduced by 50%, improving product quality.

? Assembly line efficiency increased by 30%, reducing cycle time.

? Customer complaints decreased by 35%, boosting brand reputation.

? Annual cost savings of $15 million due to reduced rework & waste.

? Conclusion: A Model for Smart Manufacturing

By integrating Lean Six Sigma, Samsung achieved faster, high-quality smartphone production with minimal waste, strengthening its market competitiveness.

The Lean Six Sigma Transformation: A Factory's Journey to Excellence

In the heart of an industrial city, PrecisionTech Electronics, a mid-sized manufacturing company, was struggling. Their once-thriving business was now plagued by delayed shipments, high defect rates, and rising costs.

The CEO, Mark Reynolds, knew something had to change. Customers were unhappy, employees were frustrated, and profits were shrinking. That's when he heard about Lean Six Sigma.

The Crisis: A Factory on the Brink

PrecisionTech manufactured circuit boards for high-end medical devices. But over the past year:

? 20% of products had defects, leading to expensive rework.

? Delivery times had slipped from 3 weeks to 6 weeks, causing lost contracts.

? Employees felt overwhelmed, constantly rushing to fix mistakes.

During a tense management meeting, Mark asked his team, "Why are we failing?"

The answers were vague—"Too much waste," "Too many defects," "Not enough time."

Mark needed real data. He brought in Emma Carter, a Lean Six Sigma Black Belt, to turn things around.

Step 1: Define the Problem

Emma began by gathering data. Using Value Stream Mapping (VSM), she uncovered the biggest issues:

? Bottlenecks in assembly line 3, causing long delays.

? High defect rates in soldering, leading to rework and scrap.

? Excess inventory, tying up cash in unused materials.

She explained to the team, "Lean Six Sigma isn't just about cutting waste—it's about improving quality, speed, and efficiency."

Step 2: Measure & Analyze – Finding the Root Causes

Using DMAIC (Define, Measure, Analyze, Improve, Control), Emma and her team:

? Tracked production times, revealing inefficiencies in machine setup.

? Used Fishbone Diagrams to find that poor soldering was due to temperature inconsistencies.

? Conducted a Pareto Analysis, showing that 80% of defects came from just two steps in production.

The biggest aha! moment came when they discovered:

? Workers were skipping machine calibrations to "save time," but it led to more defects.

? Too many unfinished circuit boards were piling up, delaying final assembly.

Step 3: Improve – The Lean Six Sigma Fix

The team implemented several Lean Six Sigma solutions:

✔ Standardized machine calibration to prevent defects.

✔ Kanban system to reduce excess inventory and ensure smooth material flow.

✔ Automated temperature control in soldering to maintain consistency.

✔ Reorganized workstations using 5S (Sort, Set in Order, Shine, Standardize, Sustain) to reduce motion waste.

At first, workers resisted the changes. "We've always done it this way," they said. But once they saw how small tweaks reduced errors and stress, they embraced the system.

Step 4: Control – Sustaining the Gains

To keep improvements in place, PrecisionTech:

? Created real-time dashboards to track defects and efficiency.

? Held weekly Kaizen meetings for continuous improvement.

? Trained employees in Lean Six Sigma, empowering them to solve problems proactively.

The Results: A Factory Reborn

Three months later, the numbers spoke for themselves:

? Defects dropped by 60%, improving product reliability.

? Delivery times shrank from 6 weeks to 2.5 weeks.

? Waste reduced by 40%, saving $2 million annually.

? Customer satisfaction skyrocketed, leading to new contracts and growth.

Mark stood in front of his team and said, "We're not just working harder—we're working smarter."

PrecisionTech was no longer just surviving—they were thriving, thanks to Lean Six Sigma.

Conclusion: A Lesson in Continuous Improvement

Lean Six Sigma isn't a one-time fix—it's a mindset. By focusing on data-driven decisions, eliminating waste, and empowering employees, any company can achieve excellence and sustained success.

Lean and ERP: How They Work Together

Lean Manufacturing and Enterprise Resource Planning (ERP) are two powerful strategies used to improve efficiency, reduce waste, and optimize business operations. However, they serve different purposes and can sometimes seem at odds with each other.

? Lean focuses on reducing waste and improving efficiency in production and business processes.

? ERP focuses on integrating and automating business functions such as inventory, procurement, finance, and production planning.

When properly integrated, Lean and ERP can complement each other, leading to better efficiency, reduced costs, and enhanced decision-making.

? How ERP Supports Lean Manufacturing

While Lean focuses on reducing waste and improving processes, ERP provides real-time data and automation to support Lean initiatives.

? Better Inventory Management → ERP helps track stock levels in real time, supporting Just-in-Time (JIT) production.

? Real-Time Decision Making → Lean requires fast responses, and ERP provides instant access to data for quick decisions.

? Automation of Routine Tasks → Lean eliminates waste; ERP reduces waste by automating processes like order processing and scheduling.

? Supply Chain Optimization → ERP ensures that suppliers deliver materials exactly when needed, aligning with Lean's pull system.

? Case Study: Lean + ERP in Action (Automotive Industry)

Company: Toyota (Known for Lean Manufacturing)

Challenge: Improve production efficiency and reduce delays.

Solution: Toyota integrated Lean principles with an ERP system to optimize scheduling, procurement, and logistics.

Results:

? Reduced production lead time by 30%.

? Lowered inventory costs by 40%.

? Improved supplier coordination for faster Just-in-Time (JIT) delivery.

? Best Practices for Integrating Lean & ERP

? Align ERP with Lean goals → Avoid overcomplicating processes with excessive automation.

? Use ERP for data-driven Lean decisions → Leverage real-time insights for continuous improvement.

? Ensure ERP supports Just-in-Time (JIT) → Optimize procurement, inventory, and scheduling.

? Train employees → Ensure teams understand how Lean and ERP work together.

? Conclusion: A Powerful Combination

By integrating Lean principles with ERP systems, companies can achieve greater efficiency, lower costs, and faster production cycles. While Lean reduces waste, ERP enhances visibility and control, making them a perfect match for modern manufacturing and business operations.

Case Study: Lean & ERP in the Education Industry

Improving University Operations with Lean & ERP

Institution: XYZ University (Example)

Challenge: Streamlining student admissions, reducing administrative waste, and optimizing resource allocation.

Solution: Implemented Lean principles to eliminate inefficiencies and an ERP system to integrate data across departments.

? The Problem: Inefficiencies in University Operations

XYZ University was struggling with:

? Delayed student admissions due to manual processes.

? Overbooked classrooms while other spaces remained underutilized.

? Slow financial processing, causing budget inefficiencies.

The administration sought a solution to reduce delays, optimize resource use, and improve student experience.

? Lean & ERP Implementation

? 1?? Lean Analysis (Identifying Waste)

✓ Used Value Stream Mapping (VSM) to track bottlenecks in student registration.

✓ Applied 5S principles to streamline administrative workflows.

✓ Identified excess paperwork and unnecessary approval steps.

? 2?? ERP System Integration

✓ Automated student enrollment, class scheduling, and faculty assignments.

✓ Linked finance, HR, and student data for real-time insights.

✓ Integrated Just-in-Time (JIT) resource allocation for classrooms and teaching staff.

? 3?? Continuous Improvement with Lean Six Sigma

✓ Used data analytics from ERP to improve resource planning.

✓ Trained staff in Kaizen (continuous improvement) to reduce inefficiencies.

? Results & Impact

? Student enrollment processing time reduced by 50%.

? Classroom utilization improved by 35%, reducing scheduling conflicts.

? Administrative costs lowered by 25% due to paperless processes.

? Improved student satisfaction, leading to higher enrollment.

? Conclusion: A Smarter Education System

By integrating Lean principles with an ERP system, XYZ University optimized administrative efficiency, student services, and resource management, creating a better experience for students and faculty.

Case Study: Lean & ERP in the Food Industry

Optimizing Food Production & Supply Chain Efficiency

Company: FreshBites Food Co. (Example)

Challenge: Reducing food waste, optimizing inventory management, and improving production efficiency.

Solution: Implemented Lean principles to eliminate inefficiencies and an ERP system to integrate supply chain, inventory, and production planning.

? The Problem: Food Waste & Supply Chain Delays

FreshBites, a mid-sized food processing company, was struggling with:

? Excess inventory leading to food spoilage and waste.

? Production bottlenecks causing delays in order fulfillment.

? Poor coordination between suppliers, production, and distribution.

To maintain profitability and sustainability, the company needed to reduce waste, streamline operations, and improve supply chain management.

? Lean & ERP Implementation

? 1?? Lean Analysis (Identifying Waste)

✓ Used Value Stream Mapping (VSM) to pinpoint inefficiencies in the supply chain.

✓ Applied Just-in-Time (JIT) principles to reduce excess inventory.

✓ Implemented 5S methodology to organize workspaces and improve production flow.

? 2?? ERP System Integration

✓ Automated real-time inventory tracking, reducing overstocking and waste.

✓ Integrated supplier and order management, ensuring smooth material flow.

✓ Implemented predictive analytics for demand forecasting, reducing spoilage.

? 3?? Continuous Improvement with Lean Six Sigma

✓ Used ERP data analytics to adjust production scheduling based on real-time demand.

✓ Improved order accuracy and on-time deliveries through process automation.

✓ Trained staff on Kaizen (continuous improvement) to maintain efficiency gains.

? Results & Impact

? Food waste reduced by 40%, improving sustainability.

? Inventory costs lowered by 30% through JIT and real-time tracking.

? Order fulfillment rate increased to 98%, enhancing customer satisfaction.

? Production efficiency improved by 25%, leading to higher profitability.

? Conclusion: A Smarter, Leaner Food Industry

By integrating Lean Manufacturing with an ERP system, FreshBites optimized food production, reduced waste, and improved supply chain coordination, creating a more sustainable and profitable business.

Case Study: Lean & ERP in the Electronics Industry

Optimizing Production and Supply Chain in an Electronics Manufacturer

Company: VoltTech Electronics (Example)

Challenge: Reducing production delays, minimizing excess inventory, and improving supply chain efficiency.

Solution: Implemented Lean principles to eliminate inefficiencies and an ERP system to integrate supply chain, inventory, and production planning.

? The Problem: Inefficient Production & Supply Chain Gaps

VoltTech, a leading manufacturer of circuit boards and electronic components, was struggling with:

? Excess raw material inventory causing high storage costs.

? Frequent production bottlenecks due to uncoordinated workflows.

? Delayed shipments because of supply chain mismanagement.

To remain competitive, the company needed to streamline production, optimize inventory management, and improve supply chain efficiency.

? Lean & ERP Implementation

? 1?? Lean Analysis (Identifying Waste)

✔ Used Value Stream Mapping (VSM) to analyze inefficiencies in material flow.

✔ Applied Just-in-Time (JIT) principles to reduce excess raw material inventory.

✔ Implemented 5S methodology to organize workstations for efficiency.

? 2?? ERP System Integration

✔ Automated real-time inventory tracking, reducing overstocking and shortages.

✔ Integrated supplier, production, and distribution data for seamless coordination.

✔ Implemented predictive analytics to forecast demand accurately.

? 3?? Continuous Improvement with Lean Six Sigma

✔ Used ERP data to adjust production schedules in real-time.

✔ Improved quality control with automated defect detection.

✔ Trained employees on Kaizen (continuous improvement) to sustain progress.

? Results & Impact

? Inventory costs reduced by 35% through JIT and ERP tracking.

? Production downtime decreased by 25%, improving efficiency.

? Order fulfillment accuracy increased to 99%, enhancing customer trust.

? Waste and rework reduced by 40%, leading to cost savings.

? Conclusion: A Smarter Electronics Manufacturer

By integrating Lean Manufacturing with an ERP system, VoltTech improved efficiency, reduced waste, and enhanced supply chain coordination, leading to higher profitability and customer satisfaction.

Case Study: Lean & ERP in the Construction Industry

Improving Project Efficiency and Cost Control in a Construction Firm

Company: BuildRight Constructions (Example)

Challenge: Reducing material waste, improving project scheduling, and enhancing supply chain management.

Solution: Implemented Lean Construction principles to eliminate inefficiencies and an ERP system to integrate project planning, inventory, and workforce management.

? The Problem: Delays, Waste, and Cost Overruns

BuildRight Constructions, a mid-sized construction firm, was facing:

? Frequent project delays due to poor scheduling and material shortages.

? Excess material waste, increasing project costs.

? Poor communication between teams, leading to errors and rework.

To remain profitable and competitive, they needed to streamline project planning, reduce waste, and improve efficiency.

? Lean & ERP Implementation

? 1?? Lean Analysis (Identifying Waste)

✔ Used Value Stream Mapping (VSM) to find inefficiencies in construction workflows.

✔ Applied Just-in-Time (JIT) principles to reduce material overordering.

✔ Implemented 5S methodology at construction sites to organize tools and materials efficiently.

? 2?? ERP System Integration

✔ Automated real-time inventory tracking to avoid shortages or excess stock.

✔ Integrated project scheduling, procurement, and workforce management.

✔ Implemented predictive analytics to optimize resource allocation.

? 3?? Continuous Improvement with Lean Six Sigma

✔ Used ERP data to improve project timelines and reduce bottlenecks.

✔ Standardized quality control processes to reduce defects and rework.

✔ Trained teams in Kaizen (continuous improvement) to sustain efficiency.

? Results & Impact

? Project completion time reduced by 30% due to better scheduling.

? Material waste decreased by 40%, leading to major cost savings.

? Labor productivity improved by 25%, reducing downtime.

? Construction rework decreased by 35%, enhancing quality and efficiency.

? Conclusion: A Smarter Construction Industry

By integrating Lean Construction principles with an ERP system, BuildRight Constructions improved project efficiency, reduced waste, and enhanced coordination, leading to faster, cost-effective, and high-quality project completion.

Lean Manufacturing & ISO 9001:2000: A Synergistic Approach

Lean Manufacturing and ISO 9001:2000 share a common goal: improving efficiency, reducing waste, and enhancing quality. While Lean focuses on eliminating non-value-added activities, ISO 9001:2000 establishes a standardized quality management system (QMS) to ensure consistent product and service quality.

When combined, Lean and ISO 9001:2000 create a powerful framework that helps organizations achieve operational excellence, customer satisfaction, and continuous improvement.

? What is ISO 9001:2000?

ISO 9001:2000 is a quality management standard that defines principles for:

? Customer Focus – Meeting customer needs and improving satisfaction.

? Process Approach – Standardizing operations to ensure quality and efficiency.

? Continuous Improvement – Using data and feedback to enhance processes.

? Fact-Based Decision Making – Using real-time data for better management.

? Integrating Lean with ISO 9001:2000

? 1?? Define & Standardize Processes – Use ISO 9001:2000 guidelines to document Lean workflows.

? 2?? Identify & Eliminate Waste – Use Lean tools like Value Stream Mapping (VSM) to remove non-value-added steps.

? 3?? Continuous Improvement (Kaizen) – Apply ISO's Plan-Do-Check-Act (PDCA) cycle with Lean's Kaizen approach.

? 4?? Improve Quality & Customer Focus – Use Lean Six Sigma and ISO quality controls for defect reduction.

? 5?? Data-Driven Decision Making – Use ERP and ISO-compliant documentation for tracking performance.

? Case Study: Lean & ISO 9001:2000 in Automotive Industry

Company: Toyota

Challenge: Improve production quality while reducing waste.

Solution:

✔ Implemented ISO 9001:2000 to ensure quality standards in production.

✔ Used Lean Manufacturing (JIT, Kanban) to reduce waste and improve efficiency.

✔ Integrated Kaizen and PDCA for continuous improvement.

Results:

? Defect rate reduced by 50%.

? Production lead time shortened by 30%.

? Customer complaints decreased by 40%.

? Conclusion: A Perfect Combination

By integrating Lean Manufacturing with ISO 9001:2000, companies can achieve higher efficiency, reduced costs, improved quality, and enhanced customer satisfaction.

Case Study: Lean & ISO 9001:2000 in the Education Industry

Enhancing Quality and Efficiency in a University

Institution: ABC University (Example)

Challenge: Improving administrative efficiency, reducing student processing delays, and ensuring high-quality education standards.

Solution: Implemented Lean principles to eliminate inefficiencies and ISO 9001:2000 to establish a quality management system (QMS) for education and administration.

? The Problem: Inefficient Administration & Lack of Standardization

ABC University faced several issues:

? Delayed student admissions due to excessive paperwork.

? Inefficient course scheduling, leading to overcrowded or underutilized classrooms.

? Lack of standardized teaching processes, causing inconsistencies in education quality.

? Slow response to student concerns due to unstructured feedback mechanisms.

To improve efficiency and quality, the university decided to implement Lean principles along with ISO 9001:2000 certification.

? Lean & ISO 9001:2000 Implementation

? 1?? Lean Analysis (Identifying Waste & Bottlenecks)

✔ Used Value Stream Mapping (VSM) to find inefficiencies in student enrollment.

✔ Applied 5S methodology to organize administrative offices and digitalize records.

✔ Implemented Just-in-Time (JIT) scheduling to optimize classroom use.

? 2?? ISO 9001:2000 Implementation

✔ Standardized student enrollment, course management, and faculty evaluation.

✔ Established clear quality objectives for teaching and student services.

✔ Created a documented process for student feedback and corrective actions.

? 3?? Continuous Improvement with Kaizen & PDCA

✔ Applied Plan-Do-Check-Act (PDCA) cycle to refine administrative processes.

✔ Conducted regular audits and faculty training for quality assurance.

✔ Integrated data-driven decision-making using an ERP system for tracking student progress.

? Results & Impact

? Student admission processing time reduced by 50%, improving experience.

? Classroom utilization improved by 40%, leading to better resource management.

? Standardized teaching practices, enhancing education quality.

? Student satisfaction increased by 30%, due to faster response times.

? Conclusion: A Lean & Quality-Focused Education System

By combining Lean principles with ISO 9001:2000, ABC University streamlined administration, improved teaching standards, and enhanced student satisfaction.

Case Study: Lean & ISO 9001:2000 in the Food Industry

Improving Quality and Efficiency in a Food Processing Company

Company: FreshDelight Foods (Example)

Challenge: Reducing food waste, improving production efficiency, and ensuring high-quality standards.

Solution: Implemented Lean Manufacturing to eliminate inefficiencies and ISO 9001:2000 to establish a standardized Quality Management System (QMS).

? The Problem: Inefficiencies in Food Production & Quality Control

FreshDelight Foods, a mid-sized packaged food manufacturer, faced:

? High food waste due to overproduction and spoilage.

? Inconsistent product quality, leading to customer complaints.

? Slow production cycles causing delayed deliveries.

? Lack of standardized hygiene and quality protocols, affecting compliance.

To maintain profitability and food safety standards, the company implemented Lean principles and ISO 9001:2000.

? Lean & ISO 9001:2000 Implementation

? 1?? Lean Analysis (Identifying Waste & Bottlenecks)

✓ Used Value Stream Mapping (VSM) to optimize raw material usage and reduce waste.

✓ Applied 5S methodology to organize workstations and ensure hygiene.

✓ Implemented Just-in-Time (JIT) production to prevent overproduction and spoilage.

? 2?? ISO 9001:2000 Implementation

✓ Standardized quality control procedures, ensuring consistent taste and safety.

✓ Implemented HACCP (Hazard Analysis and Critical Control Points) for food safety compliance.

✓ Developed a traceability system to track ingredients and finished products.

? 3?? Continuous Improvement with Kaizen & PDCA

✓ Used the Plan-Do-Check-Act (PDCA) cycle to refine production processes.

✓ Conducted regular audits and training for staff on hygiene and safety.

✓ Integrated data-driven decision-making to monitor product defects and reduce waste.

? Results & Impact

? Food waste reduced by 45%, lowering costs and improving sustainability.

? Production efficiency increased by 30%, enabling faster deliveries.

? Customer complaints decreased by 40%, due to consistent product quality.

? Compliance with food safety regulations improved, reducing legal risks.

? Conclusion: A More Efficient & Quality-Focused Food Industry

By integrating Lean Manufacturing with ISO 9001:2000, FreshDelight Foods optimized food production, ensured high-quality standards, and improved operational efficiency, leading to cost savings and customer satisfaction.

Case Study: Lean & ISO 9001:2000 in the Electronics Industry

Enhancing Quality and Efficiency in an Electronics Manufacturing Company

Company: ElectroTech Solutions (Example)

Challenge: Reducing defects, improving production efficiency, and ensuring compliance with international quality standards.

Solution: Implemented Lean Manufacturing to eliminate inefficiencies and ISO 9001:2000 to establish a standardized Quality Management System (QMS).

? The Problem: Defects, Production Delays & High Costs

ElectroTech Solutions, a mid-sized manufacturer of circuit boards and consumer electronics, faced:

? High defect rates leading to customer complaints and rework.

? Production bottlenecks causing delays in order fulfillment.

? Excess inventory of raw materials, increasing storage costs.

? Inconsistent quality control, leading to product recalls and reputational damage.

To remain competitive in the electronics market, the company adopted Lean principles alongside ISO 9001:2000 certification.

? Lean & ISO 9001:2000 Implementation

? 1?? Lean Analysis (Identifying Waste & Inefficiencies)

✓ Used Value Stream Mapping (VSM) to identify delays in assembly and testing.

✓ Applied 5S methodology to organize workstations and improve workflow efficiency.

✓ Implemented Just-in-Time (JIT) inventory management to reduce excess stock.

? 2?? ISO 9001:2000 Implementation

✓ Standardized assembly and quality control procedures to minimize defects.

✓ Implemented real-time defect tracking to detect and eliminate errors early.

✓ Established a supplier quality management system to ensure consistent raw materials.

? 3?? Continuous Improvement with Kaizen & PDCA

✓ Used Plan-Do-Check-Act (PDCA) to refine manufacturing processes.

✓ Conducted regular quality audits and employee training on ISO 9001 standards.

✓ Implemented automated testing & data-driven decision-making for quality control.

? Results & Impact

? Defect rate reduced by 50%, improving product reliability.

? Production efficiency increased by 35%, reducing lead times.

? Inventory costs lowered by 40%, thanks to JIT implementation.

? Customer complaints decreased by 45%, boosting brand reputation.

? Conclusion: A Smarter, More Efficient Electronics Manufacturer

By integrating Lean Manufacturing with ISO 9001:2000, ElectroTech Solutions optimized production, minimized defects, and improved operational efficiency, leading to higher profitability and customer satisfaction.

CHAPTER SEVEN

Agile Manufacturing

Agile Manufacturing vs Mass Manufacturing

Agile manufacturing and mass manufacturing represent two distinct approaches to production, each with its own advantages and applications. Mass manufacturing is a traditional production method that focuses on large-scale, standardized production of identical goods, often using highly automated assembly lines to maximize efficiency and minimize costs. This approach is ideal for industries that require high-volume production with minimal variation, such as automobile or consumer electronics manufacturing. In contrast, agile manufacturing is a more flexible and adaptive strategy that prioritizes responsiveness to market demands, customization, and rapid innovation. Agile manufacturing leverages advanced technologies like robotics, modular production systems, and data analytics to enable quick adjustments to design, production processes, or supply chains. While mass manufacturing emphasizes economies of scale and cost reduction, agile manufacturing focuses on adaptability and meeting diverse customer needs efficiently. As a result, companies employing agile manufacturing can quickly pivot to new products or market trends, whereas mass manufacturing excels in producing consistent, high-quality products at lower costs.

Agile Practice for Product Development: Case Studies

Agile practices in product development emphasize flexibility, iterative progress, and customer collaboration. Here are two real-world case studies showcasing how Agile methodologies have been successfully implemented in different industries.

Case Study 1: Tesla's Agile Approach to Vehicle Development

Industry: Automotive

Challenge: Traditional car manufacturing follows a rigid waterfall approach, with long development cycles and limited adaptability to technological advancements or customer feedback. Tesla needed a more dynamic approach to compete with established automakers.

Agile Implementation:

Tesla adopted an iterative design process that allowed them to continuously improve their vehicles through over-the-air (OTA) software updates.

Instead of waiting for a full product lifecycle to release improvements, Tesla gathers real-time customer data and updates vehicle software accordingly.

The company uses cross-functional teams for rapid prototyping, integrating software and hardware development simultaneously.

Results:

Faster product releases and improvements compared to traditional automakers.

Enhanced customer experience through regular feature updates.

Increased adaptability to market changes, such as introducing new autonomous driving features.

Case Study 2: Spotify's Agile Squads for Product Development

Industry: Music Streaming & Software

Challenge: As a digital music platform, Spotify needed to continuously innovate and improve user experience while scaling its platform. Traditional project management models were too slow for their fast-paced industry.

Agile Implementation:

Spotify adopted a Squad-based Agile model, where small, autonomous teams (Squads) worked on specific features like recommendations, search, and UI enhancements.

Each Squad had end-to-end responsibility for their feature, following Scrum and Kanban practices.

Regular sprint cycles ensured continuous iteration based on user feedback and data-driven insights.

Results:

Faster feature rollouts, such as personalized playlists (e.g., Discover Weekly).

Increased innovation, as teams could experiment and pivot quickly.

A scalable, self-sufficient product development framework that supported Spotify's global growth.

Conclusion

Both Tesla and Spotify demonstrate how Agile methodologies drive innovation and responsiveness in product development. Tesla's Agile approach allows continuous vehicle improvement, while Spotify's Squad-based Agile model accelerates digital innovation. These case studies highlight how Agile practices lead to better customer experiences, quicker time-to-market, and competitive advantage in dynamic industries.

Manufacturing Agile Practices

Agile manufacturing is a modern approach that focuses on flexibility, responsiveness, and efficiency in production. Unlike traditional mass manufacturing, which prioritizes economies of scale, agile manufacturing enables companies to quickly adapt to market demands, customer preferences, and technological advancements. Here are some key agile practices used in manufacturing:

1. Modular Production Systems

Manufacturing lines are designed with modular workstations that can be quickly reconfigured for different products.

This allows manufacturers to switch between product variants without significant downtime.

Example: Boeing uses modular production for assembling different aircraft models based on customer needs.

2. Lean Manufacturing & Just-in-Time (JIT) Production

Focuses on minimizing waste, reducing inventory, and ensuring materials arrive just in time for production.

Eliminates excess stock and improves efficiency.

Example: Toyota Production System (TPS) applies JIT to streamline manufacturing and reduce lead times.

3. Digital Twin & Smart Manufacturing

Uses real-time data, sensors, and AI simulations to create digital models of physical manufacturing processes.

Helps manufacturers predict issues, optimize production, and improve quality control before actual production starts.

Example: Siemens employs digital twin technology to simulate and refine production processes.

4. Agile Supply Chain Management

Supply chains are designed to be flexible and responsive, allowing manufacturers to quickly switch suppliers or adjust production levels.

Incorporates cloud-based systems and predictive analytics for real-time decision-making.

Example: Apple dynamically adjusts its supply chain to handle fluctuations in iPhone demand.

5. Cross-Functional & Self-Managing Teams

Small, autonomous teams collaborate across departments (design, production, and quality control) to make quick decisions.

Encourages continuous improvement and rapid iteration of product designs.

Example: Tesla integrates hardware and software teams to ensure seamless updates and innovations.

6. Additive Manufacturing (3D Printing)

Enables rapid prototyping and low-volume production without requiring expensive molds or tooling.

Reduces lead times and allows for on-demand manufacturing of customized parts.

Example: General Electric (GE) uses 3D printing for producing complex jet engine components.

7. Continuous Improvement & Iterative Development

Agile manufacturing promotes a culture of continuous learning and process optimization (Kaizen).

Regular feedback loops and short production cycles ensure ongoing improvements.

Example: Ford uses Agile methodologies to enhance production processes and integrate new technologies faster.

Conclusion

Agile manufacturing enables companies to produce high-quality, customized products efficiently while staying adaptable to market changes. By leveraging modular production, smart technologies, and lean principles, manufacturers can remain competitive and innovative in today's dynamic environment.

Implementing New Technology in Agile Manufacturing

Agile manufacturing thrives on flexibility, responsiveness, and continuous innovation, making the integration of new technologies essential for maintaining a competitive edge. Implementing new technology in agile manufacturing involves a structured yet adaptable approach to ensure seamless adoption without disrupting production.

Key Steps in Implementing New Technology

1. Identify the Right Technology

Assess business needs, production challenges, and customer demands.

Choose technologies that enhance flexibility, efficiency, and responsiveness.

Example: A company facing delays in supply chain management might implement AI-powered predictive analytics to optimize inventory control.

2. Pilot Testing & Iterative Development

Start with a small-scale pilot program before full implementation.

Use Agile methodologies like Scrum or Kanban to test and refine the technology in short sprints.

Example: A manufacturer introducing collaborative robots (cobots) can deploy them in a single workstation to evaluate performance before expanding.

3. Cross-Functional Collaboration

Involve design, production, IT, and supply chain teams to ensure seamless integration.

Encourage feedback loops to identify challenges and make quick adjustments.

Example: When integrating Industrial IoT (IIoT) sensors for real-time machine monitoring, collaboration between engineers and data analysts ensures proper data utilization.

4. Smart Data Integration & Digital Twins

Implement cloud-based platforms and AI-driven analytics to connect machines, processes, and supply chains.

Use Digital Twins (virtual models of production systems) to simulate and optimize before full-scale deployment.

Example: Siemens uses digital twin technology to predict failures and optimize factory layouts before physical implementation.

5. Lean & Scalable Deployment

Deploy technology in phases, ensuring minimal disruption to production.

Adopt scalable solutions that allow gradual expansion based on business needs.

Example: A company introducing 3D printing for prototyping can later scale it for small-batch production.

6. Continuous Training & Skill Development

Provide hands-on training programs for workers to adapt to new technologies.

Encourage a culture of continuous learning and upskilling.

Example: Automotive manufacturers implementing AI-driven quality inspection systems train workers to interpret AI reports and make data-driven decisions.

7. Agile Supply Chain & Vendor Collaboration

Ensure suppliers and partners are also agile-ready to support the new technology.

Establish real-time communication networks for better coordination.

Example: Tesla integrates software updates and manufacturing process changes quickly by maintaining strong digital connections with suppliers.

Technologies Transforming Agile Manufacturing

Industrial IoT (IIoT) – Enables real-time monitoring, predictive maintenance, and data-driven decision-making.

AI & Machine Learning – Improves demand forecasting, defect detection, and process automation.

3D Printing (Additive Manufacturing) – Supports rapid prototyping and custom manufacturing with minimal waste.

Digital Twin Technology – Allows simulation and optimization of production processes before real-world implementation.

Cobots (Collaborative Robots) – Enhance human-machine collaboration, increasing efficiency and safety.

Blockchain – Ensures transparent and secure supply chain management.

Conclusion

Implementing new technology in agile manufacturing requires a step-by-step, iterative approach that emphasizes pilot testing, cross-functional collaboration, and scalable deployment. By integrating AI, IoT, digital twins, and automation, manufacturers can enhance flexibility, reduce downtime, and improve overall efficiency, ensuring they stay ahead in an increasingly competitive market.

Checklist: Technology Applications for Enhancing Agility in Agile Manufacturing

Agile manufacturing relies on cutting-edge technology to improve flexibility, efficiency, and responsiveness. Below is a checklist of key technologies and their applications that enhance agility in manufacturing.

? Checklist for Implementing Agile Technology in Manufacturing

1. Smart Production & Automation

✓ Industrial IoT (IIoT) – Real-time machine monitoring, predictive maintenance.

✓ Collaborative Robots (Cobots) – Work alongside humans to enhance flexibility.

✓ Autonomous Mobile Robots (AMRs) – Adaptive material handling in dynamic environments.

✓ AI & Machine Learning – Automated defect detection, demand forecasting, and process optimization.

2. Digitalization & Connectivity

✓ Digital Twin Technology – Virtual simulations for optimizing production lines before implementation.

✓ Cloud Computing & Edge Computing – Enables real-time data processing and remote monitoring.

✓ Blockchain for Supply Chain – Enhances transparency, security, and traceability.

✓ 5G & Industrial Wireless Networks – Enables ultra-fast, low-latency data transfer for real-time communication.

3. Agile Manufacturing & Rapid Prototyping

✓ 3D Printing (Additive Manufacturing) – Supports rapid prototyping and small-batch production.

✓ Computer-Aided Design (CAD) & Simulation – Accelerates design iteration and reduces development time.

✓ Augmented Reality (AR) & Virtual Reality (VR) – Improves worker training, remote troubleshooting, and digital assembly guidance.

4. Smart Supply Chain & Inventory Management

✓ AI-Driven Demand Forecasting – Minimizes overproduction and reduces lead times.

✓ Automated Warehouse Systems – Uses AI and robotics for real-time inventory tracking and efficient logistics.

✓ Just-in-Time (JIT) & Lean Manufacturing Systems – Reduces waste and optimizes material flow.

✓ Cloud-Based ERP & MES (Manufacturing Execution System) – Streamlines production planning and real-time decision-making.

5. Workforce Empowerment & Digital Collaboration

✓ Wearable Technology & Smart Glasses – Assists workers with real-time data and guidance.

✓ Remote Monitoring & Control Systems – Enables global access to production metrics.

✓ Digital Work Instructions & AI Chatbots – Provide real-time troubleshooting and process guidance.

✓ Agile Project Management Software (e.g., Jira, Trello, Monday.com) – Enhances team collaboration and workflow tracking.

Conclusion

This checklist helps manufacturers integrate the right technology applications to enhance agility in production, reduce downtime, improve efficiency, and increase adaptability. By leveraging automation, AI, digital twins, and smart supply chains, manufacturers can stay competitive in a rapidly evolving industry. ?

Agile Technology: Make or Buy Decisions

In agile manufacturing, companies must decide whether to develop (make) technology in-house or purchase (buy) it from external suppliers. This "Make or Buy" decision is crucial for maintaining flexibility, efficiency, and cost-effectiveness in production. Agile businesses must assess multiple factors to determine the best approach based on speed, cost, expertise, and strategic advantage.

1. When to "Make" (Develop In-House Technology)

? Key Considerations:

Competitive Advantage: If the technology is a core differentiator (e.g., Tesla's proprietary battery technology).

Customization Needs: When existing solutions do not meet specific manufacturing requirements.

Data Security & IP Protection: If handling sensitive data (e.g., AI-driven analytics for process optimization).

Long-Term Cost Efficiency: If continuous improvements and adaptability are required.

? Examples of "Make" Decisions in Agile Manufacturing:

Tesla develops its own AI-driven autonomous vehicle software instead of relying on third-party providers.

Boeing creates customized digital twin models to simulate and optimize aircraft manufacturing.

2. When to "Buy" (Outsource or Purchase Technology)

? Key Considerations:

Faster Deployment: When speed-to-market is critical (e.g., integrating AI-based quality control).

Lower Initial Cost: Avoiding high R&D investment and long development timelines.

Industry-Standard Solutions Available: If off-the-shelf solutions meet requirements.

Focus on Core Business: Outsourcing non-essential but necessary functions (e.g., cloud computing services).

? Examples of "Buy" Decisions in Agile Manufacturing:

Ford integrates Google Cloud AI for predictive maintenance rather than developing its own.

Siemens adopts Autodesk CAD software for product design instead of building an in-house CAD solution.

3. Hybrid Approach: Combining "Make & Buy"

Many agile manufacturers combine both approaches by developing core technologies in-house while outsourcing supporting systems.

? Example of Hybrid Approach:

Apple buys processors from TSMC but develops its own M-series chips for better performance and integration.

BMW buys standard robotic arms but customizes AI-driven control systems in-house.

Conclusion

Agile manufacturing requires a strategic approach to the "Make or Buy" decision. Companies should develop in-house technology when it provides a competitive edge and purchase external solutions when speed, cost, and industry standards are priorities. A hybrid approach often offers the best balance between agility, innovation, and efficiency. ?

Agile Manufacturing Practices

Agile manufacturing is a flexible and responsive approach that allows manufacturers to quickly adapt to changing customer demands, technological advancements, and market conditions. It focuses on efficiency, innovation, and collaboration to enhance productivity while minimizing waste and downtime. Below are the four key Agile Manufacturing practices that drive success:

1. Modular Production Systems

? What it is:

Production is designed using modular and reconfigurable workstations that allow for quick changes between different products.

Enables mass customization without disrupting production flow.

? Example:

Boeing uses modular production to assemble different aircraft models based on customer specifications.

2. Just-in-Time (JIT) & Lean Manufacturing

? What it is:

Focuses on minimizing waste, reducing inventory costs, and increasing efficiency.

Ensures that materials and components arrive just in time for production, avoiding excess stock.

? Example:

Toyota Production System (TPS) uses JIT to streamline operations, reduce waste, and improve overall efficiency.

3. Smart Manufacturing & Digital Integration

? What it is:

Uses Industrial IoT (IIoT), AI, and real-time data analytics to monitor and optimize production.

Digital Twin technology creates virtual simulations of manufacturing processes for continuous improvements.

? Example:

Siemens employs AI-driven predictive maintenance to reduce machine downtime and enhance operational efficiency.

4. Agile Supply Chain Management

? What it is:

Ensures that the supply chain is flexible, responsive, and well-integrated with real-time monitoring.

Uses cloud-based ERP systems for dynamic adjustments in supply chain operations.

? Example:

Apple continuously adjusts its global supply chain based on real-time demand fluctuations to maintain production efficiency.

Conclusion

Agile Manufacturing combines modular production, lean principles, smart technology, and flexible supply chains to create a highly adaptable and efficient manufacturing system. By embracing real-time data, automation, and continuous improvement, manufacturers can remain competitive and responsive to market changes. ?

The Agile Factory: A Story of Innovation and Adaptability

In the bustling industrial city of NovaTech, Orion Motors, a mid-sized electric vehicle (EV) company, faced a growing challenge. Consumer preferences were shifting rapidly—customers now demanded customized EVs with unique color options, advanced self-driving features, and faster charging capabilities. Meanwhile, global supply chain disruptions made traditional mass production inefficient.

The Old Ways No Longer Worked

Orion Motors had relied on mass manufacturing, producing thousands of identical cars in long production cycles. Their rigid assembly lines and bulk inventory management made it impossible to adapt quickly. By the time they launched a new feature, competitors had already introduced the next big innovation.

The Shift to Agile Manufacturing

Determined to stay ahead, Orion Motors' CEO, Sarah, decided to embrace Agile Manufacturing. Instead of massive overhauls, the company focused on small, incremental changes using cutting-edge technology and smarter workflows.

? Step 1: Modular Production for Flexibility

Orion redesigned its factory into modular workstations, where robots and human workers could easily switch tasks.

This allowed them to produce different EV models on the same line, customizing vehicles based on customer orders.

? Step 2: Smart Technology & Real-Time Data

The company integrated Industrial IoT (IIoT) sensors to monitor production efficiency and predict equipment failures before breakdowns occurred.

They also implemented AI-driven demand forecasting, ensuring they stocked only the materials they needed—reducing waste and cost.

? Step 3: Agile Supply Chain

Instead of stockpiling parts, Orion adopted a Just-in-Time (JIT) system, ordering parts only when required.

When a chip shortage hit the industry, Orion quickly partnered with local suppliers instead of waiting for overseas shipments.

? Step 4: Continuous Improvement & Fast Prototyping

Orion introduced 3D printing to rapidly prototype new parts and test designs within days instead of months.

Engineers worked in cross-functional teams, allowing software updates and mechanical improvements to be developed simultaneously.

The Outcome: Speed, Customization, and Efficiency

Within six months, Orion Motors transformed its operations:

? Car production time decreased by 40%.

? Customers could now customize their EVs and receive delivery within weeks, not months.

? The company saved 30% on material costs by reducing excess inventory.

? Orion Motors successfully launched an industry-first self-healing battery system, ahead of its competitors.

As a result, Orion not only survived but thrived, proving that Agile Manufacturing is the key to innovation, adaptability, and long-term success in a fast-changing world. ??

This story showcases how agile principles—flexibility, smart technology, and iterative improvements—transform manufacturing, making it faster, smarter, and more customer-focused.

Agile Manufacturing: Real-Life Case Studies

Agile manufacturing enables companies to adapt quickly to market changes, reduce production time, and offer customized products efficiently. Here are three real-life case studies demonstrating how leading companies implemented Agile Manufacturing to gain a competitive edge:

? Case Study 1: Tesla – Agile Production & Over-the-Air Updates

Challenge:

Traditional automakers follow long development cycles, making it difficult to introduce rapid innovations. Tesla needed a way to quickly implement software and hardware improvements without halting production.

Agile Solution:

? Flexible Production Line – Tesla's Gigafactories use modular assembly lines that can quickly adapt to changes in production.

? AI & IoT-Driven Supply Chain – Real-time data analytics optimize material flow and minimize delays.

? Over-the-Air (OTA) Software Updates – Tesla delivers software updates to its cars remotely, improving vehicle performance without requiring physical recalls.

Results:

✔? Reduced production time per vehicle from 3 weeks to just a few days.

✔? Continuous software and hardware upgrades without disrupting operations.

✔? Achieved industry-leading production efficiency despite global supply chain disruptions.

? Case Study 2: Amazon – Agile Robotics & Warehouse Automation

Challenge:

With millions of daily orders, Amazon needed to scale operations efficiently while maintaining fast delivery speeds.

Agile Solution:

? Robotic Automation & AI-Powered Sorting – Amazon integrated Kiva Robots in its fulfillment centers, optimizing order picking and reducing human labor fatigue.

? Predictive Demand Forecasting – AI analyzes customer data to pre-stock items in nearby warehouses before customers even place an order.

? Flexible Workforce Management – Seasonal demand spikes are managed with adaptive scheduling and temporary staffing.

Results:

✓? Fulfillment times dropped from 60 minutes to under 15 minutes per order.

✓? 30% reduction in warehouse space usage due to robotic efficiency.

✓? Faster delivery speeds, with Prime Now offering 1-hour deliveries in select locations.

?? Case Study 3: Boeing – Digital Twin Technology in Aircraft Manufacturing

Challenge:

Aircraft manufacturing is complex, requiring extreme precision and zero tolerance for errors. Boeing needed to reduce defects and streamline assembly processes.

Agile Solution:

? Digital Twin Technology – Boeing uses virtual simulations to test aircraft components before physical production, eliminating costly rework.

? 3D Printing for Rapid Prototyping – Custom parts can be produced on-demand, reducing reliance on suppliers.

? Collaborative Agile Teams – Engineers, designers, and production teams work in cross-functional sprints to improve aircraft design.

Results:

✓? 20% reduction in production defects, leading to safer aircraft.

✓? Cost savings of $2 billion per year by reducing waste and inefficiencies.

✓? Faster production cycles, enabling Boeing to meet growing airline demands.

Conclusion

These case studies show how Tesla, Amazon, and Boeing leverage Agile Manufacturing to stay ahead in their industries. By adopting flexible production systems, AI-driven automation, and real-time data analytics, these companies achieve:

✓? Faster time-to-market ?

✓? Higher efficiency ?

✓? Better customization for customers ?

? Case Study: MIT's Agile Learning Factories

Challenge:

Traditional engineering and manufacturing education often focuses on theoretical learning with limited real-world application. Students graduate with knowledge but lack practical, industry-ready skills.

Agile Solution:

MIT (Massachusetts Institute of Technology) introduced an Agile Learning Lab that integrates real-world manufacturing challenges into the curriculum.

? Project-Based Learning with Agile Sprints

Students work in cross-functional teams (engineering, design, business) to solve real-world manufacturing problems.

Instead of semester-long projects, tasks are broken down into 2-4 week Agile Sprints to develop, test, and iterate solutions quickly.

? Smart Factory Simulations with Digital Twins

MIT uses Digital Twin technology to create virtual manufacturing environments where students simulate production line improvements before applying them to physical systems.

AI-driven analytics provide real-time feedback, mimicking real industry scenarios.

? Integration of 3D Printing & IoT

Students use 3D printing for rapid prototyping, just as manufacturers do in Agile Manufacturing.

IoT-enabled sensors track student-designed production processes, analyzing efficiency, waste, and optimization opportunities.

? Industry Collaboration & Just-in-Time Learning

Companies like Tesla, Boeing, and Siemens partner with MIT to provide real-world case studies, allowing students to work on active industry problems.

Instead of learning static content, students access real-time case studies and industry tools, ensuring they graduate with skills that match current industry needs.

Results & Impact

✓? 50% increase in student job placements in top manufacturing firms.

✓? Faster learning cycles, allowing students to prototype, test, and iterate solutions within weeks rather than months.

✓? Stronger collaboration with industry, ensuring students are workforce-ready upon graduation.

✓? Reduced skill gap between academia and industry, creating more adaptable engineers.

Conclusion

Agile Manufacturing principles are reshaping education by moving from rigid, theoretical learning to hands-on, iterative, and industry-aligned training. Schools and universities implementing Agile Learning Labs, Digital Twins, and Smart Manufacturing tools create students who are better prepared for modern, technology-driven industries. ?

Agile Manufacturing in the Food Industry: Case Study of McDonald's & Nestlé

The food industry is evolving rapidly, with changing consumer demands, supply chain disruptions, and the need for sustainability and efficiency. Agile Manufacturing allows food companies to adapt quickly, reduce waste, and introduce new products faster.

? Case Study 1: McDonald's – Agile Supply Chain & Customization

Challenge:

McDonald's needed to offer personalized menu options while maintaining its fast service and global consistency. Additionally, supply chain disruptions required a flexible, resilient approach.

Agile Solution:

? Modular Production System (Made-to-Order)

McDonald's shifted from mass production to an on-demand assembly model.

Instead of pre-making burgers, orders are assembled fresh using just-in-time inventory to reduce waste.

? AI-Driven Demand Forecasting

AI monitors real-time sales data to predict demand fluctuations and adjust ingredient supply accordingly.

Smart kiosks suggest customized meal options based on customer preferences and past orders.

? Dynamic Supply Chain & Local Sourcing

McDonald's partners with local farmers to reduce transportation costs and adapt to regional ingredient availability.

Cloud-based ERP systems allow for real-time inventory adjustments across global locations.

Results:

✓? 30% reduction in food waste due to smarter inventory management.

✓? Faster service times despite increased menu customization.

✓? Increased sales through personalized menu recommendations.

? Case Study 2: Nestlé – Agile Product Innovation & Smart Manufacturing

Challenge:

Nestlé needed to accelerate new product development and reduce production costs while maintaining high-quality food safety standards.

Agile Solution:

? Digital Twin Technology for Production Optimization

Nestlé implemented virtual factory simulations to test new production techniques before applying them to real factories.

AI-driven predictive maintenance helped prevent machine breakdowns, reducing downtime.

? Rapid Product Development & 3D Food Printing

Instead of taking years to develop new products, Nestlé uses rapid prototyping and consumer testing in Agile Sprints.

3D printing of chocolate and plant-based foods allows faster testing of new recipes.

? Smart Packaging & AI-Powered Quality Control

Nestlé integrated IoT sensors in packaging to monitor freshness and detect contamination.

AI-powered computer vision detects defects in packaging 10x faster than human workers.

Results:

✓? 50% faster product development cycles, allowing Nestlé to launch new items ahead of competitors.

✓? 20% reduction in production costs through predictive maintenance and energy efficiency.

✓? Safer and higher-quality food due to AI-powered inspection systems.

Conclusion

McDonald's and Nestlé showcase how Agile Manufacturing helps food companies stay competitive by:

✓? Adapting to customer demands faster (e.g., personalized menus).

✓? Reducing waste and improving efficiency (e.g., JIT inventory & AI forecasting).

✓? Accelerating product innovation (e.g., digital twins & 3D food printing).

Agile Manufacturing in Healthcare: Case Study of 3D-Printed Medical Devices & Personalized Medicine

Agile manufacturing is revolutionizing healthcare by enabling faster production, customization, and efficiency in medical equipment, pharmaceuticals, and patient care. The demand for personalized treatments, rapid medical innovations, and supply chain flexibility has driven the healthcare industry to adopt agile methods.

? Case Study 1: 3D Printing for Medical Devices (Johnson & Johnson)

Challenge:

Traditional manufacturing of medical devices like prosthetics, implants, and surgical tools takes months to produce and often lacks customization for individual patients. Johnson & Johnson needed a faster, patient-specific approach.

Agile Solution:

? 3D Printing for On-Demand Medical Devices

Johnson & Johnson implemented additive manufacturing (3D printing) to produce custom implants and prosthetics tailored to individual patients.

Surgeons can now scan a patient's body and 3D print surgical tools designed specifically for their anatomy.

? Agile Prototyping & Rapid Testing

Instead of waiting months for traditional device approvals, J&J uses agile iterative prototyping to test and refine new designs within weeks.

? Localized Micro-Factories

The company opened small, decentralized manufacturing hubs near hospitals, allowing on-site production of critical devices, reducing delays.

Results:

✓? 50% faster production of patient-specific implants.

✓? 30% cost reduction due to localized manufacturing.

✓? Better patient outcomes with custom-fitted medical devices.

? Case Study 2: Personalized Medicine & AI-Driven Drug Manufacturing (Moderna & Pfizer)

Challenge:

Traditional vaccine and drug development takes years, making it difficult to respond quickly to global health crises like COVID-19. Moderna & Pfizer needed a faster, flexible approach to vaccine production.

Agile Solution:

? AI-Powered Drug Discovery

Moderna used AI & machine learning to analyze billions of potential mRNA sequences, speeding up vaccine development.

Instead of lengthy lab testing, AI predicts which formulations will work best, reducing trial-and-error cycles.

? Modular Manufacturing for Rapid Scaling

Pfizer built modular mRNA vaccine production units that can be quickly reconfigured to produce new vaccines if a virus mutates.

These units allow vaccines to be manufactured globally without building new factories from scratch.

? Continuous Manufacturing Instead of Batch Processing

Traditional drug manufacturing works in batches, leading to inefficiencies.

Moderna & Pfizer adopted continuous manufacturing, producing vaccines in a non-stop flow, reducing delays.

Results:

✓? COVID-19 vaccines were developed & mass-produced in under a year, an industry first.

✓? 70% reduction in production time compared to traditional methods.

✓? Future pandemics can be tackled faster, as mRNA platforms are adaptable.

Conclusion

The healthcare industry is embracing Agile Manufacturing through 3D printing, AI-driven drug discovery, and modular production. Companies like Johnson & Johnson, Moderna, and Pfizer have demonstrated that agility leads to:

✓? Faster time-to-market for life-saving treatments

✓? Customization & personalization for better patient outcomes

✓? More resilient & efficient healthcare supply chains

CHAPTER EIGHT

Sustainable Manufacturing

1. Competitive Strategy

Competitive strategy refers to the long-term action plans that businesses implement to gain a competitive advantage in their industry. It is based on the principles proposed by Michael Porter and involves:

Cost Leadership: Offering products/services at the lowest possible cost.

Differentiation: Creating unique products or services that offer superior value.

Focus Strategy: Targeting a specific market segment with either cost leadership or differentiation.

A company must align its competitive strategy with market needs, technological advancements, and resource availability to sustain its position.

2. Manufacturing Strategies

Manufacturing strategy defines how a company's production system supports its overall business strategy. It involves decisions about:

Process Choice: Job shop, batch production, mass production, or continuous flow.

Technology Utilization: Implementation of automation, robotics, and AI.

Quality Management: Using Lean, Six Sigma, or TQM to improve product quality.

Supply Chain Integration: Coordinating suppliers, logistics, and production systems.

Sustainability Initiatives: Reducing waste, energy consumption, and emissions.

A well-defined manufacturing strategy ensures efficiency, cost reduction, and customer satisfaction.

3. Strategic Improvement Programme in Sustainable Manufacturing

Sustainable manufacturing focuses on minimizing environmental impact while maintaining profitability. Developing a strategic improvement programme includes:

(A) Identifying Key Areas for Improvement

Energy efficiency

Waste reduction

Sustainable sourcing

Circular economy principles (recycling, remanufacturing)

(B) Implementing Sustainable Practices

Lean Manufacturing: Reducing waste and increasing efficiency.

Green Supply Chain Management: Partnering with eco-friendly suppliers.

Eco-Design: Developing products with sustainable materials.

Carbon Footprint Reduction: Using renewable energy and optimizing logistics.

(C) Setting Performance Metrics

Carbon emissions per unit of production

Waste reduction percentage

Energy savings achieved

Compliance with environmental regulations

(D) Continuous Improvement & Innovation

Investing in R&D for green technologies

Implementing smart manufacturing (IoT, AI)

Employee training for sustainable practices

By integrating competitive strategy with sustainable manufacturing, companies can ensure long-term profitability while meeting environmental and social responsibilities.

1. Cost Leadership Strategy – Walmart

Case Study: Walmart's Low-Cost Strategy

Background

Walmart is a global retail giant known for its low prices, efficient supply chain, and large-scale operations.

Competitive Strategy Applied

Economies of Scale: Walmart purchases in bulk, reducing costs per unit.

Efficient Supply Chain Management: Uses advanced logistics, automation, and supplier negotiations to keep inventory costs low.

Cost-Cutting Measures: Self-checkout kiosks, minimal store decor, and strategic store locations reduce overhead costs.

Impact

Walmart remains a market leader with low pricing as its key value proposition.

Despite competition from Amazon, Walmart retains customers with everyday low pricing (EDLP).

Lesson: Cost leadership works best when a company can achieve high efficiency and pass cost savings to customers.

2. Differentiation Strategy – Apple Inc.

Case Study: Apple's Premium Branding

Background

Apple is a technology company that focuses on innovation, design, and brand loyalty.

Competitive Strategy Applied

Premium Product Design: Apple products feature sleek, user-friendly designs.

Innovation & R&D: Apple invests heavily in developing new technologies (e.g., Face ID, M1 chips).

Ecosystem Lock-in: Seamless integration between Apple devices (iPhone, Mac, iPad, Apple Watch).

Brand Loyalty & Marketing: Strong brand identity and customer experience (Apple Stores, Genius Bar).

Impact

Apple commands high profit margins despite premium pricing.

Loyal customers continue to buy Apple products despite competition.

Lesson: Differentiation is successful when a company offers unique value that customers are willing to pay a premium for.

3. Focus Strategy – Tesla (Niche Market Domination)

Case Study: Tesla's Electric Vehicle Market Domination

Background

Tesla entered the automotive industry focusing exclusively on electric vehicles (EVs).

Competitive Strategy Applied

Niche Market Selection: Focused on high-performance electric cars for early adopters.

Technology Leadership: Developed superior battery technology and self-driving capabilities.

Direct-to-Consumer Sales Model: No dealerships; sells online and through Tesla showrooms.

Sustainability & Brand Perception: Marketed as an environmentally conscious brand.

Impact

Tesla disrupted the auto industry and forced traditional manufacturers to accelerate EV development.

The company expanded from a niche market to a broader audience with affordable models (e.g., Model 3).

Lesson: Focus strategy works when a company dominates a niche before expanding into the mainstream market.

The Tale of Three Bakeries ??

In a bustling town called Marketville, three bakeries competed for customers: Budget Bakes, Gourmet Delights, and Special Treats. Each one had a different strategy to win over the town's residents.

1. The Cost Leader – Budget Bakes ?

Owner: Tom

Strategy: Cost Leadership (Low prices, high efficiency)

Tom wanted to offer the most affordable bread and pastries in town. To achieve this, he:

? Bought ingredients in bulk at discounted prices.

? Used efficient baking machines to speed up production.

? Hired a few skilled workers instead of many, reducing labor costs.

? Focused on simple, everyday baked goods without fancy decorations.

Because of this, Budget Bakes sold the cheapest bread in Marketville, attracting budget-conscious families and students.

Lesson: Tom succeeded by keeping costs low and passing the savings to customers, just like Walmart does in retail.

2. The Differentiator – Gourmet Delights ?

Owner: Sarah

Strategy: Differentiation (Premium quality, unique offerings)

Sarah believed that people would pay more for something special. To stand out, she:

? Used organic, high-quality ingredients.

? Created unique recipes (like lavender-infused croissants ?).

? Designed beautiful cakes and pastries for weddings and events.

? Built a cozy bakery with an elegant café setting.

Because of this, Gourmet Delights became the go-to place for people looking for premium, artisan baked goods. Even though it was expensive, customers loved the experience and quality.

Lesson: Sarah thrived by offering something unique, just like Apple differentiates itself with premium design and innovation.

3. The Focus Player – Special Treats ?

Owner: Raj

Strategy: Focus Strategy (Targeting a niche market)

Raj saw an opportunity that others missed – catering to health-conscious customers. His bakery specialized in:

? Gluten-free, vegan, and keto-friendly baked goods.

? Using natural sweeteners instead of sugar.

? Partnering with gyms and yoga studios to promote his products.

? Selling only a limited variety, but excelling in that niche.

Because of this, Special Treats became the favorite spot for fitness enthusiasts, people with dietary restrictions, and health-conscious individuals.

Lesson: Raj succeeded by focusing on a specific group of customers, just like Tesla initially targeted EV enthusiasts before expanding.

Moral of the Story

To win in business, you must decide:

1?? Will you compete on price like Budget Bakes?

2?? Will you offer unique value like Gourmet Delights?

3?? Will you target a niche market like Special Treats?

Choosing the right competitive strategy is the key to success!

1. Lean Manufacturing – Toyota

Case Study: Toyota Production System (TPS)

Background

Toyota revolutionized manufacturing with its Lean Manufacturing approach, known as the Toyota Production System (TPS). This system focuses on eliminating waste (Muda), improving efficiency, and continuously enhancing production processes.

Manufacturing Strategy Applied

Just-in-Time (JIT) Production: Toyota produces only what is needed, reducing inventory costs.

Kaizen (Continuous Improvement): Employees at all levels contribute to process improvement.

Automation with a Human Touch (Jidoka): Machines detect defects automatically and stop production to prevent quality issues.

Standardized Work: Processes are optimized and consistently followed to minimize variation.

Impact

? Reduced production costs and waste.

? Improved efficiency and product quality.

? Inspired global manufacturers to adopt Lean Manufacturing principles.

? Lesson: Lean Manufacturing helps businesses eliminate waste, improve efficiency, and deliver quality products at lower costs.

2. Agile Manufacturing – Zara

Case Study: Zara's Fast Fashion Model

Background

Zara, a leading fashion retailer, adopted an Agile Manufacturing strategy to quickly respond to changing fashion trends.

Manufacturing Strategy Applied

Flexible Supply Chain: Zara produces small batches and quickly adjusts production based on demand.

Proximity Manufacturing: Most production occurs in Spain and nearby countries, reducing lead times.

Data-Driven Decision-Making: Zara uses real-time sales data to decide which designs to produce.

Rapid Prototyping: Designs go from concept to stores in 2-3 weeks, compared to the industry average of 6 months.

Impact

? Zara responds to trends faster than competitors, reducing unsold inventory.

? Higher profit margins by reducing overproduction and markdowns.

? Customer satisfaction due to frequently updated collections.

? Lesson: Agile Manufacturing allows companies to adapt quickly to market changes and customer demands.

3. Mass Customization – Dell

Case Study: Dell's Build-to-Order Model

Background

Dell disrupted the PC industry with its Mass Customization approach, allowing customers to customize their computers based on preferences.

Manufacturing Strategy Applied

Build-to-Order (BTO) Model: Computers are assembled only after an order is placed, reducing excess inventory.

Direct-to-Customer Sales: Eliminated middlemen and allowed customers to configure their PCs online.

Modular Design: Standardized components enabled quick assembly and customization.

Efficient Supply Chain Management: Dell kept low inventory levels and relied on Just-in-Time (JIT) procurement.

Impact

? Customers received personalized products without increasing costs.

? Reduced inventory costs and improved efficiency.

? Gained a competitive advantage over traditional PC manufacturers like HP and IBM.

? Lesson: Mass Customization enables companies to offer personalized products while maintaining efficiency and cost control.

4. Sustainable Manufacturing – Tesla

Case Study: Tesla's Green Manufacturing Approach

Background

Tesla is known for pioneering Sustainable Manufacturing in the automotive industry.

Manufacturing Strategy Applied

Gigafactories: Large-scale production facilities focused on efficiency and renewable energy use.

Vertical Integration: Tesla manufactures its batteries, motors, and software in-house to reduce dependency on suppliers.

Renewable Energy Usage: Gigafactories are powered by solar and wind energy.

Closed-Loop Recycling: Tesla recycles batteries and other materials to minimize waste.

Sustainable Materials: Focuses on eco-friendly materials in car production.

Impact

? Reduced carbon footprint in vehicle production.

? Lower dependency on external suppliers, increasing production efficiency.

? Strengthened Tesla's brand as a leader in sustainability.

? Lesson: Sustainable Manufacturing is a long-term strategy that reduces environmental impact while improving efficiency and brand value.

1. Manufacturing Strategy in Business Success Strategy Formation

Business success strategy formation involves defining how a company competes in the market, and manufacturing strategy aligns production capabilities with this vision.

Key Roles of Manufacturing Strategy in Business Success

1?? Competitive Advantage: A well-defined manufacturing strategy helps a company gain a cost, quality, or innovation advantage.

2?? Operational Efficiency: Lean and agile manufacturing reduce waste, optimize resource use, and improve responsiveness.

3?? Market Responsiveness: Flexible manufacturing systems help companies adapt to changing customer demands and trends.

4?? Cost Leadership or Differentiation: Manufacturing decisions (e.g., automation, supply chain efficiency) impact whether a business competes on low cost or high differentiation.

5?? Innovation & Technology Adoption: The use of smart manufacturing (AI, IoT, robotics) helps companies maintain leadership in their industry.

? Example: Zara's fast fashion model relies on an agile manufacturing strategy to deliver trendy clothing in record time, supporting its overall business strategy of speed and responsiveness.

2. Manufacturing Strategy Formulation in Sustainable Manufacturing

What is Sustainable Manufacturing?

Sustainable manufacturing focuses on minimizing environmental impact while maintaining profitability and social responsibility. It ensures that production processes are efficient, eco-friendly, and resource-conscious.

Steps to Formulate a Sustainable Manufacturing Strategy

(A) Define Sustainability Goals

Companies must set clear sustainability objectives, such as:

Reducing carbon emissions (e.g., using renewable energy in factories).

Minimizing waste (e.g., circular economy practices).

Enhancing energy efficiency (e.g., smart automation to reduce power consumption).

Improving worker well-being (e.g., ethical labor practices).

? Example: Unilever aims for net-zero carbon emissions by 2039 and has redesigned its manufacturing plants to be energy-efficient.

(B) Implement Sustainable Manufacturing Practices

1?? Lean & Green Manufacturing: Reducing waste, improving energy efficiency, and optimizing processes.

2?? Eco-friendly Materials: Using biodegradable or recycled materials in production.

3?? Circular Economy Approach: Designing products for reuse, recycling, and remanufacturing.

4?? Smart Manufacturing & IoT: Using real-time data and automation to optimize production and reduce waste.

5?? Green Supply Chain Management: Partnering with suppliers who follow sustainable practices.

? Example: Tesla's Gigafactories use solar energy and closed-loop battery recycling, aligning manufacturing with sustainability goals.

(C) Integrate Sustainability Metrics in Performance Measurement

Companies should track:

Carbon footprint reduction per unit of production.

Waste and energy consumption.

Sustainable sourcing compliance.

Customer perception of green products.

? Example: Patagonia, a sustainable clothing brand, measures the environmental impact of its materials and production processes to continuously improve sustainability.

Conclusion

A well-formulated sustainable manufacturing strategy not only helps businesses reduce environmental impact but also enhances efficiency, brand reputation, and long-term profitability.

Key Takeaways:

Align manufacturing with overall business success strategy.

Implement green production practices for sustainability.

Use technology & automation to optimize resource use.

Track sustainability performance metrics to improve continuously.

The Green Factory: A Tale of Business Success and Sustainable Manufacturing

Once upon a time, in the city of Indusville, three friends—Leo, Aisha, and Vikram—decided to start a business. They had a shared passion for sustainability and wanted to build a company that produced eco-friendly furniture.

Step 1: Business Success Strategy Formation

Before setting up their factory, they had to decide:

? Who are their target customers?

? How will they compete—low-cost, premium quality, or niche market?

? How can they ensure long-term profitability and sustainability?

After brainstorming, they came up with their business strategy:

? Target Market: Urban eco-conscious consumers and offices looking for sustainable furniture.

? Competitive Strategy: Differentiation – Unique, high-quality furniture made from recycled materials.

? Sustainability Commitment: Use renewable energy, reduce waste, and adopt green manufacturing.

? Lesson: A well-defined business strategy provides direction for manufacturing decisions.

Step 2: Manufacturing Strategy Formulation

With their business strategy set, they needed a manufacturing strategy that aligned with it.

Leo, who had expertise in operations, suggested:

? Lean Manufacturing – Minimize waste by using recycled wood and optimizing production.

? Energy Efficiency – Install solar panels in the factory to reduce electricity costs.

? Smart Automation – Use AI-powered machines to reduce production errors and improve efficiency.

Aisha, an expert in marketing, insisted on:

? Customizable Products – Allow customers to choose designs, making them feel involved.

? Eco-Friendly Branding – Promote the sustainability factor in marketing.

Vikram, a finance expert, ensured:

? Cost Control – Bulk purchasing of sustainable raw materials to reduce expenses.

? Supply Chain Sustainability – Partnering with green-certified suppliers.

? Lesson: The manufacturing strategy must support the business goal—in this case, sustainability and quality differentiation.

Step 3: Implementing the Manufacturing Strategy

Their factory, GreenFurn, was set up with:

? Sustainable Materials: 90% recycled wood and biodegradable components.

? Renewable Energy: Solar power covered 80% of their energy needs.

? Zero-Waste Policy: Leftover materials were reused or recycled.

With these manufacturing strategies, their business became:

? Cost-Efficient – Lower energy and material costs improved profitability.

? Competitive – Their furniture was unique and in demand among eco-conscious buyers.

? Sustainable – Their factory's carbon footprint was 50% lower than competitors.

Soon, they received a government sustainability award, and large office chains partnered with them for eco-friendly furniture.

The Outcome: Business Success Through Strategic Manufacturing

GreenFurn's Success Formula:

? Business Strategy (What to do?) → Market leadership through sustainable, high-quality furniture.

? Manufacturing Strategy (How to do it?) → Lean, sustainable, and automated production.

? Execution (Doing it right!) → Smart technology, waste reduction, and customer customization.

Moral of the Story

A company's business success depends on choosing the right manufacturing strategy. Sustainability, efficiency, and innovation help businesses not only reduce costs and waste but also gain a competitive edge.

Structured Strategy Formulation: A Step-by-Step Approach

What is Structured Strategy Formulation?

Structured strategy formulation is a systematic process of developing a clear and actionable business strategy by analyzing internal and external factors, setting objectives, and designing an implementation plan.

It ensures that an organization aligns its vision, goals, and resources effectively to achieve competitive advantage and long-term success.

? Key Steps in Structured Strategy Formulation

Step 1: Defining Vision, Mission, and Objectives

✔ Vision Statement – Defines where the company wants to be in the long term.

✔ Mission Statement – Explains why the company exists and what it does.

✔ Strategic Objectives – Measurable goals aligned with the vision (e.g., market expansion, revenue growth, sustainability).

? Example: Tesla's vision is "to create the most compelling car company of the 21st century by driving the world's transition to electric vehicles."

Step 2: Environmental Analysis (SWOT & PESTEL)

✔ Internal Analysis (SWOT) – Strengths, Weaknesses, Opportunities, and Threats.

✔ External Analysis (PESTEL) – Political, Economic, Social, Technological, Environmental, and Legal factors affecting the business.

? Example: A company manufacturing electric cars might analyze:

? Strengths – Strong R&D, brand reputation.

? Weaknesses – High production costs.

? Opportunities – Rising demand for EVs.

? Threats – Competition from new startups.

Step 3: Identifying Competitive Strategy (Porter's Generic Strategies)

Companies must choose how they will compete:

1?? Cost Leadership – Producing goods at a lower cost than competitors (e.g., Walmart).

2?? Differentiation – Offering unique, high-quality products (e.g., Apple).

3?? Focus Strategy – Targeting a niche market with specialized products (e.g., Tesla initially targeting luxury EV buyers).

? Example: Zara uses "cost leadership + differentiation" by offering trendy designs quickly at affordable prices.

Step 4: Setting Strategic Initiatives & Action Plans

✔ Resource Allocation – Deciding how to allocate capital, workforce, and technology.

✔ Technology & Innovation Plan – Integrating AI, automation, or digital transformation.

✔ Sustainability & Ethical Considerations – Implementing green practices.

? Example: A manufacturing company may set a goal to reduce waste by 30% through automation and increase production efficiency by 20%.

Step 5: Strategy Implementation & Performance Monitoring

✔ Key Performance Indicators (KPIs) – Measuring success (e.g., profit margins, market share, sustainability impact).

✔ Balanced Scorecard Approach – Evaluating strategy effectiveness through:

Financial performance

Customer satisfaction

Internal processes

Innovation & growth

? Example: Amazon tracks customer satisfaction and delivery speed as KPIs for logistics strategy success.

? Why is Structured Strategy Formulation Important?

? Ensures a clear direction for business growth.

? Aligns resources, processes, and goals.

? Helps mitigate risks by analyzing external challenges.

? Improves decision-making based on data-driven insights.

Case Study: Structured Strategy Formulation at Tesla

Tesla is a great example of structured strategy formulation, where a clear, systematic approach helped the company disrupt the automotive industry and become a leader in sustainable transportation.

? Step 1: Defining Vision, Mission & Objectives

? Vision Statement:

"To create the most compelling car company of the 21st century by driving the world's transition to electric vehicles."

? Mission Statement:

"To accelerate the world's transition to sustainable energy."

? Strategic Objectives:

? Market Domination – Become the world's leading EV manufacturer.

? Sustainability – Reduce carbon footprint and promote renewable energy.

? Innovation Leadership – Advance battery technology and autonomous driving.

? Step 2: Environmental Analysis (SWOT & PESTEL)

SWOT Analysis

? Strengths:

Cutting-edge battery technology.

Strong brand and loyal customer base.

Direct-to-consumer sales model (no dealerships).

? Weaknesses:

High production costs.

Supply chain dependency on lithium and rare metals.

? Opportunities:

Rising demand for electric vehicles (EVs) worldwide.

Government incentives for clean energy.

? Threats:

Increasing competition from Rivian, Lucid, and legacy automakers (Ford, GM, etc.).

Shortages of raw materials (e.g., lithium for batteries).

PESTEL Analysis

✓ Political – Government incentives for EV adoption.

✓ Economic – Rising fuel prices increasing EV demand.

✓ Social – Consumers becoming environmentally conscious.

✓ Technological – Advances in battery and AI-driven autonomous driving.

✓ Environmental – Carbon emissions reduction focus.

✓ Legal – Strict regulations for emissions and vehicle safety.

? Step 3: Identifying Competitive Strategy (Porter's Generic Strategies)

Tesla's Competitive Strategy:

? Differentiation Strategy – Unique, high-performance EVs with cutting-edge technology.

? Cost Leadership (Long-term Goal) – Lowering battery production costs via Gigafactories.

? Vertical Integration – Tesla manufactures its own batteries and software, unlike competitors.

? Example:

Tesla's Gigafactories help reduce costs by producing batteries in-house, rather than depending on external suppliers.

? Step 4: Setting Strategic Initiatives & Action Plans

? Strategic Initiatives

? Expand Gigafactories to increase production and lower costs.

? Invest in R&D for next-gen battery technology.

? Improve autonomous driving AI to lead in self-driving technology.

? Scale up solar energy & battery storage solutions (Tesla Powerwall).

? Example:

Tesla's 4680 battery cell innovation significantly reduces costs and increases range, aligning with its strategy.

? Step 5: Strategy Implementation & Performance Monitoring

Key Performance Indicators (KPIs)

✓ EV market share growth (Tesla leads with over 60% market share in the U.S.).

✓ Cost per kWh of battery production (target: below \$100/kWh).

✓ Reduction in carbon footprint from Tesla's Gigafactories.

✓ Autopilot safety metrics to ensure AI-driven cars are safer than human-driven vehicles.

? Example:

Tesla tracks sales growth and sustainability impact to measure business success and continuously refine its strategy.

? Conclusion: How Structured Strategy Formulation Led to Tesla's Success

✓ Clear vision & mission aligned all efforts.

✓ Environmental analysis helped Tesla anticipate market trends.

✓ Differentiation strategy positioned Tesla as a high-tech, eco-friendly brand.

✓ Strategic initiatives (Gigafactories, AI, battery R&D) ensured sustainable growth.

✓ Data-driven performance monitoring kept Tesla ahead of competitors.

Key Takeaway:

A well-structured strategy formulation process helped Tesla transform from a niche EV startup to a global leader in sustainable transportation. ??

The Rise of EcoTech: A Story of Structured Strategy Formulation

Chapter 1: The Visionary Dream

In the bustling city of NeoVille, three friends—Alex, Priya, and Omar—had a dream. They wanted to build a sustainable technology company that would create eco-friendly smartphones using recycled materials and energy-efficient designs.

But having a dream wasn't enough. They needed a structured strategy to turn their vision into reality.

Chapter 2: Defining the Vision, Mission & Objectives

One evening, the trio sat down in a coffee shop to answer some critical questions:

? Vision – "To revolutionize the smartphone industry with sustainable, ethical, and innovative products."

? Mission – "To design and manufacture high-quality smartphones using eco-friendly materials, ensuring fair labor practices and energy-efficient production."

? Objectives:

? Launch their first sustainable smartphone within 18 months.

? Achieve 50% lower carbon footprint than traditional smartphones.

? Capture 10% of the premium eco-conscious market within 5 years.

Chapter 3: Environmental Analysis (SWOT & PESTEL)

Before starting production, they analyzed the market and industry trends using SWOT and PESTEL frameworks.

SWOT Analysis

? Strengths:

Unique eco-friendly smartphone concept.

Strong team with tech and business expertise.

? Weaknesses:

High initial production costs.

Limited brand recognition.

? Opportunities:

Rising demand for sustainable products.

Government green energy incentives.

? Threats:

Competition from big tech companies.

Supply chain risks for recycled materials.

PESTEL Analysis

✓ Political – Government grants for sustainable startups.

✓ Economic – Growing market for eco-conscious consumers.

✓ Social – Customers demanding ethical and sustainable products.

✓ Technological – Advances in solar-powered batteries.

✓ Environmental – Need for e-waste reduction.

✓ Legal – Strict regulations on electronics recycling.

With this analysis, they realized that timing was perfect—the world was ready for an eco-friendly smartphone! ??

Chapter 4: Choosing the Competitive Strategy

The team then debated how they would compete.

Alex suggested Cost Leadership:

"We could make cheap eco-phones and sell in bulk!"

Priya argued for Differentiation:

"No! Let's create a premium smartphone that people will love for its sustainability and design!"

Omar proposed a Focus Strategy:

"Why not target eco-conscious tech lovers who care about sustainability?"

After long discussions, they chose a combination of Differentiation and Focus Strategy:

? High-end, eco-friendly smartphones with recycled materials and solar-powered charging.

? Targeting sustainability-conscious professionals willing to pay for a premium ethical product.

Chapter 5: Strategic Initiatives & Action Plan

With a clear strategy, they mapped out their action plan:

? R&D Investment – Develop energy-efficient processors and recycled materials.

? Sustainable Supply Chain – Partner with ethical suppliers for fair labor practices.

? Factory Setup – Use solar-powered manufacturing units.

? Marketing Plan – Brand EcoTech as "The World's First Truly Sustainable Smartphone."

? They also set Key Performance Indicators (KPIs):

? Carbon footprint reduction per unit.

? Customer satisfaction and brand loyalty.

? Market share growth in the premium segment.

Chapter 6: Execution & Monitoring

EcoTech launched its first product—the EcoPhone X—within 18 months. ?

Tech reviewers loved it! ?

Customers praised the sustainable materials and energy efficiency.

Investors saw huge potential and provided funding for further expansion.

By continuously tracking their KPIs and adapting their strategy, EcoTech grew rapidly. Within five years, they had:

? Captured 15% of the premium eco-tech market (exceeding their goal!).

? Reduced production carbon footprint by 60%.

? Expanded to Europe and North America.

The Moral of the Story

A structured strategy formulation helped EcoTech go from an idea to a market leader.

? Key Takeaways:

✔ A clear vision and mission drive success.

✔ SWOT & PESTEL analysis reveal market opportunities.

✔ Choosing the right competitive strategy is crucial.

✔ Well-planned execution turns ideas into reality.

✔ Measuring performance (KPIs) ensures long-term success.

And that's how EcoTech changed the world, one sustainable smartphone at a time! ??

Sustainable Manufacturing System Design Options

A sustainable manufacturing system focuses on reducing waste, energy consumption, and environmental impact while maintaining high productivity and economic feasibility. The design of a sustainable manufacturing system involves choosing the right processes, materials, and technologies to minimize the carbon footprint while ensuring long-term competitiveness.

? Key Sustainable Manufacturing System Design Options

1?? Lean Manufacturing (Waste Reduction)

Concept: Eliminate waste (materials, energy, time) to improve efficiency and sustainability.

Key Strategies:

? Just-in-Time (JIT) Production – Reduces excess inventory and waste.

? Kaizen (Continuous Improvement) – Small, ongoing changes to improve efficiency.

? Value Stream Mapping (VSM) – Identifies and eliminates inefficiencies in the process.

? Example: Toyota has implemented Lean Manufacturing to minimize waste and reduce production costs, making its processes more eco-friendly.

2?? Circular Manufacturing (Closed-Loop Systems)

Concept: Design products for reuse, remanufacturing, and recycling to create a closed-loop production system.

Key Strategies:

? Product Life Extension – Make products durable and repairable.

? Remanufacturing – Reusing components from old products.

? Recycling Materials – Designing products that can be easily recycled.

? Example: Philips has developed a circular economy model for its healthcare equipment, ensuring that devices are refurbished and reused instead of being discarded.

3?? Green Manufacturing (Eco-Friendly Processes)

Concept: Use clean energy sources and eco-friendly materials to reduce environmental impact.

Key Strategies:

? Renewable Energy Integration – Solar, wind, or bioenergy for production.

? Biodegradable & Sustainable Materials – Using plant-based plastics or recyclable metals.

? Water & Energy Efficiency – Smart sensors and automation to reduce consumption.

? Example: Tesla's Gigafactories run on solar and wind energy, reducing reliance on fossil fuels.

4?? Smart & Digital Manufacturing (Industry 4.0)

Concept: Use AI, IoT, and automation to optimize resource usage and minimize waste.

Key Strategies:

? AI & Machine Learning – Predictive maintenance to reduce machine downtime.

? IoT Sensors – Monitor and optimize energy and material usage.

? Digital Twins – Simulate production processes to identify inefficiencies before implementation.

? Example: Siemens' "Factory of the Future" uses AI and IoT to reduce material waste and energy consumption by up to 30%.

5?? Additive Manufacturing (3D Printing for Sustainability)

Concept: On-demand, layer-by-layer production to minimize material waste and transportation emissions.

Key Strategies:

? Localized Production – Reduces transportation impact.

? Material Efficiency – Uses only the required material, minimizing waste.

? Biodegradable & Recyclable Printing Materials – Sustainable filaments and resins.

? Example: Adidas uses 3D printing to manufacture sustainable, lightweight shoes, reducing material waste by 50%.

Conclusion

The best sustainable manufacturing system design depends on the industry, product type, and environmental goals. Companies often combine multiple approaches to achieve maximum efficiency and sustainability.

Case Study: Tesla's Sustainable Manufacturing System ??

Tesla has revolutionized the automotive industry by designing a sustainable manufacturing system that integrates lean principles, green energy, circular economy practices, and Industry 4.0 technologies.

? Step 1: Lean Manufacturing – Reducing Waste

? Strategy: Tesla adopted Just-in-Time (JIT) production and automation to reduce waste in manufacturing.

? Gigafactories use robotic automation to minimize material loss.

? AI-driven predictive maintenance reduces machine downtime.

? Battery production is optimized to use fewer raw materials.

? Result: Tesla reduced production waste by 30% and improved efficiency in battery assembly lines.

? Step 2: Circular Manufacturing – Recycling & Reuse

? Strategy: Tesla follows a closed-loop system for battery production and recycling.

? Old Tesla batteries are recycled and repurposed in new vehicles.

? Tesla partners with battery recycling companies to recover lithium, cobalt, and nickel.

? Battery life extension strategies ensure long-term use.

? Result: 92% of Tesla's battery materials are recycled and reused, reducing mining impact.

? Step 3: Green Manufacturing – Renewable Energy Use

? Strategy: Tesla's Gigafactories run on solar and wind energy, reducing reliance on fossil fuels.

? Gigafactory Nevada generates solar power for its operations.

? Energy-efficient robots optimize production with minimal energy use.

? Tesla's Powerpack storage system stores excess renewable energy.

? Result: Tesla's factories operate with 100% renewable energy, cutting CO_2 emissions drastically.

? Step 4: Smart Manufacturing – AI & IoT Optimization

? Strategy: Tesla integrates AI, IoT sensors, and digital twins to enhance efficiency.

? AI-driven quality control detects manufacturing defects early.

? IoT sensors monitor real-time energy and material usage.

? Digital twin simulations predict and resolve production bottlenecks.

? Result: Tesla reduced manufacturing defects by 50% and improved energy efficiency by 25%.

? Step 5: 3D Printing for Sustainability

? Strategy: Tesla incorporates additive manufacturing (3D printing) for rapid prototyping and sustainable parts production.

? 3D-printed parts help Tesla test vehicle components before mass production.

? Recycled materials are used for 3D printing parts.

? Reduces supply chain dependency and shipping emissions.

? Result: Tesla cuts material waste by 40% in the R&D process.

? Conclusion: Why Tesla's Strategy Works

✓ Integrated Approach – Combines lean, green, circular, smart, and 3D manufacturing.

✓ Data-Driven – Uses AI and IoT for real-time optimization.

✓ Sustainability at Scale – Gigafactories reduce environmental impact worldwide.

Tesla's manufacturing system proves that sustainability and profitability can coexist when a company strategically designs its operations.

Approaches to Strategy Formulation

Strategy formulation is the process of defining an organization's direction and making decisions on how to allocate resources to achieve long-term objectives. There are several approaches to strategy formulation, depending on the business environment, competitive landscape, and organizational goals.

? 1. Prescriptive vs. Descriptive Approaches

? Prescriptive (Planned) Approach

Strategy is formulated before implementation.

Based on analysis, planning, and structured decision-making.

Follows a top-down approach where leaders decide and employees execute.

? Example: Toyota's Lean Manufacturing Strategy was meticulously planned to eliminate waste and improve efficiency before implementation.

? Descriptive (Emergent) Approach

Strategy evolves over time based on real-world changes.

Encourages flexibility and adaptation rather than rigid planning.

Often follows a bottom-up approach, incorporating employee insights.

? Example: Amazon started as an online bookstore but adapted to market changes, becoming the world's largest e-commerce platform.

? 2. Major Strategy Formulation Approaches

1?? Classical Approach (Rational Planning Model)

? Concept: Strategy is a logical, step-by-step process where leaders analyze the environment and choose the best course of action.

Key Steps:

? Define mission & objectives.

? Conduct SWOT analysis.

? Identify competitive advantage.

? Develop a detailed action plan.

? Best for: Stable environments where long-term planning is possible.

? Example: McDonald's global expansion strategy follows structured market analysis before entering new regions.

2?? Evolutionary Approach (Survival of the Fittest)

? Concept: Strategy emerges from market competition—companies that adapt survive, while others fail.

Key Features:

? Firms experiment with different strategies.

? The most profitable approach wins over time.

? Emphasizes cost reduction, efficiency, and performance.

? Best for: Highly competitive industries where firms must continuously evolve.

? Example: Netflix evolved from DVD rentals to streaming by adapting to technological advancements.

3?? Processual Approach (Learning & Adaptation)

? Concept: Strategy is shaped by experience, learning, and internal culture rather than pure analysis.

Key Features:

? Focuses on continuous learning and employee insights.

? Small, incremental changes lead to long-term transformation.

? Strategy is influenced by organizational culture & politics.

? Best for: Uncertain environments where rapid change is required.

? Example: Google allows employees to spend 20% of their time on innovation projects, leading to products like Gmail and Google Maps.

4?? Systemic Approach (Societal & Cultural Influence)

? Concept: Strategy is shaped by culture, values, regulations, and social expectations.

Key Features:

? Business decisions align with social, ethical, and legal factors.

? Success depends on understanding regional markets and consumer behavior.

? Government policies and cultural differences shape the strategy.

? Best for: Global businesses that need to adapt to local markets.

? Example: McDonald's customizes menus (vegetarian in India, McArabia in the Middle East) to match local cultures.

? Conclusion

No one-size-fits-all strategy exists! The best approach depends on:

✓ Industry type (Stable vs. dynamic)

✓ Competitive landscape (High competition vs. niche markets)

✓ Company culture & resources (Structured vs. flexible approach)

Realization of New Strategies and System Designs

The realization of new strategies or system designs involves turning a formulated strategy into a practical and operational plan. This process requires effective execution, adaptation, and continuous monitoring to ensure long-term success.

? Key Steps in Realizing New Strategies & System Designs

1?? Strategy Validation & Feasibility Analysis

? Market & Competitive Analysis – Ensure the new strategy aligns with external opportunities and threats.

? Feasibility Study – Assess financial, technological, and operational feasibility.

? Risk Assessment – Identify potential challenges and develop mitigation plans.

? Example: Before launching the iPhone, Apple conducted extensive feasibility studies to ensure the product would succeed in the competitive mobile market.

2?? Resource Allocation & Capability Building

? Human Resources – Train employees to align with the new strategy.

? Technology & Infrastructure – Upgrade systems to support new processes.

? Financial Investment – Allocate budgets for R&D, marketing, and production.

? Example: Tesla's Gigafactories required massive investments in battery technology, renewable energy infrastructure, and automation to realize its sustainability strategy.

3?? Implementation Planning & Execution

? Develop a Roadmap – Break down the strategy into clear phases with milestones.

? Pilot Testing – Start with small-scale trials before full implementation.

? Change Management – Communicate and engage stakeholders to reduce resistance.

? Example: Amazon Go (cashier-less stores) was first tested in select locations before being scaled up worldwide.

4?? Performance Monitoring & Continuous Improvement

? Key Performance Indicators (KPIs) – Track success metrics (e.g., cost savings, customer satisfaction).

? Feedback Loops – Collect real-time feedback from customers and employees.

? Iterate & Optimize – Make continuous improvements based on insights.

? Example: Netflix continuously refines its recommendation algorithm using customer data to improve user experience and engagement.

? Conclusion

The realization of new strategies or system designs requires a structured approach, from feasibility analysis to continuous improvement. Companies that successfully implement strategic changes focus on resource alignment, stakeholder engagement, and adaptability.

CHAPTER NINE

Intelligent Manufacturing

Concepts of Competitive Strategy and Manufacturing Strategies

1. Competitive Strategy

Competitive strategy refers to the long-term approach an organization adopts to gain a competitive advantage in the market. It determines how a company differentiates itself from competitors and attracts customers.

There are three main types of competitive strategies (Michael Porter's Generic Strategies):

Cost Leadership – Competing by offering the lowest cost in the industry while maintaining acceptable quality.

Differentiation – Offering unique products or services that stand out in the market.

Focus (Niche Strategy) – Targeting a specific market segment with either cost leadership or differentiation.

Other strategic approaches include:

Blue Ocean Strategy – Creating a new, uncontested market space rather than competing in an existing one.

Hybrid Strategy – Combining cost leadership and differentiation for a competitive edge.

2. Manufacturing Strategies

Manufacturing strategy aligns production capabilities with business goals and competitive strategy. It focuses on key areas such as cost, quality, flexibility, and delivery.

There are four major types of manufacturing strategies:

Make-to-Stock (MTS) – Producing in advance based on demand forecasts.

Make-to-Order (MTO) – Manufacturing only after receiving customer orders.

Assemble-to-Order (ATO) – Producing parts in advance and assembling them when an order is placed.

Engineer-to-Order (ETO) – Designing and manufacturing based on customer specifications.

Key elements of manufacturing strategy:

Lean Manufacturing – Reducing waste and improving efficiency.

Agile Manufacturing – Enhancing responsiveness to market changes.

Mass Customization – Combining efficiency with product personalization.

Technology & Automation – Utilizing robotics, AI, and Industry 4.0 for production.

Development of a Strategic Improvement Programme

A Strategic Improvement Programme (SIP) is a structured plan to enhance business and manufacturing performance. It involves:

Assessing Current Performance

Identify strengths, weaknesses, opportunities, and threats (SWOT analysis).

Benchmark against competitors and industry best practices.

Setting Strategic Goals

Define clear, measurable objectives (e.g., reducing production costs by 10%, improving product quality by 15%).

Identifying Improvement Areas

Focus on process efficiency, product quality, supply chain management, and workforce skills.

Implementing Key Initiatives

Lean Six Sigma for waste reduction.

Total Quality Management (TQM) for customer satisfaction.

Digital transformation using IoT and AI-driven analytics.

Monitoring and Continuous Improvement

Establish Key Performance Indicators (KPIs).

Use Plan-Do-Check-Act (PDCA) cycles for ongoing refinement.

Adapt to changing market demands and technological advancements.

Competitive Strategy and Manufacturing Strategies in the Food Industry

The food industry is highly competitive, requiring businesses to develop strong strategies to stay ahead. Below is how competitive strategy and manufacturing strategy apply, along with a strategic improvement programme tailored for food production.

1. Competitive Strategies in the Food Industry

Businesses in the food sector can adopt different strategies based on their market positioning:

a) Cost Leadership

Large-scale food manufacturers (e.g., Nestlé, Coca-Cola) focus on mass production to reduce costs.

Use of efficient supply chains, bulk purchasing, and process automation.

Example: McDonald's achieves cost leadership through standardization and bulk procurement.

b) Differentiation

Creating unique flavors, organic ingredients, or premium-quality products.

Example: Ben & Jerry's differentiates with unique ice cream flavors and ethical sourcing.

c) Focus (Niche Market Strategy)

Targeting a specific customer base, such as vegan, gluten-free, or organic foods.

Example: Beyond Meat specializes in plant-based meat alternatives.

d) Hybrid Strategy

Combining low costs with differentiation.

Example: Costco's Kirkland brand offers high-quality food products at affordable prices.

2. Manufacturing Strategies in the Food Industry

Manufacturing strategies in food production focus on efficiency, safety, and quality.

a) Make-to-Stock (MTS)

Mass production of staple food products (e.g., canned goods, snacks, beverages).

Requires demand forecasting to avoid overproduction and waste.

b) Make-to-Order (MTO)

Customized food production, common in restaurants or specialty food companies.

Example: Bespoke meal-prep services create personalized meals based on customer preferences.

c) Assemble-to-Order (ATO)

Used in fast-food chains where components (buns, patties, sauces) are pre-made and assembled when ordered.

Example: Subway assembles sandwiches based on customer selection.

d) Engineer-to-Order (ETO)

Custom-designed food products, such as wedding cakes or personalized health food plans.

3. Developing a Strategic Improvement Programme for the Food Industry

A Strategic Improvement Programme (SIP) helps food businesses enhance production efficiency, quality, and customer satisfaction.

Step 1: Assess Current Performance

Conduct SWOT analysis to identify strengths, weaknesses, opportunities, and threats.

Analyze production efficiency, ingredient sourcing, and waste levels.

Step 2: Set Strategic Goals

Reduce food waste by 20% within a year.

Improve production speed while maintaining quality.

Implement new technology (e.g., AI for demand forecasting).

Step 3: Identify Key Improvement Areas

Process efficiency: Introduce lean manufacturing and automation.

Food safety: Upgrade quality control procedures and compliance with regulations (e.g., FDA, HACCP).

Sustainability: Use eco-friendly packaging, reduce water usage.

Supply chain optimization: Source locally to reduce costs and improve freshness.

Step 4: Implement Key Initiatives

Lean Six Sigma for minimizing waste and optimizing resources.

Smart food manufacturing: AI-driven monitoring of food quality.

Sustainable practices: Recycling food waste and reducing plastic usage.

Step 5: Monitor and Continuously Improve

Track Key Performance Indicators (KPIs) such as production output, defect rate, and energy consumption.

Use Plan-Do-Check-Act (PDCA) cycles for ongoing refinement.

Stay updated with consumer trends, such as plant-based diets and healthier eating.

Conclusion

For a food business, a combination of cost efficiency, quality focus, and sustainability is key to success. By implementing a structured improvement programme, food manufacturers can optimize production, meet customer demands, and remain competitive.

Applying competitive strategy and manufacturing strategies in the food industry for the education sector can be highly beneficial, especially for school meal programs, university cafeterias, and educational food initiatives. Here's how these concepts can be tailored:

1. Competitive Strategy for Food in Education

a) Cost Leadership (Affordable Meals for Students)

Schools and universities often operate on tight budgets, requiring cost-efficient meal production.

Bulk purchasing, centralized kitchens, and automated food preparation can reduce costs.

Example: Public school lunch programs using government-subsidized ingredients.

b) Differentiation (Health & Nutrition Focus)

Offering organic, locally sourced, or customized dietary options can set an institution apart.

Nutritional transparency and student involvement in menu design.

Example: University dining halls offering plant-based, allergen-free, or gourmet meal options.

c) Focus/Niche Strategy (Specialized Dietary Needs)

Schools catering to specific dietary groups (e.g., vegetarian, halal, gluten-free).

Example: Schools offering allergy-friendly kitchens for students with food sensitivities.

d) Hybrid Strategy (Affordable & Healthy Meals)

A mix of cost efficiency and differentiation by providing budget-friendly, nutritious meals.

Example: Meal programs that balance cost while offering fresh, high-quality ingredients.

2. Manufacturing Strategies for Food in Education

a) Make-to-Stock (MTS) – Standardized School Meal Prep

Pre-made meals prepared in bulk and stored for daily service.

Requires demand forecasting to prevent food waste.

Example: Packaged school lunches distributed across multiple campuses.

b) Make-to-Order (MTO) – Personalized Meal Choices

Cafeteria-style dining with customizable options for students.

Example: University dining halls offering made-to-order meals (e.g., salad bars, sandwich stations).

c) Assemble-to-Order (ATO) – Prepped Ingredients, Final Assembly at Service

Preparing ingredients in advance and assembling based on demand.

Example: Burrito bars or pasta stations in college dining halls.

d) Engineer-to-Order (ETO) – Custom Nutrition Plans

Tailored meal plans for students with medical or athletic dietary needs.

Example: Sports nutrition programs for student-athletes.

3. Strategic Improvement Programme for Food in Education

Step 1: Assess Current Performance

Analyze meal costs, student satisfaction surveys, and waste levels.

Identify inefficiencies in food preparation, delivery, and quality control.

Step 2: Set Strategic Goals

Reduce food waste by 30% through better inventory management.

Improve meal quality while maintaining affordability.

Enhance sustainability by sourcing local ingredients.

Step 3: Identify Key Improvement Areas

Streamline food prep through automation and central kitchens.

Upgrade food safety measures (HACCP compliance).

Improve nutritional content by offering balanced meal plans.

Step 4: Implement Key Initiatives

Introduce smart food tracking systems for better inventory control.

Use Lean Six Sigma to cut waste and improve efficiency.

Partner with local farmers and suppliers to support sustainability.

Step 5: Monitor and Continuously Improve

Track KPIs: meal costs per student, waste reduction, and satisfaction rates.

Use feedback loops to adjust menus and operations.

Regularly review health guidelines and adapt menus accordingly.

Conclusion

By combining cost efficiency, quality, and sustainability, food programs in educational institutions can offer nutritious, appealing, and affordable meals while maintaining operational efficiency.

Manufacturing Strategy in Business Success: Strategy Formation and Formulation in Intelligent Manufacturing

Manufacturing strategy plays a crucial role in business success by aligning production capabilities with overall business goals. In the era of intelligent manufacturing, companies leverage advanced technologies such as AI, IoT, robotics, and automation to optimize production efficiency and gain a competitive edge.

1. Manufacturing Strategy and Business Success

A manufacturing strategy defines how a company produces goods efficiently while maintaining quality, flexibility, and cost control. It impacts business success by:

? Reducing Costs – Streamlining processes and eliminating waste.

? Improving Quality – Implementing precision manufacturing and automated quality control.

? Enhancing Agility – Responding quickly to market changes with flexible production.

? Driving Innovation – Using technology to create unique, high-value products.

? Sustainability – Reducing energy consumption and waste in production.

2. Strategy Formation in Intelligent Manufacturing

Intelligent Manufacturing (IM) integrates AI, IoT, cloud computing, big data, and automation to enhance production.

Key Steps in Strategy Formation:

? Step 1: Industry & Market Analysis

Assess customer demand, market trends, and competitor strategies.

Identify technological advancements that can improve manufacturing efficiency.

? Step 2: Define Business Goals

Align manufacturing strategy with cost, quality, flexibility, and sustainability goals.

Example: A company may prioritize AI-driven production optimization to reduce energy costs.

? Step 3: Choose the Right Manufacturing Model

Traditional vs. Smart Manufacturing:

Traditional: Labor-intensive, fixed processes.

Smart Manufacturing: AI-driven, flexible, data-optimized.

Batch vs. Continuous Production:

Batch: Small, varied production runs (e.g., customized food products).

Continuous: Large-scale production (e.g., beverage production lines).

? Step 4: Invest in Intelligent Manufacturing Technologies

IoT Sensors: Real-time monitoring of equipment & quality.

AI & Machine Learning: Predictive maintenance, demand forecasting.

Robotic Process Automation (RPA): Faster, more precise assembly.

Digital Twins: Simulating production before physical implementation.

? Step 5: Performance Measurement & Continuous Improvement

Implement KPIs such as production uptime, defect rates, and energy efficiency.

Use Lean Six Sigma and PDCA (Plan-Do-Check-Act) cycles for continuous optimization.

Framework for Strategy Formulation

1?? Define Strategic Objectives – Align production goals with business vision.

2?? Assess Current Capabilities – Evaluate technology, workforce, and supply chain.

3?? Select Smart Manufacturing Tools – Identify AI, IoT, automation solutions.

4?? Implement & Test – Gradual deployment of intelligent systems.

5?? Measure & Optimize – Continuous improvement through data analytics.

4. Conclusion

A well-formulated manufacturing strategy is critical for business success, especially in the era of intelligent manufacturing. By integrating automation, AI, and real-time data analytics, businesses can:

? Increase efficiency while reducing costs.

? Enhance quality control with AI-powered defect detection.

? Improve flexibility to adapt to demand changes.

? Ensure sustainability through eco-friendly production methods.

Intelligent Manufacturing Strategies in the Food Industry

The food industry is evolving with the adoption of intelligent manufacturing (IM), integrating AI, IoT, robotics, automation, and big data to improve efficiency, quality, and sustainability. These strategies help food manufacturers reduce waste, enhance safety, and meet changing consumer demands.

1. Importance of Intelligent Manufacturing in Food Production

? Benefits of Smart Manufacturing in Food Industry

✔ Higher Efficiency – Automated production lines reduce errors and downtime.

✔ Improved Food Safety – AI-powered quality checks prevent contamination.

✔ Cost Reduction – Predictive maintenance and demand forecasting lower expenses.

✔ Sustainability – Smart factories optimize energy and water use.

✔ Customization – AI-driven production allows for personalized nutrition and packaging.

2. Manufacturing Strategies for Intelligent Food Production

(A) Make-to-Stock (MTS) – Mass Production with Smart Forecasting

? AI-driven demand prediction helps prevent overproduction and waste.

? Automated packaging and sorting systems speed up output.

? Example: Large food manufacturers (Nestlé, PepsiCo) use IoT sensors to optimize batch production.

(B) Make-to-Order (MTO) – Custom Food Manufacturing

? AI-powered production lines adjust recipes in real-time based on orders.

? Smart ingredient dispensers improve consistency.

? Example: Meal prep companies (e.g., Freshly, HelloFresh) use AI to create personalized meals.

(C) Assemble-to-Order (ATO) – Quick-Service Food Processing

? Automated ingredient dispensers streamline fast food assembly.

? AI-powered cooking robots ensure consistency in cooking times.

? Example: McDonald's AI-driven kitchen automation adjusts fryer settings based on demand.

(D) Engineer-to-Order (ETO) – Personalized Nutrition & Functional Foods

? AI-based food formulation creates specialized products (e.g., keto, vegan).

? Smart 3D food printing for custom dietary needs.

? Example: Personalized protein bars or medical nutrition for hospitals and athletes.

3. Strategy Formation for Smart Food Manufacturing

Step 1: Assess Market & Technology Trends

Use big data analytics to identify food trends (e.g., plant-based, sugar-free).

Evaluate automation and AI adoption in competitors' operations.

Step 2: Define Strategic Goals

? Reduce food waste by 30% through AI-driven inventory management.

? Increase production speed by 20% with robotic automation.

? Improve food traceability for 100% transparency using blockchain.

Step 3: Choose the Right Intelligent Manufacturing Technologies

Step 4: Implement & Optimize Smart Manufacturing

? Pilot AI-driven systems in food production lines.

? Use digital twins to simulate processes before full-scale implementation.

? Train workforce on intelligent automation tools.

Step 5: Monitor and Improve

? Use Key Performance Indicators (KPIs):

✓ Energy consumption per unit of food produced.

✓ Waste reduction percentage.

✓ Production uptime vs. downtime.

4. Future Trends in Intelligent Food Manufacturing

? AI-driven sensory evaluation for taste and texture optimization.

? Smart robotic kitchens that prepare meals autonomously.

? Sustainable protein production (lab-grown meat, algae-based proteins).

? Hyper-personalized nutrition with DNA-based meal planning.

Conclusion

By implementing intelligent manufacturing, food companies can increase efficiency, improve quality, and reduce costs while delivering safe, customized, and sustainable food products.

Intelligent Manufacturing in the Education Industry

Intelligent Manufacturing (IM) in education goes beyond traditional factory settings—it involves using AI, IoT, robotics, and automation to enhance learning environments, optimize resource management, and prepare students for Industry 4.0. Schools, universities, and vocational training centers can integrate smart manufacturing concepts to improve learning outcomes and efficiency.

1. Why Intelligent Manufacturing Matters in Education

? Enhances Practical Learning – AI-driven labs & simulation tools help students understand real-world manufacturing.

? Optimizes Resource Management – Smart inventory tracking for lab materials reduces waste.

? Prepares Future Workforce – Training students on automation, AI, and robotics bridges the skills gap.

? Personalized Education – AI-driven adaptive learning customizes manufacturing training based on student progress.

? Sustainability & Efficiency – Smart classrooms reduce energy use and integrate sustainable practices.

2. Applications of Intelligent Manufacturing in Education

(A) Smart Manufacturing Labs & AI-Driven Learning

? IoT-based sensors in workshops for real-time monitoring of machinery.

? AI-powered tutoring systems for manufacturing concepts (e.g., CNC machining, 3D printing).

? VR/AR-based simulations for hands-on learning in smart factories.

? Example: Digital twin technology allows students to simulate manufacturing processes before real-world application.

(B) Robotics & Automation in Technical Training

? Robotic arms and cobots (collaborative robots) for hands-on training.

? Smart CNC and additive manufacturing (3D printing) labs.

? Example: University engineering programs using AI-driven robotics labs to teach automation.

(C) AI & Big Data in Curriculum Personalization

? AI-driven adaptive learning platforms adjust lessons based on student performance.

? Smart learning analytics predict skill gaps and recommend training.

? Example: Industry 4.0-aligned courses using AI to design personalized training for future engineers.

(D) Intelligent Campus & Smart Infrastructure

? AI-driven scheduling systems optimize lab and classroom usage.

? IoT-based energy management reduces electricity costs.

? Example: Universities implementing smart campuses with automated lighting and lab resource tracking.

3. Strategy Formation for Intelligent Manufacturing in Education

Step 1: Identify Key Objectives

? Improve student engagement through immersive technologies (AR/VR).

? Reduce resource waste by 20% using AI-driven inventory tracking.

? Increase Industry 4.0 readiness with smart factory simulation tools.

Step 2: Select Smart Technologies for Education

Step 3: Implement & Integrate Smart Learning Solutions

? Develop smart factory labs for hands-on training.

? Use AI-based assessment tools to track student performance.

? Partner with industry to integrate real-world manufacturing case studies.

Step 4: Monitor & Optimize Learning Outcomes

? Key Performance Indicators (KPIs):

✔ Student skill development in automation & AI.

✔ Reduction in lab material waste via smart tracking.

✔ Increased job placements in smart manufacturing sectors.

4. Future Trends in Intelligent Manufacturing Education

? AI-powered teacher assistants for personalized learning.

? Blockchain-based certifications for Industry 4.0 skills.

? Digital twins for real-time industrial simulations.

? Cyber-physical learning environments for smart factory training.

Conclusion

Integrating intelligent manufacturing into education prepares students for the future of work, enhances learning efficiency, and bridges the gap between academia and industry.

Intelligent Manufacturing in the Automotive Industry

The automotive industry is at the forefront of Intelligent Manufacturing (IM), integrating AI, IoT, robotics, automation, and big data to enhance production, quality control, and supply chain management. This approach increases efficiency, reduces costs, and enables the production of advanced vehicles, including electric and autonomous cars.

1. Why Intelligent Manufacturing Matters in Automotive Industry

? Higher Efficiency – AI-driven predictive maintenance reduces downtime.

? Improved Quality – Automated defect detection enhances safety.

? Cost Reduction – Smart supply chain management optimizes inventory.

? Customization – AI-powered production lines enable personalized vehicles.

? Sustainability – Smart factories optimize energy and reduce waste.

2. Key Applications of Intelligent Manufacturing in Automotive

(A) Smart Factories & AI-Driven Production

? IoT sensors track production data in real-time for process optimization.

? AI-based predictive maintenance prevents unexpected machine failures.

? Robotic automation enhances precision in assembly lines.

? Example: Tesla's Gigafactories use AI-driven robotics for EV production.

(B) Automation & Robotics in Car Manufacturing

? Cobots (collaborative robots) work alongside humans for assembly tasks.

? Automated welding & painting systems ensure precision and speed.

? Example: BMW & Ford use AI-driven robots for assembling car components.

(C) AI & Big Data for Quality Control

? AI-powered vision systems detect manufacturing defects in real-time.

? Machine learning models predict potential failures before they occur.

? Example: Toyota uses AI-powered quality inspection systems to reduce defects.

(D) Intelligent Supply Chain & Smart Logistics

? Blockchain for supply chain transparency ensures ethical sourcing of materials.

? AI-driven demand forecasting optimizes parts inventory.

? Example: Volkswagen uses digital twins for supply chain optimization.

(E) 3D Printing & Additive Manufacturing

? Rapid prototyping reduces design and testing time.

? Lightweight custom parts enhance fuel efficiency in EVs.

? Example: Ford uses 3D printing for rapid prototyping & spare parts production.

3. Strategy Formation for Intelligent Automotive Manufacturing

Step 1: Define Strategic Goals

? Increase production efficiency by 20% through AI-driven automation.

? Reduce manufacturing defects by 30% with smart quality control.

? Cut energy consumption by 15% using IoT-based smart factories.

Step 2: Select Key Smart Manufacturing Technologies

Step 3: Implement & Optimize Smart Automotive Manufacturing

? Deploy AI-driven robotics in assembly lines.

? Use digital twins to simulate production before implementation.

? Integrate IoT for predictive maintenance and energy efficiency.

Step 4: Measure & Improve Performance

? Key Performance Indicators (KPIs):

✔ Production uptime vs. downtime (predictive maintenance efficiency).

✔ Defect rate reduction through AI-powered quality control.

✔ Cost savings & energy efficiency improvements.

4. Future Trends in Intelligent Automotive Manufacturing

? AI-driven generative design for lightweight vehicle structures.

? Fully autonomous smart factories with minimal human intervention.

? Hyper-personalized vehicles using AI-driven customization.

? Sustainable car production with recycled & biodegradable materials.

Conclusion

Intelligent Manufacturing is revolutionizing the automotive industry by improving efficiency, reducing costs, and enabling high-tech vehicle production.

Intelligent Manufacturing Roadmap for an Automotive Company

This roadmap provides a step-by-step guide to implementing Intelligent Manufacturing (IM) in an automotive company. It includes strategy formation, key technologies, and execution phases to optimize efficiency, reduce costs, and improve quality.

? Step 1: Define Business Objectives & Goals

Before implementing smart manufacturing, it's crucial to identify key goals for the company.

? Increase production efficiency by 20% using AI & robotics.

? Reduce manufacturing defects by 30% through automated quality control.

? Lower energy consumption by 15% with IoT-driven smart factories.

? Enhance supply chain transparency with blockchain & AI.

? Speed up vehicle customization using AI-driven production.

? Step 2: Select Key Intelligent Manufacturing Technologies

? Step 3: Develop an Implementation Plan

? Phase 1: Digital Foundation (0-6 months)

? Upgrade IT infrastructure – Cloud-based systems & cybersecurity.

? Integrate IoT sensors in production lines for real-time monitoring.

? Train workforce on AI, robotics, and smart manufacturing tools.

? Phase 2: Automation & AI Integration (6-12 months)

? Deploy robotic automation in assembly, welding, and painting.

? Use AI-driven predictive maintenance to reduce machine downtime.

? Implement AI-based quality control for defect detection.

? Phase 3: Smart Factory Optimization (12-24 months)

? Adopt digital twins for production and supply chain simulation.

? Integrate blockchain for transparent material sourcing.

? Optimize energy efficiency using AI and IoT-based energy monitoring.

? Phase 4: Continuous Improvement & Expansion (24+ months)

? Leverage AI-powered generative design for lightweight and efficient car components.

? Develop a hyper-personalized vehicle production line with AI-driven customization.

? Expand intelligent manufacturing to electric & autonomous vehicle production.

? Step 4: Monitor & Optimize Performance

? Key Performance Indicators (KPIs):

✔ Production Efficiency: Cycle time reduction & automation success rate.

✔ Quality Improvement: Defect rate decrease using AI inspection.

✔ Cost Savings: Energy consumption & waste reduction.

✔ Supply Chain Transparency: Blockchain adoption rate.

✔ Worker Productivity: Training completion & AI adoption by employees.

? Step 5: Scale & Innovate for the Future

? Sustainability: Implement green manufacturing with smart waste reduction.

? EV & Autonomous Car Focus: Optimize production for electric & self-driving vehicles.

? AI-Powered R&D: Develop next-gen vehicle components using AI and 3D printing.

? Conclusion: Transforming Automotive Production with Intelligent Manufacturing

By following this roadmap, your automotive company can transition into an Industry 4.0 leader, improving efficiency, reducing costs, and pioneering smart, sustainable, and high-tech vehicle production.

Structured Strategy Formulation in Intelligent Manufacturing

Intelligent Manufacturing (IM) requires a well-structured strategy formulation process to integrate AI, IoT, robotics, big data, and automation into production. This structured approach ensures alignment with business objectives, optimizes operations, and enhances competitiveness.

? 1. What is Structured Strategy Formulation?

Structured strategy formulation in Intelligent Manufacturing follows a systematic, data-driven process to define objectives, analyze challenges, and implement smart solutions. It includes:

✓ Data-Driven Decision-Making – Using AI & analytics for strategic insights.

✓ Integration of Smart Technologies – Ensuring seamless adoption of AI, IoT, automation, etc.

✓ Competitive Positioning – Enhancing efficiency, quality, and customization capabilities.

✓ Scalability & Flexibility – Adapting to industry changes and future innovations.

? 2. Steps for Structured Strategy Formulation in Intelligent Manufacturing

? Step 1: Define Vision & Objectives

Start by setting clear, measurable goals aligned with business growth and technological advancements.

? Increase production efficiency by 20% using smart automation.

? Reduce waste and energy consumption by 15% with IoT-based monitoring.

? Enhance product quality with AI-driven defect detection.

? Optimize supply chain through blockchain and predictive analytics.

? Enable mass customization with AI-powered flexible manufacturing.

? Step 2: Analyze Industry Trends & Internal Capabilities

? External Analysis (Industry 4.0 Trends & Competitor Benchmarking)

✓ Study emerging technologies like AI-driven robotics, digital twins, and smart factories.

✓ Evaluate competitors' adoption of intelligent automation and data-driven manufacturing.

? Internal Analysis (Capability Assessment & Readiness Check)

✓ Conduct a technology gap analysis to identify missing capabilities.

✓ Assess workforce skills and training needs for smart manufacturing.

✓ Review existing production infrastructure for scalability.

? Step 3: Identify Key Smart Manufacturing Technologies

? Step 4: Develop Implementation Roadmap

? Short-Term (0-6 months) – Digital Infrastructure Setup

? Upgrade IT systems for AI & IoT integration.

? Deploy IoT sensors for real-time monitoring.

? Train workforce on smart manufacturing tools.

? Mid-Term (6-18 months) – Automation & AI Integration

? Introduce robotic automation in production lines.

? Implement AI-driven predictive maintenance.

? Deploy digital twins for process optimization.

? Long-Term (18+ months) – Smart Factory & Continuous Innovation

? Scale AI & IoT solutions across all production units.

? Develop mass customization capabilities with flexible manufacturing.

? Expand intelligent manufacturing for new product lines (e.g., EVs, medical devices, etc.).

? Step 5: Monitor Performance & Optimize

Use Key Performance Indicators (KPIs) to measure success and refine the strategy.

✓ Production Efficiency: Cycle time & automation impact.

✓ Defect Rate Reduction: AI-powered quality control results.

✓ Cost Savings: Energy consumption & waste reduction.

✓ Supply Chain Transparency: Blockchain adoption rate.

✓ Workforce Productivity: Training completion & AI adoption rates.

? 3. Future-Proofing the Strategy

? Adopt AI-powered generative design for innovative product development.

? Expand sustainable manufacturing through smart waste reduction.

? Invest in hyper-personalized production using AI-driven customization.

? Integrate quantum computing for next-gen intelligent manufacturing models.

? Conclusion: A Systematic Approach to Intelligent Manufacturing

Structured strategy formulation ensures a step-by-step, data-driven transformation in intelligent manufacturing. By aligning AI, IoT, automation, and robotics with business goals, companies can achieve efficiency, quality, and sustainability in Industry 4.0.

Structured Strategy Formulation for Intelligent Manufacturing in the Food Industry

The food industry is undergoing a transformation with Intelligent Manufacturing (IM), integrating AI, IoT, robotics, and automation to enhance efficiency, safety, and sustainability. A structured strategy formulation ensures a systematic, data-driven approach to implementing these technologies.

? 1. Defining Vision & Objectives

? Increase production efficiency by 20% using automation & AI.

? Enhance food safety with real-time IoT monitoring & AI-based quality control.

? Reduce waste by 30% through smart inventory & predictive analytics.

? Optimize energy & water usage for sustainable food processing.

? Enable mass customization using AI-driven flexible manufacturing.

? 2. Industry Analysis & Readiness Check

? External Analysis (Trends & Competitive Landscape)

✓ Adoption of AI-powered quality inspection in food packaging.

✓ Use of IoT sensors to monitor temperature & humidity in supply chains.

✓ Growing demand for personalized nutrition & on-demand food production.

✓ Emphasis on sustainability & food traceability with blockchain.

? Internal Analysis (Technology & Workforce Assessment)

✓ Evaluate current automation levels in food processing & packaging.

✓ Identify gaps in AI, IoT, and robotics adoption.

✓ Assess workforce training needs for operating intelligent systems.

✓ Ensure compliance with food safety regulations (FDA, HACCP, etc.).

? 3. Selecting Key Intelligent Manufacturing Technologies

? 4. Developing an Implementation Roadmap

? Phase 1: Digital Foundation (0-6 Months)

? Install IoT sensors for real-time monitoring of food processing.

? Upgrade IT infrastructure to support AI & automation.

? Implement AI-driven demand forecasting for supply chain optimization.

? Phase 2: Automation & AI Integration (6-18 Months)

? Deploy robotic automation in food processing & packaging.

? Use AI-powered quality control for detecting contamination & defects.

? Adopt blockchain for transparent food traceability.

? Phase 3: Smart Factory Optimization (18+ Months)

? Develop digital twins for optimizing food production efficiency.

? Integrate 3D food printing for customized food production.

? Expand intelligent manufacturing to new product lines (e.g., personalized nutrition, plant-based foods).

? 5. Measuring Performance & Continuous Improvement

? Key Performance Indicators (KPIs):

✓ Production Efficiency: AI-driven cycle time & automation impact.

✓ Food Safety Compliance: Reduction in contamination risks using AI.

✓ Waste Reduction: Lower food spoilage with smart inventory systems.

✓ Sustainability Metrics: Energy & water usage optimization.

✓ Supply Chain Transparency: Blockchain implementation rate.

? **6. Future-Proofing the Strategy**

? Adopt AI-powered food formulation for personalized nutrition.

? Expand sustainable packaging solutions using smart biodegradable materials.

? Integrate quantum computing for optimizing complex food processing algorithms.

? Leverage fully autonomous smart factories with minimal human intervention.

? Conclusion: A Systematic Approach to Smart Food Manufacturing

By implementing a structured strategy for intelligent manufacturing, food companies can enhance safety, efficiency, and sustainability while meeting consumer demands for transparency & customization.

Structured Strategy Formulation for Intelligent Manufacturing in the Dairy Industry ??

The dairy industry is evolving with Intelligent Manufacturing (IM) to improve efficiency, food safety, sustainability, and traceability. A structured strategy formulation ensures a systematic, data-driven approach to integrating AI, IoT, robotics, and automation into dairy processing and distribution.

? **1. Defining Vision & Objectives**

? Increase production efficiency by 25% using automation & AI.

? Enhance milk safety with real-time IoT monitoring & AI-based quality control.

? Reduce dairy waste by 30% through smart inventory & predictive analytics.

? Optimize energy & water usage to make dairy processing more sustainable.

? Ensure 100% supply chain transparency using blockchain traceability.

? **2. Industry Analysis & Readiness Check**

? External Analysis (Trends & Competitive Landscape)

✔ Growing adoption of AI-powered milk quality testing.

✔ Use of IoT sensors for real-time temperature and bacterial monitoring.

✔ Demand for sustainable dairy processing & packaging.

✔ Increased focus on personalized dairy products (lactose-free, fortified milk, etc.).

? Internal Analysis (Technology & Workforce Assessment)

✔ Evaluate current automation levels in milk processing & packaging.

✔ Identify gaps in AI, IoT, and robotics adoption.

✔ Assess workforce training needs for intelligent manufacturing tools.

✔ Ensure compliance with food safety regulations (FDA, HACCP, FSSAI, etc.).

? **3. Selecting Key Intelligent Manufacturing Technologies**

? **4. Developing an Implementation Roadmap**

? **Phase 1: Digital Foundation (0-6 Months)**

? Deploy IoT sensors in milk collection, storage, and transportation.

? Upgrade IT infrastructure for AI-driven quality analysis.

? Implement AI-based demand forecasting for dairy inventory optimization.

? **Phase 2: Automation & AI Integration (6-18 Months)**

? Introduce robotic automation in pasteurization & packaging.

? Use AI-powered defect detection for milk quality control.

? Implement blockchain for transparent dairy product traceability.

? **Phase 3: Smart Dairy Optimization (18+ Months)**

? Adopt digital twins to simulate & optimize dairy processing.

? Develop 3D-printed dairy alternatives (e.g., plant-based milk proteins).

? Expand intelligent manufacturing to new dairy product lines (e.g., lactose-free, fortified milk).

? **5. Measuring Performance & Continuous Improvement**

? Key Performance Indicators (KPIs):

✔ Production Efficiency: AI-driven cycle time & automation impact.

✔ Milk Safety Compliance: Reduction in bacterial contamination risks using AI.

✔ Dairy Waste Reduction: Lower spoilage rates with smart storage.

✔ Sustainability Metrics: Energy & water consumption optimization.

✔ Supply Chain Transparency: Blockchain implementation rate.

? 6. Future-Proofing the Strategy

? AI-powered dairy formulation for personalized milk & cheese products.

? Sustainable dairy packaging using biodegradable smart materials.

? Quantum computing for optimizing complex dairy processing models.

? Fully autonomous smart dairy plants with minimal human intervention.

? Conclusion: Smart Dairy Manufacturing for the Future

By following this structured intelligent manufacturing strategy, dairy companies can achieve higher efficiency, improved product quality, and sustainability, ensuring cost savings and competitive advantage in the evolving food industry.

Structured Strategy Formulation for Intelligent Manufacturing in the Education Industry ??

Intelligent Manufacturing (IM) in the education industry involves integrating AI, IoT, robotics, automation, and data-driven decision-making to enhance learning environments, skill development, and operational efficiency in educational institutions. A structured strategy ensures a systematic, scalable, and sustainable transformation.

? 1. Defining Vision & Objectives

? Enhance technical education with hands-on learning in smart factories.

? Implement AI-driven adaptive learning for manufacturing courses.

? Create real-world Industry 4.0 labs for skill-based training.

? Reduce operational costs by automating administrative and facility management tasks.

? Develop digital twins of manufacturing processes for virtual learning.

? Integrate intelligent automation into research & development centers.

? 2. Industry & Institutional Analysis

? External Analysis (Education Trends & Industry Demand)

✔ Rising demand for Industry 4.0-ready workforce in smart factories.

✔ Universities and training centers shifting towards AI, IoT, and robotics-based learning.

✔ Growing adoption of simulation tools, VR, and AR for manufacturing education.

✔ Emphasis on hands-on training through digital twins & smart labs.

? Internal Analysis (Capability & Readiness Check)

✔ Assess current education infrastructure for Industry 4.0 compatibility.

✔ Identify gaps in AI, robotics, and smart automation courses.

✔ Evaluate faculty & student readiness for intelligent manufacturing technologies.

✔ Review partnerships with industries for real-world project collaboration.

? 3. Selecting Key Intelligent Manufacturing Technologies for Education

? 4. Developing an Implementation Roadmap

? Phase 1: Digital Foundation (0-6 Months)

? Set up IoT-enabled smart labs for real-time data collection & automation training.

? Introduce AI-based adaptive learning for Industry 4.0 education.

? Upgrade IT infrastructure to support digital manufacturing simulations.

? Phase 2: Integration & Practical Application (6-18 Months)

? Implement robotics & automation labs for hands-on student training.

? Deploy digital twins for virtual factory simulations.

? Use blockchain for secure student credentials & project documentation.

? Phase 3: Smart Campus & Industry Collaboration (18+ Months)

? Integrate AI-driven learning assistants for personalized education.

? Expand VR-based manufacturing training for immersive learning.

? Develop partnerships with industries for real-world manufacturing projects.

? 5. Measuring Performance & Continuous Improvement

? Key Performance Indicators (KPIs):

✓ Student Learning Outcomes: Industry 4.0 skill proficiency improvement.

✓ Lab Efficiency: Increase in hands-on practical training hours.

✓ Technology Adoption Rate: AI, robotics, and IoT implementation in curriculum.

✓ Industry Collaboration: Number of partnerships & internships in smart manufacturing.

✓ Student Employability: Percentage of graduates placed in Industry 4.0 roles.

? 6. Future-Proofing the Strategy

? AI-powered virtual instructors for manufacturing skill development.

? Sustainable smart campuses with AI-driven resource optimization.

? Collaborative innovation hubs for university-industry co-research.

? Fully autonomous learning factories integrated with intelligent automation.

? Conclusion: The Future of Intelligent Manufacturing in Education

A structured strategy for Intelligent Manufacturing in education ensures technological integration, hands-on training, and industry readiness, preparing students for the future of smart factories and Industry 4.0.

Approaches to Strategy Formulation in Intelligent Manufacturing ???

Intelligent Manufacturing (IM) involves integrating AI, IoT, automation, robotics, and data analytics to optimize production, improve efficiency, and ensure sustainability. Strategy formulation in IM requires a structured, adaptable, and data-driven approach to align with industry needs, technological advancements, and competitive pressures.

Here are key approaches to strategy formulation in Intelligent Manufacturing:

? 1. Classical Approach (Planned Strategy)

? Focus: Long-term planning based on market analysis and competitive positioning.

? Steps:

Define mission, vision, and long-term goals for IM adoption.

Conduct SWOT analysis (Strengths, Weaknesses, Opportunities, Threats).

Develop a structured roadmap for technology adoption (AI, IoT, automation).

Implement in phases with key performance indicators (KPIs).

? Best for: Large enterprises with stable market conditions.

? Example: Siemens systematically planning & implementing Industry 4.0 solutions.

? 2. Adaptive Approach (Emergent Strategy)

? Focus: Flexibility and continuous adaptation to technological changes.

? Steps:

Start with pilot projects for AI & automation in manufacturing.

Use real-time data & AI insights to refine strategies dynamically.

Encourage cross-functional teams to experiment & iterate on innovations.

? Best for: Fast-changing industries, SMEs, and startups.

? Example: Tesla continuously refining manufacturing processes with AI-driven automation.

? 3. Evolutionary Approach (Incremental Strategy)

? Focus: Gradual improvements in IM based on small-scale changes.

? Steps:

Begin with process automation (e.g., robotics for repetitive tasks).

Gradually integrate AI-driven predictive maintenance.

Expand IoT-enabled real-time monitoring across supply chains.

? Best for: Businesses transitioning from traditional to smart manufacturing.

? Example: Foxconn gradually upgrading assembly lines with intelligent robotics.

? 4. Disruptive Approach (Innovative Strategy)

? Focus: Transformational change through breakthrough technologies.

? Steps:

Identify new business models enabled by IM (e.g., mass customization, digital twins).

Leverage AI-powered autonomous systems to redefine production.

Adopt blockchain for transparent supply chain management.

? Best for: Companies aiming for industry leadership & radical innovation.

? Example: Amazon's fully automated warehouses revolutionizing logistics.

? 5. Agile Approach (Lean & Data-Driven Strategy)

? Focus: Rapid iterations, real-time analytics, and lean manufacturing.

? Steps:

Implement IoT & AI-driven analytics for continuous feedback.

Use machine learning models to optimize production dynamically.

Apply Kaizen & Lean principles for efficiency gains.

? Best for: Manufacturers focusing on cost reduction & agile decision-making.

? Example: Toyota's smart manufacturing integrating AI & IoT for lean production.

? 6. Hybrid Approach (Integrated Strategy)

? Focus: Combining multiple approaches for a balanced strategy.

? Steps:

Use classical planning for long-term vision.

Apply adaptive & agile strategies for emerging tech adoption.

Incorporate evolutionary & disruptive elements for sustained competitiveness.

? Best for: Large-scale enterprises with diverse product lines.

? Example: GE's digital transformation blending planned, adaptive, and disruptive strategies.

? Conclusion: Choosing the Right Approach

The choice of strategy formulation approach in Intelligent Manufacturing depends on:

? Company size & industry dynamics

? Technology readiness & investment capacity

? Competitive positioning & innovation goals

Approaches to Strategy Formulation in Intelligent Manufacturing for the Food Industry ???

Intelligent Manufacturing (IM) in the food industry focuses on automation, AI-driven quality control, IoT-based traceability, and sustainable production. A structured strategy formulation ensures efficiency, safety, and adaptability in food processing, packaging, and distribution.

? 1. Classical Approach (Planned Strategy)

? Best for: Large food processing companies with stable markets.

? Strategy:

Long-term planning for smart food production.

AI-powered quality control for reducing food contamination risks.

IoT-enabled cold chain logistics for perishable goods.

Blockchain for traceability to meet food safety regulations.

? Example: Nestlé systematically implementing AI & blockchain for supply chain transparency.

? 2. Adaptive Approach (Emergent Strategy)

? Best for: Startups and companies in rapidly changing food tech.

? Strategy:

Start with small-scale automation pilots in food packaging.

Use real-time AI insights to optimize production dynamically.

Implement flexible manufacturing for personalized food products.

? Example: Impossible Foods adapting AI-based plant-based food formulation.

? 3. Evolutionary Approach (Incremental Strategy)

? Best for: Traditional food manufacturers transitioning to IM.

? Strategy:

Introduce smart sensors for food storage monitoring.

Upgrade batch processing systems with automation.

Implement AI-driven waste reduction in food production.

? Example: PepsiCo gradually optimizing manufacturing using AI and robotics.

? 4. Disruptive Approach (Innovative Strategy)

? Best for: Companies aiming for revolutionary changes in food production.

? Strategy:

Develop 3D-printed food solutions for mass customization.

Use AI-powered flavor profiling for new product development.

Create fully automated cloud kitchens for smart food service.

? Example: Amazon Fresh using AI-powered robotic fulfillment for food distribution.

? 5. Agile Approach (Lean & Data-Driven Strategy)

? Best for: Companies optimizing costs while improving efficiency.

? Strategy:

Implement AI-based demand forecasting to minimize food waste.

Use IoT-enabled smart factories to reduce energy consumption.

Apply Lean & Six Sigma to streamline food processing.

? Example: Coca-Cola using AI for lean manufacturing & supply chain optimization.

? 6. Hybrid Approach (Integrated Strategy)

? Best for: Large-scale food enterprises combining multiple strategies.

? Strategy:

Use classical strategy for long-term food safety & sustainability goals.

Apply adaptive approaches for emerging AI innovations.

Incorporate disruptive technologies like food robotics & blockchain.

? Example: Danone using a hybrid model for smart dairy processing & sustainability.

? Conclusion: Choosing the Right Approach

The best strategy depends on:

✔ Company size & product type

✔ Market dynamics & regulatory requirements

✔ Technology readiness & innovation goals

Approaches to Strategy Formulation in Intelligent Manufacturing for the Education Industry ??

Intelligent Manufacturing (IM) in the education industry involves integrating AI, robotics, IoT, digital twins, and automation into technical education, vocational training, and research. A structured strategy formulation ensures that educational institutions can equip students with Industry 4.0 skills, enhance learning experiences, and collaborate with industries for innovation.

? 1. Classical Approach (Planned Strategy)

? Best for: Universities and institutions with structured, long-term development goals.

? Strategy:

Develop a 10-year roadmap for integrating IM in education.

Invest in smart manufacturing labs with AI & robotics.

Partner with industries for internships & real-world projects.

Design AI-based adaptive learning modules for IM courses.

? Example: MIT systematically implementing AI & digital twins in manufacturing education.

? 2. Adaptive Approach (Emergent Strategy)

? Best for: Educational institutions in rapidly evolving tech environments.

? Strategy:

Start with pilot projects in IM-based training programs.

Use real-time AI insights to improve teaching methodologies.

Implement modular curriculum updates based on industry needs.

? Example: Technical Universities in Germany continuously updating their Industry 4.0 programs based on emerging technologies.

? 3. Evolutionary Approach (Incremental Strategy)

? Best for: Traditional institutions transitioning to IM-based education.

? Strategy:

Begin with automation & robotics in existing technical courses.

Introduce IoT-enabled smart classrooms and virtual labs.

Gradually incorporate AI-powered simulations for practical training.

? Example: Indian Institutes of Technology (IITs) gradually introducing IM in engineering courses.

? 4. Disruptive Approach (Innovative Strategy)

? Best for: Institutions aiming to lead in IM education.

? Strategy:

Develop fully autonomous smart campuses with AI-driven operations.

Create AI-powered digital instructors for personalized learning.

Establish virtual reality-based manufacturing training.

? Example: Stanford University pioneering AI-driven education in manufacturing.

? 5. Agile Approach (Lean & Data-Driven Strategy)

? Best for: Institutions optimizing costs while ensuring cutting-edge learning.

? Strategy:

Use AI-driven analytics to refine teaching methods.

Implement digital twins for real-time learning in smart factories.

Apply Lean principles to improve education delivery efficiency.

? Example: Singapore's Smart Learning Institutes integrating AI & IoT in technical training.

? 6. Hybrid Approach (Integrated Strategy)

? Best for: Large universities and multi-disciplinary institutions.

? Strategy:

Use classical planning for long-term IM education integration.

Apply adaptive strategies to keep up with technological advancements.

Incorporate disruptive innovations for cutting-edge research and training.

? Example: Harvard's Innovation Labs integrating AI, IoT, and IM research.

? Conclusion: Choosing the Right Approach

The best strategy depends on:

✓ Type of institution (university, technical school, online education, etc.)

✓ Technological readiness & funding availability

✓ Industry collaboration & market demand for IM skills

Approaches to Strategy Formulation in Intelligent Manufacturing for the Automotive Industry ??

Intelligent Manufacturing (IM) in the automotive industry involves leveraging AI, robotics, IoT, digital twins, blockchain, and automation to enhance production efficiency, reduce costs, improve vehicle quality, and enable smart factories. A well-defined strategy formulation ensures that automakers, suppliers, and R&D centers can adapt to evolving technologies and market demands.

? 1. Classical Approach (Planned Strategy)

? Best for: Established automakers with stable operations.

? Strategy:

Develop a 10-year roadmap for IM integration.

Invest in AI-driven predictive maintenance for production lines.

Standardize automation & robotics across all manufacturing plants.

Implement blockchain-based supply chain tracking for transparency.

? Example: Toyota's Smart Factories using planned AI-driven lean production.

? 2. Adaptive Approach (Emergent Strategy)

? Best for: Companies in dynamic markets (EVs, autonomous vehicles).

? Strategy:

Launch pilot projects for AI & IoT-enabled production lines.

Use real-time AI insights to refine manufacturing efficiency.

Continuously adjust IM adoption plans based on new technology developments.

? Example: Tesla's Gigafactories rapidly adapting AI & automation for battery and EV production.

? 3. Evolutionary Approach (Incremental Strategy)

? Best for: Traditional automakers transitioning to IM.

? Strategy:

Start with robotic process automation (RPA) for assembly lines.

Introduce AI-based defect detection systems.

Expand IoT-enabled smart sensors for predictive maintenance.

? Example: Ford gradually implementing AI-based quality control systems.

? 4. Disruptive Approach (Innovative Strategy)

? Best for: Companies aiming for industry leadership in IM.

? Strategy:

Develop fully autonomous smart factories with AI-driven production.

Use 3D printing for vehicle prototyping & parts production.

Integrate digital twins for real-time vehicle testing & design.

? Example: Rivian & Lucid Motors using disruptive AI & automation in EV production.

? 5. Agile Approach (Lean & Data-Driven Strategy)

? Best for: Companies optimizing manufacturing costs and efficiency.

? Strategy:

Use AI-driven demand forecasting to minimize production waste.

Implement machine learning models to optimize logistics & supply chains.

Apply lean manufacturing principles with real-time data analytics.

? Example: BMW's smart factories leveraging AI for efficiency and sustainability.

? 6. Hybrid Approach (Integrated Strategy)

? Best for: Large automotive enterprises with diverse product lines.

? Strategy:

Use classical planning for long-term IM integration.

Apply adaptive strategies for emerging AI & IoT innovations.

Integrate disruptive technologies like smart robotics & digital twins.

? Example: Volkswagen Group blending planned, adaptive, and disruptive IM strategies.

? Conclusion: Choosing the Right Approach

The best strategy depends on:

✓ Company size (OEMs, suppliers, startups, etc.)

✓ Technology readiness & investment capacity

✓ Market dynamics (EVs, autonomous vehicles, sustainability)

Realization of New Strategies & System Designs in Intelligent Manufacturing ???

The realization of new strategies and system designs in Intelligent Manufacturing (IM) involves integrating AI, IoT, robotics, digital twins, cloud computing, and smart automation to improve efficiency, flexibility, and sustainability.

This process consists of four key phases: Conceptualization, System Design, Implementation, and Continuous Improvement.

? 1. Conceptualization: Defining New Strategies

? Objective: Identify key challenges, opportunities, and goals for IM.

? Key Steps:

Conduct market & industry analysis (Industry 4.0 & 5.0 trends).

Perform SWOT analysis (Strengths, Weaknesses, Opportunities, Threats).

Define KPIs (Key Performance Indicators) for IM adoption.

Select a strategy approach (planned, adaptive, disruptive, etc.).

? Example: Tesla's Gigafactories started with a vision of AI-driven automated production.

? 2. System Design: Creating the Intelligent Manufacturing Model

? Objective: Develop an integrated digital & physical manufacturing system.

? Key Steps:

Design smart factory architecture with AI, IoT, and robotics.

Implement cyber-physical systems (CPS) for real-time monitoring.

Integrate digital twins for virtual testing & optimization.

Develop modular, scalable production layouts.

? Example: Siemens' Digital Factory uses digital twins for real-time system optimization.

? 3. Implementation: Deploying the Intelligent Manufacturing System

? Objective: Deploy and integrate smart technologies into manufacturing operations.

? Key Steps:

Automate production lines with AI-driven robotics & autonomous systems.

Use IoT-enabled sensors for real-time data collection & predictive maintenance.

Implement AI-powered decision-making systems for dynamic process optimization.

Establish cloud-based industrial control for remote operations.

? Example: BMW's Smart Factory integrates AI for quality control & predictive maintenance.

? 4. Continuous Improvement: Enhancing and Scaling

? Objective: Optimize and refine intelligent manufacturing processes over time.

? Key Steps:

Use machine learning & data analytics for continuous optimization.

Apply Lean & Six Sigma methodologies for efficiency improvements.

Conduct regular AI-driven audits to identify areas for automation & cost reduction.

Expand IM capabilities to new product lines & market segments.

? Example: Amazon Robotics continuously enhances warehouse automation for efficiency.

? Conclusion: Realizing IM Strategies Successfully

To realize new strategies & system designs in Intelligent Manufacturing:

✓ Align strategy with industry needs & future trends

✓ Design flexible & scalable smart factory models

✓ Ensure seamless AI, IoT, and automation integration

✓ Adopt an iterative, data-driven improvement approach

CHAPTER TEN

Smart Manufacturing

Various Smart Manufacturing Techniques ???

Smart Manufacturing (SM) integrates AI, IoT, robotics, cloud computing, and data analytics to enhance efficiency, flexibility, and productivity in manufacturing. These technologies enable real-time monitoring, predictive maintenance, automation, and intelligent decision-making.

Here are some of the most impactful Smart Manufacturing Techniques:

1. Internet of Things (IoT) in Manufacturing ?

? What it does:

Connects machines, sensors, and systems for real-time data collection.

Enables remote monitoring & control of production processes.

Improves supply chain visibility with smart inventory management.

? Example: GE's Brilliant Factory uses IoT to optimize production efficiency.

2. Artificial Intelligence (AI) & Machine Learning (ML) ?

? What it does:

AI-powered predictive maintenance prevents unexpected failures.

ML-driven process optimization improves efficiency & reduces waste.

AI-enabled quality control systems detect defects in real time.

? Example: BMW's AI-powered quality inspection ensures defect-free production.

3. Digital Twins & Simulation ?

? What it does:

Creates virtual replicas of physical assets for simulation & testing.

Enables real-time process monitoring & predictive analytics.

Helps manufacturers optimize workflows & reduce downtime.

? Example: Siemens Digital Factory uses digital twins for process optimization.

4. Robotics & Automation ??

? What it does:

Uses collaborative robots (cobots) for precision manufacturing.

Automates assembly lines, welding, painting, and packaging.

Reduces labor costs & improves consistency in production.

? Example: Tesla's Gigafactory employs AI-driven robotics for EV manufacturing.

5. Additive Manufacturing (3D Printing) ??

? What it does:

Enables on-demand, customized part production.

Reduces material waste compared to traditional manufacturing.

Accelerates prototyping & product development cycles.

? Example: Airbus uses 3D printing to manufacture aircraft parts with less material waste.

6. Cloud Computing & Edge Computing ?

? What it does:

Stores & processes manufacturing data in the cloud for global access.

Uses edge computing for real-time data processing closer to production sites.

Enhances collaboration between factories & supply chains.

? Example: Amazon Web Services (AWS) IoT helps manufacturers with cloud-based data analytics.

7. Blockchain for Supply Chain Transparency ?

? What it does:

Ensures end-to-end visibility in supply chain operations.

Provides secure, tamper-proof tracking of materials & products.

Improves traceability & compliance with industry regulations.

? Example: Nestlé & Walmart use blockchain for food supply chain tracking.

8. Augmented Reality (AR) & Virtual Reality (VR) in Manufacturing ??

? What it does:

Uses AR for assembly instructions & remote troubleshooting.

Applies VR for immersive training & factory simulations.

Enhances worker productivity & safety with real-time guidance.

? Example: Boeing uses AR glasses to assist workers in aircraft wiring tasks.

9. Cyber-Physical Systems (CPS) & Smart Sensors ?

? What it does:

Combines physical machines with digital controls for automation.

Uses smart sensors to monitor temperature, pressure, and equipment health.

Enables self-optimizing production lines based on real-time data.

? Example: Siemens' Industry 4.0 plants use CPS for intelligent automation.

10. Lean & Six Sigma with AI Optimization ?

? What it does:

Applies AI-driven Lean & Six Sigma techniques to eliminate waste.

Uses real-time data analytics to enhance manufacturing efficiency.

Improves production speed, accuracy, and sustainability.

? Example: Toyota's Smart Manufacturing System integrates Lean AI techniques.

? Conclusion: The Future of Smart Manufacturing

Smart Manufacturing enables:

✓ Higher efficiency & reduced costs

✓ Real-time monitoring & predictive maintenance

✓ Customization & flexibility in production

✓ Improved product quality & sustainability

Supply Chain Management (SCM) Explained ???

Supply Chain Management (SCM) is the process of planning, managing, and optimizing the flow of goods, services, information, and finances from raw material suppliers to the final customer. It ensures efficiency, cost reduction, and customer satisfaction.

? Key Components of Supply Chain Management

1. Planning & Demand Forecasting ?

? Uses AI & big data to predict demand trends.

? Helps in inventory optimization to prevent overstocking/shortages.

? Aligns supply chain with market trends & customer preferences.

? Example: Amazon's AI-driven demand forecasting optimizes inventory levels across warehouses.

2. Procurement & Supplier Management ?

? Identifies reliable suppliers for raw materials & components.

? Uses blockchain for transparency & secure transactions.

? Negotiates cost-effective contracts with suppliers.

? Example: Apple's global supplier ecosystem ensures efficient procurement & component sourcing.

3. Manufacturing & Production ?

? Optimizes factory operations with Lean & Six Sigma.

? Uses IoT sensors & AI for real-time quality control.

? Applies Just-In-Time (JIT) manufacturing to reduce waste.

  ? Example: Toyota's Lean Manufacturing System minimizes waste & enhances productivity.

4. Inventory & Warehouse Management ?

? Uses AI-powered warehouse robots for faster sorting & storage.

? Implements RFID & barcode scanning for real-time tracking.

? Applies cloud-based inventory management for data-driven decisions.

  ? Example: Walmart's smart warehouses use AI & robotics for inventory automation.

5. Logistics & Distribution ?

? Uses route optimization algorithms for faster delivery.

? Employs autonomous trucks & drones for last-mile delivery.

? Implements real-time GPS tracking for shipments.

  ? Example: DHL & FedEx use AI-driven logistics for real-time delivery tracking.

6. Customer Service & Returns (Reverse Logistics) ?

? Uses AI-powered chatbots for customer inquiries.

? Implements automated returns processing for defective/damaged products.

? Enhances customer satisfaction with fast dispute resolution.

  ? Example: Zara's flexible return policy improves customer satisfaction through AI-driven returns.

? Modern Trends in Supply Chain Management

1. AI & Machine Learning in SCM ?

? AI predicts demand fluctuations & optimizes supply chain efficiency.

? Automates warehouse management & inventory tracking.

2. Blockchain for Transparency ?

? Ensures secure transactions & fraud prevention.

? Improves traceability of raw materials & finished goods.

3. IoT & Smart Sensors ?

? Provides real-time tracking of shipments & goods.

? Detects temperature, humidity, and storage conditions.

4. Sustainability & Green Supply Chains ?

? Uses eco-friendly transportation & packaging.

? Reduces carbon footprint & waste.

5. Cloud Computing in SCM ☁?

? Enables real-time data sharing across the supply chain.

? Improves collaboration between suppliers, manufacturers & retailers.

? Conclusion: Why SCM Matters?

✓ Reduces costs & improves efficiency

✓ Ensures on-time delivery & customer satisfaction

✓ Enhances transparency & risk management

✓ Adapts to market changes & disruptions

? Key Components of Food Supply Chain Management

1. Demand Forecasting & Procurement ?

? Uses AI & big data analytics to predict food demand.

? Optimizes procurement of raw ingredients from local & global suppliers.

? Reduces food waste by aligning production with demand trends.

  ? Example: McDonald's uses AI to predict sales and adjust ingredient orders accordingly.

2. Supplier Management & Quality Control ?

? Selects certified & ethical suppliers to ensure food safety.

? Uses IoT sensors to monitor ingredient quality in real time.

? Implements blockchain for supplier transparency & traceability.

  ? Example: Nestlé uses blockchain to track ingredients from farm to table.

3. Smart Manufacturing & Food Processing ?

? Uses AI-driven automation for sorting, processing, and packaging.

? Applies IoT sensors for real-time monitoring of food production.

? Implements robotic systems to improve speed & hygiene in processing plants.

  ? Example: Coca-Cola's AI-driven bottling plants optimize production efficiency.

4. Cold Chain Logistics & Storage ❄??

? Uses IoT temperature sensors to track perishable goods.

? Implements AI-driven route optimization for faster delivery.

? Uses automated warehouses for food storage & inventory tracking.

  ? Example: Walmart uses IoT sensors to monitor food freshness during transportation.

5. Retail & Distribution ?

? Uses AI-based demand forecasting to stock stores efficiently.

? Implements smart vending machines & automated checkouts.

? Uses real-time tracking to prevent food spoilage.

  ? Example: Amazon Fresh uses AI-driven warehouse & delivery logistics for faster food delivery.

6. Food Safety & Traceability ?

? Implements blockchain for end-to-end transparency.

? Uses AI-powered cameras to detect contamination.

? Applies digital twins for real-time supply chain monitoring.

  ? Example: IBM Food Trust (used by Walmart & Nestlé) tracks food origins using blockchain.

7. Sustainability & Waste Reduction ???

? Uses AI to optimize packaging for minimal waste.

? Implements biodegradable & recyclable materials.

? Uses food waste tracking systems to minimize losses.

  ? Example: Unilever's AI-driven sustainability program reduces food waste across its supply chain.

  ? Smart Technologies in Food SCM

  ? AI & Machine Learning → Predicts demand & optimizes logistics.

? IoT Sensors → Tracks food temperature & quality in real time.

? Blockchain → Ensures transparency & food safety compliance.

? Robotics & Automation → Enhances processing & packaging efficiency.

? Cloud Computing → Provides real-time data access for all supply chain partners.

  ? Conclusion: Why Smart SCM Matters in Food Industry?

  ✔ Reduces food waste & improves sustainability

✔ Ensures food safety & regulatory compliance

✔ Improves efficiency & lowers transportation costs

✔ Enhances customer trust & transparency

Key Components of Education Supply Chain Management (SCM) ??

Education Supply Chain Management (SCM) ensures that educational institutions receive the right resources—such as textbooks, technology, and learning materials—efficiently and cost-effectively. With the rise of digital learning, e-learning platforms, and AI-driven education, SCM in education is evolving to include smart technologies for better resource planning and distribution.

? 1. Demand Forecasting & Resource Planning ?

? Uses AI & data analytics to predict student enrollment trends.

? Aligns budget planning with resource needs (books, laptops, lab equipment).

? Ensures cost-efficient procurement of educational materials.

    ? Example: Universities use AI-driven forecasting to predict student supply needs for each semester.

? 2. Procurement & Supplier Management ?

    ? Selects reliable suppliers for textbooks, digital tools, and lab equipment.

? Uses blockchain for secure transactions & transparent supplier tracking.

? Ensures quality control for educational materials.

    ? Example: Amazon Education partners with institutions for bulk book & tech supply.

? 3. Logistics & Distribution ?

    ? Ensures timely delivery of learning materials to schools & universities.

? Uses AI-driven logistics to optimize delivery routes for efficiency.

? Implements smart inventory tracking for school supplies.

    ? Example: Google for Education ships Chromebooks & digital tools based on school demand trends.

? 4. Digital Learning Infrastructure & IT Support ?

    ? Deploys cloud-based education platforms (Google Classroom, Moodle, Blackboard).

? Uses IoT for smart classrooms & interactive learning tools.

? Ensures cybersecurity & data privacy for online learning.

    ? Example: Microsoft Teams for Education manages digital learning supply chains worldwide.

? 5. Facility & Campus Management ?

    ? Manages physical infrastructure (classrooms, labs, libraries).

? Uses IoT sensors for energy efficiency & smart facility management.

? Implements predictive maintenance for school assets.

    ? Example: Smart campuses use AI to optimize classroom scheduling & maintenance.

? 6. Teacher & Staff Supply Chain ??

    ? Ensures timely hiring & training of educators.

? Uses AI-driven HR systems for faculty planning.

? Aligns teacher-to-student ratios for quality education.

    ? Example: AI-powered HR systems help universities optimize staffing needs.

? 7. Sustainability & Waste Reduction ?

    ? Uses digital textbooks & e-learning to reduce paper waste.

? Implements sustainable procurement policies for eco-friendly school supplies.

? Uses smart recycling & waste management systems on campuses.

    ? Example: Universities adopt digital libraries & green procurement strategies to reduce waste.

? Smart Technologies in Education SCM

    ? AI & Data Analytics → Predicts student resource needs.

? Blockchain → Secures supply chain transactions & improves transparency.

? IoT & Smart Sensors → Optimizes facility management & security.

? Cloud Computing → Enhances online learning access & resource distribution.

? Robotics & Automation → Supports logistics & smart campus operations.

    ? Why Smart SCM Matters in Education?

    ✔ Ensures timely & cost-efficient resource allocation

✔ Enhances learning experience through smart technology

✔ Reduces waste & promotes sustainability

✔ Improves teacher & student satisfaction

Key Components of Electronics Supply Chain Management (SCM) ???

The electronics industry relies on global sourcing, just-in-time manufacturing, and high-tech logistics to manage complex supply chains. From raw materials to finished products like smartphones, semiconductors, and consumer electronics, efficiency, resilience, and speed are critical.

Smart supply chain management in electronics integrates AI, IoT, blockchain, automation, and predictive analytics to enhance efficiency, cost control, and risk management.

? 1. Demand Forecasting & Market Analysis ?

? Uses AI & data analytics to predict demand for electronic products.

? Aligns manufacturing capacity with market trends.

? Reduces overproduction & component shortages.

? Example: Apple's AI-driven demand prediction optimizes iPhone production.

? 2. Raw Material Procurement & Supplier Management ?

? Sources semiconductors, rare earth metals, and circuit components.

? Uses blockchain for secure & transparent supplier tracking.

? Ensures multi-supplier strategies to avoid shortages & geopolitical risks.

? Example: TSMC & Samsung diversify their semiconductor supply chain to reduce risks.

? 3. Manufacturing & Assembly ?

? Uses smart factories with robotics & AI automation.

? Implements Just-In-Time (JIT) & Lean manufacturing to reduce waste.

? Uses IoT sensors for real-time production monitoring.

? Example: Foxconn automates iPhone assembly with AI-driven robotics.

? 4. Logistics & Distribution ?

? Uses AI-powered route optimization for global shipping.

? Implements real-time GPS tracking for components & finished products.

? Ensures cold-chain logistics for temperature-sensitive semiconductors.

? Example: Tesla optimizes logistics with AI-driven supply chain analytics.

? 5. Inventory & Warehouse Management ?

? Uses automated warehouses & AI-powered inventory tracking.

? Implements RFID & barcode scanning for real-time stock visibility.

? Reduces excess stock & component shortages.

? Example: Amazon's AI-driven warehouses optimize inventory for electronics.

? 6. Product Lifecycle & Reverse Logistics ?

? Ensures efficient handling of defective & end-of-life electronics.

? Implements electronics recycling & refurbishment programs.

? Uses AI-based diagnostics for faster repairs.

? Example: Apple's trade-in & recycling program reuses components efficiently.

? 7. Sustainability & Risk Management ?

? Uses eco-friendly materials & energy-efficient production.

? Implements circular economy principles for electronics reuse.

? Monitors geopolitical risks affecting semiconductor supply chains.

? Example: Intel and NVIDIA adopt green manufacturing & sustainable sourcing policies.

? Smart Technologies in Electronics SCM

? AI & Machine Learning → Predicts demand & optimizes logistics.

? Blockchain → Ensures supplier transparency & component tracking.

? IoT & Smart Sensors → Monitors production efficiency in real time.

? Cloud Computing → Improves global supply chain visibility.

? Robotics & Automation → Enhances manufacturing precision & speed.

? Why Smart SCM Matters in Electronics?

✔ Reduces costs & increases supply chain resilience

✔ Ensures timely production & component availability

✔ Improves product quality & reduces defects

✔ Enhances sustainability & regulatory compliance

Supply Chain Management (SCM) Strategy for Consumer Electronics ???

The consumer electronics supply chain is complex, involving global sourcing, just-in-time production, rapid product cycles, and sustainability challenges. Companies like Apple, Samsung, and Sony use AI, IoT, blockchain, and automation to optimize their supply chains for efficiency, cost savings, and risk management.

? Key Components of Consumer Electronics SCM

1. Demand Forecasting & Market Trends ?

? Uses AI & big data to predict sales trends.

? Helps prevent overproduction or component shortages.

? Aligns supply chain strategies with seasonal demand (e.g., holiday shopping).

? Example: Apple's AI-driven demand prediction ensures optimal iPhone production before launches.

2. Raw Material Sourcing & Supplier Management ?

? Sources semiconductors, batteries, displays, and rare earth metals.

? Uses blockchain for supplier transparency & ethical sourcing.

? Implements multi-supplier strategies to reduce risks from geopolitical issues.

? Example: Tesla & Samsung diversify their chip supply to avoid semiconductor shortages.

3. Smart Manufacturing & Assembly ?

? Uses AI-powered robotics for precision assembly (e.g., circuit board soldering).

? Implements Just-In-Time (JIT) manufacturing to reduce excess inventory.

? Uses IoT sensors for real-time production monitoring & defect detection.

? Example: Foxconn's smart factories automate iPhone & PlayStation assembly.

4. Logistics & Distribution ?

? Uses AI-powered route optimization for fast & cost-effective shipping.

? Implements real-time GPS tracking for components & finished products.

? Ensures cold-chain logistics for temperature-sensitive microchips.

? Example: Amazon & Apple optimize global distribution using AI-driven logistics.

5. Inventory & Warehouse Management ?

? Uses automated warehouses with AI-based inventory tracking.

? Implements RFID & barcode scanning for real-time stock updates.

? Reduces excess stock & component shortages through AI-driven forecasting.

? Example: Amazon's AI-powered fulfillment centers process electronics orders efficiently.

6. Product Lifecycle & Reverse Logistics ?

? Ensures fast & efficient repair and refurbishment programs.

? Implements trade-in programs for old devices to encourage circular economy.

? Uses AI-based diagnostics for remote troubleshooting.

? Example: Apple's trade-in program refurbishes old iPhones for resale or recycling.

7. Sustainability & ESG Compliance ?

? Uses eco-friendly materials & promotes energy-efficient production.

? Implements electronic waste recycling programs.

? Uses renewable energy sources in production facilities.

? Example: Sony & Samsung adopt green manufacturing for eco-friendly product lines.

? Smart Technologies in Consumer Electronics SCM

? AI & Machine Learning → Predicts demand & optimizes logistics.

? Blockchain → Ensures transparency in component sourcing.

? IoT & Smart Sensors → Tracks production efficiency in real time.

? Cloud Computing → Enhances supply chain collaboration.

? Robotics & Automation → Improves precision in manufacturing.

? Why Smart SCM Matters in Consumer Electronics?

✓ Reduces production costs & increases efficiency

✓ Ensures timely product launches & availability

✓ Improves product quality & customer satisfaction

✓ Enhances sustainability & regulatory compliance

? How Blockchain Works in Inventory Management?

1. Decentralized Ledger for Inventory Tracking ?

? Every inventory update is recorded on a secure blockchain ledger.

? Prevents data tampering & ensures all transactions are verifiable.

? Provides real-time visibility across warehouses, suppliers, and retailers.

? Example: Walmart & IBM Food Trust use blockchain to track food inventory and prevent spoilage.

2. Smart Contracts for Automated Transactions ?

? Smart contracts trigger automatic reordering when stock reaches low levels.

? Automates payments to suppliers once goods are delivered & verified.

? Reduces manual errors & paperwork.

? Example: Amazon uses blockchain-based smart contracts for automated supplier payments.

3. Supply Chain Transparency & Authentication ?

? Ensures authenticity of products (prevents counterfeiting in electronics, pharmaceuticals, etc.).

? Provides traceability of inventory from supplier to end consumer.

? Customers can verify product authenticity & ethical sourcing.

? Example: Louis Vuitton & LVMH use blockchain to verify luxury goods authenticity.

4. Integration with IoT for Real-Time Monitoring ?

? IoT devices track temperature, humidity, and location of inventory.

? Blockchain stores real-time IoT data securely & permanently.

? Ensures cold-chain logistics for perishable goods (food, vaccines, etc.).

? Example: Pfizer tracks COVID-19 vaccines using blockchain & IoT sensors.

5. Fraud Prevention & Loss Reduction ?

? Prevents inventory theft & misreporting by securing transaction records.

? Reduces fake returns & supplier fraud with immutable tracking.

? Detects anomalies in supply chain movement using AI & blockchain analytics.

? Example: Maersk & IBM's TradeLens blockchain reduces fraud in global shipping.

? Industries Benefiting from Blockchain Inventory Management

? Retail → Prevents stockouts & overstocking (e.g., Amazon, Walmart).

? Electronics → Ensures genuine parts & secure supply chains (e.g., Samsung, Apple).

? Automotive → Tracks vehicle parts authenticity & maintenance history.

? Food Industry → Monitors expiration dates & prevents food waste.

? Pharmaceuticals → Ensures proper storage & prevents counterfeit drugs.

? Why Blockchain is the Future of Inventory Management?

✓ 100% Transparency & Security → Eliminates fraud & unauthorized stock changes.

✓ Real-Time Supply Chain Visibility → Enhances tracking across global networks.

✓ Automated Inventory Control → Reduces human errors & processing time.

✓ Better Compliance & Sustainability → Ensures ethical sourcing & regulatory adherence.

Blockchain-Based Inventory Management for the Shipping Industry ???

The shipping industry relies on global supply chains, real-time tracking, and secure transactions to ensure smooth operations. Blockchain technology enhances inventory management, cargo tracking, fraud prevention, and logistics efficiency by providing a decentralized, tamper-proof ledger for tracking shipments across borders.

? Key Benefits of Blockchain in Shipping Inventory Management

? Real-Time Cargo Tracking → Prevents lost shipments & delays.

? Smart Contracts for Automated Payments → Reduces manual paperwork.

? Fraud & Theft Prevention → Ensures transparency in cargo movement.

? Integration with IoT & GPS → Tracks shipment location & environmental conditions.

? Reduces Supply Chain Delays → Eliminates inefficiencies & customs bottlenecks.

? Enhanced Security & Compliance → Prevents counterfeit products & tax fraud.

? How Blockchain Works in Shipping Inventory Management?

1. Decentralized Ledger for Cargo Tracking ?

? Every shipment transaction is recorded on a blockchain ledger for transparency.

? All stakeholders (suppliers, logistics companies, customs, and buyers) access real-time inventory data.

? Reduces errors in shipment documentation (Bills of Lading, Invoices, etc.).

? Example: Maersk & IBM's TradeLens blockchain platform tracks global cargo shipments securely.

2. Smart Contracts for Automated Shipping Transactions ?

? Smart contracts trigger automatic payments when cargo reaches its destination.

? Automates customs clearance & document verification.

? Reduces manual errors & speeds up shipment processing.

? Example: Hapag-Lloyd & Ocean Network Express (ONE) use blockchain smart contracts to speed up port transactions.

3. Secure & Transparent Inventory Management ?

? Ensures accurate stock levels in warehouses and shipping ports.

? Prevents counterfeit goods & fraudulent shipping records.

? Improves supply chain traceability for high-value cargo.

? Example: FedEx uses blockchain to enhance package tracking & reduce lost shipments.

4. IoT & GPS Integration for Real-Time Monitoring ?

? IoT sensors track temperature, humidity, and location of sensitive shipments.

? GPS data is stored on the blockchain ledger for real-time tracking.

? Ensures cold-chain logistics for perishable goods (food, medicine, vaccines).

? Example: Pfizer & Moderna use blockchain with IoT sensors to track COVID-19 vaccine shipments.

5. Fraud Prevention & Security ?

? Prevents cargo theft & supply chain manipulation.

? Blockchain-based digital identities ensure only authorized parties handle shipments.

? Reduces illegal shipments & tax evasion with tamper-proof tracking.

? Example: Port of Rotterdam uses blockchain to reduce fraud in shipping transactions.

? Blockchain Use Cases in Shipping

? Ocean Freight → Automates Bills of Lading & customs clearance.

? Air Cargo → Tracks real-time inventory & prevents lost shipments.

? Warehousing & Ports → Uses blockchain for secure inventory records.

? Supply Chain Logistics → Ensures fast, paperless, and secure shipments.

? Why Blockchain is the Future of Shipping?

✔ 100% Transparency & Security → Eliminates fraud & unauthorized cargo handling.

✔ Real-Time Inventory & Shipment Tracking → Improves global logistics efficiency.

✔ Automated Transactions & Customs Clearance → Reduces delays & paperwork.

✔ Better Compliance & Environmental Monitoring → Ensures regulatory adherence.

Blockchain-Based Inventory Management Strategy for the Pharmaceutical Industry ???

The pharmaceutical industry faces challenges like counterfeit drugs, supply chain inefficiencies, compliance regulations, and cold-chain logistics. Blockchain technology ensures secure, transparent, and real-time tracking of pharmaceutical inventory, improving patient safety and regulatory compliance.

? Key Benefits of Blockchain in Pharmaceutical Inventory Management

? Prevents Counterfeit Drugs → Tracks drug authenticity from production to patient.

? Real-Time Inventory Visibility → Reduces drug shortages & overstocking.

? Smart Contracts for Automated Compliance → Ensures regulatory adherence.

? Secure Cold-Chain Monitoring → Protects temperature-sensitive drugs & vaccines.

? Prevents Drug Theft & Diversion → Tracks shipments across the supply chain.

? Fast & Paperless Transactions → Reduces inefficiencies in supply chain management.

? How Blockchain Works in Pharmaceutical Inventory Management?

1. Decentralized Ledger for Drug Tracking ?

? Each batch of drugs is recorded on a secure blockchain ledger with a unique identifier.

? Ensures end-to-end traceability from manufacturers → wholesalers → hospitals → patients.

? Helps regulatory bodies (FDA, WHO, etc.) track drug movement to prevent illegal distribution.

? Example: Pfizer & Merck use blockchain to trace medicine distribution securely.

2. Smart Contracts for Automated Compliance & Transactions ?

? Automates supplier payments & restocking when inventory reaches low levels.

? Ensures drugs meet FDA, WHO, and GMP regulations before shipment.

? Prevents fraud in clinical trials & drug recalls with tamper-proof records.

? Example: Novartis uses blockchain-based smart contracts for regulatory compliance & drug supply tracking.

3. Cold-Chain Logistics & IoT Integration ??

? IoT sensors track temperature, humidity, and location of sensitive drugs.

? Blockchain records real-time data to prevent vaccine spoilage & quality degradation.

? Ensures compliance with Good Distribution Practices (GDP) for pharmaceuticals.

? Example: Moderna & IBM use blockchain with IoT sensors to monitor COVID-19 vaccine shipments.

4. Fraud Prevention & Drug Authentication ?

? Prevents fake drugs from entering the supply chain (a $200B global issue).

? Uses blockchain-based QR codes & RFID tags for drug authentication.

? Enables patients & pharmacies to verify drug legitimacy via blockchain.

? Example: Walmart & IBM's blockchain-based Drug Verification System prevents counterfeit medicine sales.

5. Inventory Optimization & Warehouse Management ?

? Uses AI-powered demand forecasting to optimize stock levels.

? Tracks expiration dates to reduce medicine waste.

? Enables real-time inventory monitoring across global warehouses.

? Example: Roche & Bayer use blockchain for AI-driven pharmaceutical inventory control.

? Implementation Roadmap for Blockchain in Pharma SCM

? Phase 1: Pilot Program & Stakeholder Collaboration (0-6 months)

? Identify key stakeholders: Manufacturers, Distributors, Regulators, Pharmacies.

? Develop a blockchain prototype for real-time drug tracking.

? Integrate IoT sensors & AI for inventory forecasting.

? Phase 2: Smart Contracts & Regulatory Compliance (6-12 months)

? Implement smart contracts for automated supplier payments & restocking.

? Ensure compliance with FDA, WHO, EU MDR, and GMP regulations.

? Set up blockchain-based QR codes for drug authentication.

? Phase 3: Full-Scale Deployment & AI Integration (12-24 months)

? Deploy blockchain across global warehouses & distribution centers.

? Train employees, pharmacies, and regulators on blockchain use.

? Use AI & predictive analytics for inventory optimization & demand forecasting.

? Why Blockchain is the Future of Pharma Supply Chains?

✓ Eliminates counterfeit drugs & improves patient safety

✓ Ensures end-to-end traceability & compliance

✓ Reduces inventory costs & prevents medicine shortages

✓ Improves transparency & efficiency in global pharma supply chains

Blockchain-Based Inventory Management Strategy for the Retail Industry ????

The retail industry faces challenges like stock discrepancies, counterfeit products, supply chain inefficiencies, and slow restocking processes. Blockchain technology provides a transparent, secure, and real-time inventory management system, improving stock accuracy, fraud prevention, and overall operational efficiency.

? Key Benefits of Blockchain in Retail Inventory Management

? Real-Time Stock Visibility → Reduces stockouts & overstocking.

? Prevents Counterfeit Products → Ensures product authenticity & brand trust.

? Smart Contracts for Automated Restocking → Streamlines supplier payments & order fulfillment.

? Faster & More Secure Supply Chain → Reduces delays & inefficiencies in logistics.

? Better Consumer Transparency → Customers can verify product origin & ethical sourcing.

? Fraud Prevention & Loss Reduction → Tracks goods from warehouse to checkout.

? How Blockchain Works in Retail Inventory Management?

1. Decentralized Ledger for Real-Time Stock Tracking ?

? Every product is recorded on a blockchain ledger with a unique identifier.

? Provides real-time inventory updates across stores, warehouses, and suppliers.

? Reduces stock errors caused by mismanagement, theft, or supply chain disruptions.

? Example: Walmart & IBM's blockchain tracks food & retail products for real-time inventory monitoring.

2. Smart Contracts for Automated Supplier Transactions ?

? Smart contracts automatically reorder stock when inventory runs low.

? Automates supplier payments & invoicing based on pre-set agreements.

? Reduces manual order processing errors & payment delays.

? Example: Amazon & Alibaba use smart contracts for automatic supplier payments & restocking.

3. Supply Chain Transparency & Product Authentication ?

? Ensures authenticity of branded products (prevents counterfeiting).

? Tracks products from manufacturer to retailer for ethical sourcing & sustainability.

? Consumers can verify product details using blockchain-based QR codes.

? Example: Louis Vuitton & Nike use blockchain to verify product authenticity & fight counterfeiting.

4. Fraud Prevention & Secure Transactions ?

? Reduces inventory shrinkage due to theft or internal fraud.

? Uses blockchain-based RFID & IoT sensors to track product movement.

? Prevents fake returns & unauthorized discounts at checkout.

? Example: Target & Home Depot use blockchain to reduce fraudulent product returns.

5. AI & IoT Integration for Demand Forecasting ?

? AI-driven analytics predict demand & optimize inventory levels.

? IoT sensors track product movement & storage conditions in real time.

? Ensures efficient warehouse management & automated stock replenishment.

? Example: Zara & H&M use AI + blockchain for real-time inventory optimization.

? Implementation Roadmap for Blockchain in Retail SCM

? Phase 1: Pilot Program & Inventory Digitization (0-6 months)

? Identify key retail partners: suppliers, warehouses, logistics, & stores.

? Implement blockchain-based inventory tracking for select product lines.

? Develop smart contracts for automated supplier payments.

? Phase 2: Full-Scale Integration & AI Optimization (6-12 months)

? Expand blockchain system across all stores & warehouses.

? Train staff & suppliers on blockchain-based inventory management.

? Integrate AI & IoT sensors for demand forecasting & real-time tracking.

? Phase 3: Customer-Facing Blockchain Benefits (12-24 months)

? Launch blockchain-based product authentication (QR codes for customers).

? Ensure seamless supplier collaboration using real-time smart contracts.

? Scale blockchain implementation for omnichannel retail operations.

? Why Blockchain is the Future of Retail Supply Chains?

✔ Eliminates counterfeit goods & improves customer trust

✔ Ensures real-time stock accuracy & supply chain efficiency

✔ Automates supplier transactions & reduces human errors

✔ Improves consumer experience through transparency & faster restocking

Blockchain-Based Inventory Management Strategy for the Education Industry ???

The education sector requires efficient inventory management for handling textbooks, lab equipment, digital devices, classroom supplies, and campus resources. Blockchain technology provides a secure, transparent, and decentralized system to track inventory, prevent theft, reduce waste, and streamline procurement.

? Key Benefits of Blockchain in Educational Inventory Management

? Real-Time Asset Tracking → Ensures accurate stock levels & reduces losses.

? Prevents Theft & Misuse → Tracks inventory movement across campuses.

? Smart Contracts for Automated Procurement → Simplifies order processing & supplier payments.

? Reduces Administrative Workload → Automates inventory audits & reporting.

? Transparency & Compliance → Prevents misallocation of education funds.

? Enhanced Digital Resource Management → Secures e-books, software licenses, & learning materials.

? How Blockchain Works in Education Inventory Management?

1. Decentralized Ledger for Real-Time Inventory Tracking ?

? Every item (books, laptops, lab materials) is registered on a blockchain with a unique ID.

? Tracks who checked out an item, when, and where it was last used.

? Reduces inventory loss, theft, and mismanagement.

? Example: A university uses blockchain to track science lab equipment & prevent loss.

2. Smart Contracts for Automated Procurement ?

? Automates ordering, restocking, and payments when supply levels are low.

? Ensures transparent vendor selection & budget allocation.

? Reduces manual paperwork & procurement fraud.

? Example: A school district uses blockchain smart contracts to automate textbook purchases.

3. Secure Management of Digital Learning Resources ?

? Stores e-books, software licenses, & research papers securely on the blockchain.

? Prevents unauthorized sharing of paid educational resources.

? Ensures students & teachers have verifiable access to licensed materials.

? Example: A university uses blockchain to manage digital textbook licenses for students.

4. Campus Asset & Resource Allocation ?

? Tracks classroom furniture, projectors, sports gear, and IT assets.

? Ensures fair distribution of resources across multiple campuses.

? Reduces waste & unnecessary purchases.

? Example: A school uses blockchain to track shared lab equipment across multiple buildings.

5. Compliance, Auditing & Budget Transparency ?

? Maintains tamper-proof records of inventory-related transactions.

? Helps schools & universities track inventory spending & prevent fraud.

? Simplifies annual audits & government compliance reporting.

? Example: A public university uses blockchain for transparent tracking of education funds.

? Implementation Roadmap for Blockchain in Education Inventory Management

? Phase 1: Pilot Program & Inventory Digitization (0-6 months)

? Identify key stakeholders: administrators, teachers, procurement teams.

? Develop a blockchain-based inventory tracking system for a specific department.

? Implement RFID/barcode scanning for asset tracking.

? Phase 2: Smart Contracts & Full-Scale Deployment (6-12 months)

? Automate inventory restocking & supplier payments with smart contracts.

? Expand blockchain tracking to all school/university assets.

? Train staff on using blockchain for inventory audits & reporting.

? Phase 3: AI & IoT Integration for Optimization (12-24 months)

? Use AI-driven analytics to optimize inventory purchases & usage patterns.

? Integrate IoT sensors for real-time asset tracking (e.g., lab equipment).

? Ensure full-scale blockchain adoption across all campuses.

? Why Blockchain is the Future of Education Inventory Management?

✔ Prevents inventory mismanagement & budget fraud

✔ Enhances transparency in procurement & asset tracking

✔ Reduces losses & ensures efficient resource distribution

✔ Automates inventory restocking & compliance reporting

Blockchain-Based Inventory Management Strategy for the Food Industry ???

The food industry faces challenges like supply chain inefficiencies, food fraud, contamination risks, perishability, and regulatory compliance. Blockchain technology ensures secure, real-time tracking of food inventory, enhancing transparency, safety, and efficiency across the supply chain.

? Key Benefits of Blockchain in Food Inventory Management

? Prevents Food Fraud & Counterfeit Products → Ensures food authenticity & quality.

? Real-Time Inventory Tracking → Reduces food waste & optimizes stock levels.

? Smart Contracts for Automated Supplier Payments → Enhances efficiency in procurement.

? Food Safety & Compliance → Ensures adherence to HACCP, FDA, and FSMA regulations.

? Cold-Chain Monitoring → Maintains temperature-sensitive food quality.

? Faster Recall Management → Quickly identifies contaminated products.

? How Blockchain Works in Food Inventory Management?

1. Decentralized Ledger for Food Traceability ?

? Each food product is recorded on a blockchain ledger with a unique identifier.

? Tracks food movement from farm → supplier → distributor → retailer → consumer.

? Helps in verifying organic, halal, or non-GMO certifications.

? Example: Walmart & IBM use blockchain to track leafy greens from farm to shelf in seconds.

2. Smart Contracts for Automated Inventory Management ?

? Automates restocking orders when inventory is low.

? Processes supplier payments only after order verification.

? Reduces supply chain fraud & manual paperwork.

? Example: Nestlé uses blockchain smart contracts for supplier payments based on verified deliveries.

3. Cold-Chain Monitoring for Perishable Goods ??

? IoT sensors monitor temperature, humidity, and freshness of food products.

? Blockchain records real-time data to prevent spoilage.

? Ensures compliance with HACCP & FDA cold storage regulations.

? Example: Carrefour uses blockchain to track the cold chain of dairy & meat products.

4. Food Safety & Recall Management ?

? Tracks batch numbers & expiration dates for quick recalls.

? Prevents contaminated food from reaching consumers.

? Reduces brand liability in foodborne illness cases.

? Example: Tyson Foods uses blockchain to improve food recall response time.

5. AI & Blockchain for Demand Forecasting ?

? Uses AI-driven analytics to predict food demand.

? Reduces overstocking & food waste.

? Ensures optimal stock distribution across stores & warehouses.

? Example: Kroger integrates AI with blockchain to optimize food inventory.

? Implementation Roadmap for Blockchain in Food Inventory Management

? Phase 1: Pilot Program & Supplier Collaboration (0-6 months)

? Identify key stakeholders: farmers, suppliers, distributors, retailers.

? Implement blockchain-based inventory tracking for perishable goods.

? Develop smart contracts for automated supplier payments.

? Phase 2: Full-Scale Integration & AI Optimization (6-12 months)

? Expand blockchain tracking to all food products & warehouses.

? Train supply chain participants on blockchain-based inventory management.

? Integrate AI for predictive stock replenishment.

? Phase 3: Consumer Transparency & Global Expansion (12-24 months)

? Launch blockchain-based QR codes for product traceability.

? Ensure seamless compliance with global food safety standards.

? Scale blockchain adoption across multiple retail chains & food suppliers.

? Why Blockchain is the Future of Food Inventory Management?

✔ Prevents counterfeit & fraudulent food labeling

✔ Ensures real-time traceability & safety compliance

✔ Reduces food waste & supply chain inefficiencies

✔ Optimizes procurement & supplier management

Plant Digitization: Transforming Manufacturing with Smart Technologies ??

Plant digitization refers to the integration of digital technologies, automation, and data-driven systems into manufacturing plants to enhance efficiency, productivity, and decision-making. This transformation is a key component of Industry 4.0, enabling real-time monitoring, predictive maintenance, smart production, and end-to-end supply chain visibility.

? Key Elements of Plant Digitization

1. Industrial Internet of Things (IIoT) ??

? Connects machines, sensors, and devices for real-time data collection.

? Enhances remote monitoring & predictive maintenance.

? Enables machine-to-machine (M2M) communication for automated workflows.

? Example: A smart factory using IoT-enabled sensors to monitor equipment health.

2. Digital Twin Technology ???

? Creates a virtual replica of the physical plant for real-time simulation & optimization.

? Helps in predictive analytics & scenario testing before real-world execution.

? Improves quality control & process efficiency.

? Example: Airbus uses digital twins to optimize aircraft production processes.

3. Artificial Intelligence & Machine Learning ??

? AI-driven predictive analytics for demand forecasting & quality control.

? ML algorithms optimize production scheduling & resource allocation.

? AI-powered computer vision detects defects & ensures product quality.

? Example: BMW uses AI for automated quality inspection in car manufacturing.

4. Cloud & Edge Computing ☁???

? Cloud-based platforms store & process vast amounts of production data.

? Edge computing enables real-time data analysis at the factory floor.

? Ensures faster decision-making & reduced downtime.

? Example: Siemens uses cloud computing for global factory operations monitoring.

5. Smart Robotics & Automation ??

? Collaborative robots (cobots) work alongside humans to improve efficiency.

? Automated assembly lines, packaging, and logistics reduce manual errors.

? Robotics enhance precision & speed in repetitive manufacturing tasks.

? Example: Tesla's Gigafactories use advanced robotics for electric vehicle assembly.

6. Blockchain for Secure & Transparent Operations ??

? Provides tamper-proof records of production, inventory, and supply chain.

? Ensures compliance, traceability, and fraud prevention.

? Smart contracts automate supplier transactions & quality verification.

? Example: Nestlé uses blockchain to track food production & sourcing.

7. Augmented Reality (AR) & Virtual Reality (VR) ????

? AR-assisted maintenance & training for factory workers.

? VR simulations for production line optimization.

? Enhances worker safety & operational efficiency.

? Example: Boeing uses AR glasses to guide assembly technicians.

? Benefits of Plant Digitization

✓ Increased Productivity → Automation speeds up production & reduces errors.

✓ Cost Reduction → AI & predictive maintenance cut downtime & repair costs.

✓ Enhanced Quality Control → AI-powered inspections reduce defects.

✓ Better Supply Chain Management → Real-time tracking & blockchain ensure transparency.

✓ Sustainability & Energy Efficiency → Smart sensors optimize resource usage.

Customized Plant Digitization Strategy for the Automotive Industry ??

Plant digitization in the automotive industry enhances production efficiency, quality control, and supply chain transparency through advanced technologies such as Industrial IoT, AI-driven automation, digital twins, and blockchain. This transformation is key to achieving smart manufacturing and intelligent production.

? Key Components of Automotive Plant Digitization

1. Industrial Internet of Things (IIoT) ??

? Sensors and IoT devices monitor equipment performance, production status, and material flow in real time.

? Helps in predictive maintenance, reducing machine downtime and repair costs.

? Enables automated data collection for quality checks and efficiency analysis.

? Example: Toyota uses IoT sensors to monitor robotic arms and optimize production lines.

2. Digital Twin Technology ???

? Creates a real-time virtual replica of an automotive manufacturing plant.

? Simulates production scenarios to optimize workflows, reduce waste, and improve energy efficiency.

? Enhances rapid prototyping and testing of new car designs before physical manufacturing.

? Example: BMW leverages digital twins to design and optimize production plants.

3. Artificial Intelligence (AI) & Machine Learning (ML) ??

? AI-driven predictive analytics forecasts demand, supply chain risks, and machine failures.

? ML algorithms optimize production scheduling, workforce allocation, and material usage.

? AI-powered computer vision detects defects in car parts and enhances quality control.

    ? Example: Tesla uses AI for automated quality inspection of vehicle assembly.

4. Smart Robotics & Automation ??

    ? Collaborative robots (cobots) work alongside human workers to increase production speed.

? Autonomous mobile robots (AMRs) handle material movement across the factory.

? Robotics streamline assembly, welding, painting, and quality inspection processes.

    ? Example: Ford integrates AI-powered robots for automated car assembly and painting.

5. Blockchain for Supply Chain & Inventory Management ??

    ? Tracks car components from raw materials to finished vehicles with immutable blockchain records.

? Ensures transparency in supplier transactions, reducing counterfeiting and fraud.

? Smart contracts automate parts procurement, payments, and compliance tracking.

    ? Example: Volkswagen uses blockchain to track ethical sourcing of raw materials like cobalt.

6. Augmented Reality (AR) & Virtual Reality (VR) ????

    ? AR overlays guide factory workers during complex assembly tasks, reducing errors.

? VR training programs prepare workers for new manufacturing technologies.

? Improves worker safety and operational efficiency by providing real-time guidance.

    ? Example: Audi trains factory employees using VR simulations of assembly line operations.

7. Cloud & Edge Computing ☁???

    ? Cloud-based platforms store and analyze massive amounts of production data.

? Edge computing enables real-time processing of factory data at the source, improving decision-making.

? Ensures seamless data integration across multiple automotive plants.

    ? Example: Mercedes-Benz uses cloud-based AI analytics for predictive maintenance.

? Implementation Roadmap for Automotive Plant Digitization

? Phase 1: IoT & Automation Integration (0-6 months)

    ? Install IoT sensors and smart robotics in key production areas.

? Begin predictive maintenance using AI-based analytics.

? Implement automated assembly line monitoring for defect detection.

? Phase 2: Digital Twin & Blockchain Implementation (6-12 months)

    ? Develop a digital twin of the manufacturing plant for process optimization.

? Use blockchain for supplier transactions and parts traceability.

? Deploy AR-based maintenance and training systems.

? Phase 3: Full-Scale AI & Smart Factory Optimization (12-24 months)

    ? Integrate AI-driven demand forecasting and workflow optimization.

? Expand automation in logistics, warehousing, and supply chain.

? Ensure full-scale connectivity across all production plants.

? Why Digitization is the Future of Automotive Manufacturing?

    ✔ Increases efficiency & production speed through automation.

✔ Enhances quality control with AI-driven defect detection.

✔ Reduces operational costs & downtime with predictive maintenance.

✔ Improves supply chain transparency with blockchain tracking.

✔ Optimizes worker safety & training using AR and VR.

Customized Plant Digitization Strategy for the Food Industry ??

Plant digitization in the food industry enhances efficiency, food safety, traceability, and cost optimization by integrating IoT, AI-driven automation, blockchain, robotics, and digital twins into production and supply chain processes.

? **Key Components of Food Industry Plant Digitization**

1. Industrial Internet of Things (IIoT) for Food Processing ??

? IoT sensors monitor temperature, humidity, and production efficiency.

? Real-time tracking of food quality and shelf life to minimize spoilage.

? Smart equipment predicts machine failures, reducing downtime.

? Example: Nestlé uses IoT to track production efficiency and ensure food quality.

2. AI & Machine Learning for Process Optimization ??

? AI-driven predictive maintenance ensures minimal machine breakdowns.

? Smart analytics optimize ingredient usage, reducing food waste.

? AI-powered vision systems detect defects in food packaging.

? Example: PepsiCo uses AI for real-time defect detection in chips production.

3. Digital Twin for Virtual Food Production Simulation ???

? Creates a real-time digital replica of the food plant for process testing.

? Optimizes energy use, production scheduling, and logistics.

? Helps in scaling up recipes and improving efficiency before real-world execution.

? Example: Coca-Cola uses digital twins to optimize beverage production.

4. Blockchain for Food Safety & Traceability ??

? Tracks ingredients from farm to factory to retailer with immutable records.

? Ensures compliance with HACCP, FDA, FSMA, and ISO 22000 food safety standards.

? Enhances recall efficiency by pinpointing contaminated batches in seconds.

? Example: Walmart & IBM use blockchain to track leafy greens from farm to store.

5. Robotics & Automation for Smart Food Processing ??

? Automated sorting & packaging reduce human error and labor costs.

? Robotic arms improve efficiency in food handling, mixing, and cutting.

? Autonomous mobile robots (AMRs) transport materials within the plant.

? Example: Tyson Foods uses robotic butchers to enhance meat processing efficiency.

6. Augmented Reality (AR) & Virtual Reality (VR) for Training & Quality Control ????

? AR-powered maintenance guides technicians for quick equipment repairs.

? VR training programs educate workers on food safety & hygiene practices.

? Reduces human error in quality checks and production monitoring.

? Example: Kraft Heinz uses AR for real-time production monitoring.

7. Cloud & Edge Computing for Real-Time Food Production Data ☁???

? Cloud-based platforms store production and inventory data for real-time monitoring.

? Edge computing enables faster data processing on-site, reducing response time.

? Optimizes supply chain logistics, food inventory levels, and production efficiency.

? Example: Unilever uses cloud computing for global factory operations tracking.

? **Implementation Roadmap for Food Industry Plant Digitization**

? **Phase 1: IoT & AI Integration (0-6 months)**

? Install IoT sensors to track temperature, humidity, and energy consumption.

? Deploy AI-driven predictive maintenance for food processing equipment.

? Implement smart automation in food sorting & packaging.

? **Phase 2: Blockchain & Digital Twin Deployment (6-12 months)**

? Use blockchain for ingredient traceability & supplier authentication.

? Create a digital twin of the food plant to simulate process improvements.

? Introduce AR-powered maintenance tools for factory workers.

? **Phase 3: Full-Scale AI & Robotics Implementation (12-24 months)**

? Expand AI-powered demand forecasting to reduce food waste.

? Deploy robotics in food handling & warehouse automation.

? Ensure full integration of digitized production across all supply chain partners.

? Why Digitization is the Future of the Food Industry?

✔ Enhances food safety & regulatory compliance

✔ Reduces food waste & operational costs

✔ Improves production efficiency & quality control

✔ Strengthens traceability & recall management

✔ Optimizes inventory & supply chain logistics

Customized Plant Digitization Strategy for the Education Industry ??

Plant digitization in the education industry focuses on modernizing vocational training, research labs, and manufacturing facilities within educational institutions using smart technologies, automation, and AI-driven systems. This enhances hands-on learning, operational efficiency, and real-time monitoring in educational manufacturing environments.

? Key Components of Plant Digitization for the Education Industry

1. Smart IoT-Enabled Learning Labs & Workshops ??

? IoT sensors track machine usage, maintenance needs, and student interaction.

? Real-time data collection optimizes equipment availability and usage patterns.

? Automated alerts ensure machine safety and compliance in workshops.

? Example: A technical university integrates IoT to monitor CNC machines and 3D printers in a training lab.

2. Digital Twin for Virtual Plant Training & Experimentation ???

? Creates virtual models of real-world manufacturing plants for immersive learning.

? Enables students to test production scenarios before working on physical equipment.

? Helps optimize research and development projects in education-based manufacturing units.

? Example: An engineering institute develops a digital twin of an automotive assembly line for student training.

3. AI-Powered Predictive Maintenance & Smart Scheduling ??

? AI algorithms predict equipment failures, reducing downtime and repair costs.

? Smart scheduling tools allocate workshop resources efficiently based on student needs.

? AI-driven insights improve curriculum design by analyzing machine usage trends.

? Example: A polytechnic institute uses AI to predict wear and tear in robotic arms used for training.

4. Robotics & Automation for Hands-On Training ??

? Collaborative robots (cobots) help students learn automation and robotics.

? AI-driven robotic systems simulate real-world factory conditions.

? Automates repetitive educational tasks like material handling in workshops.

? Example: A vocational training center integrates robotic assembly lines for student learning.

5. Blockchain for Secure Student-Certification & Equipment Access ??

? Stores tamper-proof academic records, certifications, and student achievements.

? Ensures secure access control for lab equipment using blockchain-based authentication.

? Tracks research projects and intellectual property in education-based innovation labs.

? Example: A technical university uses blockchain for verifiable student certifications in Industry 4.0 training.

6. Augmented Reality (AR) & Virtual Reality (VR) for Immersive Training ????

? AR/VR-based modules offer interactive, hands-on learning experiences in a virtual environment.

? AR overlays guide students through complex machine operations & troubleshooting.

? Enhances distance learning for technical subjects like manufacturing and automation.

? Example: An institute uses VR headsets to train students on factory safety protocols.

7. Cloud & Edge Computing for Remote Learning & Data Management ☁???

? Cloud-based learning platforms store digital lessons, manuals, and real-time factory data.

? Edge computing enables real-time data processing in smart workshops.

? Supports remote access to simulations, IoT dashboards, and digital twins.

? Example: A university offers cloud-based access to real-time plant data for students studying industrial automation.

? Implementation Roadmap for Plant Digitization in Education

? Phase 1: IoT & AI Integration in Learning Labs (0-6 months)

? Install IoT sensors in vocational training equipment.

? Use AI-based predictive maintenance for lab machines.

? Implement smart scheduling for lab access and machine usage.

? Phase 2: Digital Twin & Blockchain for Secure Learning (6-12 months)

? Develop digital twins of lab environments for virtual training.

? Deploy blockchain for secure student certification & equipment access.

? Introduce AR-powered maintenance and troubleshooting for students.

? Phase 3: Full-Scale AI & Robotics Implementation (12-24 months)

? Expand AI-driven student analytics & personalized learning paths.

? Deploy robotics in training programs for hands-on automation experience.

? Ensure full integration of smart plant technologies across all educational workshops.

? Why Digitization is the Future of Education in Manufacturing?

✓ Enhances practical learning with real-world industrial exposure

✓ Reduces equipment downtime and optimizes lab usage

✓ Improves student certification security with blockchain

✓ Enables remote and immersive learning with AR/VR

✓ Prepares students for Industry 4.0 with AI-driven training

? Predictive Maintenance (PdM) Explained

Predictive maintenance (PdM) is a data-driven maintenance approach that uses IoT sensors, AI, and machine learning to predict equipment failures before they occur. Unlike reactive maintenance (fixing after failure) or preventive maintenance (scheduled servicing), PdM minimizes downtime and maintenance costs by fixing equipment only when needed, based on real-time data.

? Key Technologies in Predictive Maintenance

1. Internet of Things (IoT) Sensors ??

? Vibration sensors detect abnormal machine movements.

? Temperature sensors track overheating in machinery.

? Acoustic sensors analyze sound patterns for early fault detection.

? Oil analysis sensors check lubrication quality to prevent wear and tear.

? Example: A factory uses IoT sensors to track motor vibrations, preventing failures in advance.

2. Artificial Intelligence (AI) & Machine Learning ??

? AI analyzes historical and real-time machine data to detect failure patterns.

? Machine learning improves prediction accuracy over time.

? AI-powered anomaly detection systems trigger maintenance alerts.

? Example: Airlines use AI to predict jet engine failures before takeoff, improving safety and reducing delays.

3. Digital Twin for Virtual Machine Simulation ???

? Creates a real-time digital replica of machines for simulation.

? Helps manufacturers test different maintenance strategies before applying them.

? Reduces downtime by identifying weak points in equipment.

? Example: Automotive plants use digital twins to simulate wear-and-tear on robotic arms.

4. Big Data & Cloud Computing ☁??

? Cloud storage enables real-time monitoring of global machine networks.

? Big data analytics identifies maintenance trends across multiple locations.

? Allows remote maintenance decision-making via cloud dashboards.

? Example: A food processing company tracks factory equipment performance across multiple sites using cloud analytics.

? Benefits of Predictive Maintenance

✔ Reduces unplanned downtime by up to 50%

✔ Lowers maintenance costs by 10-40%

✔ Extends equipment lifespan

✔ Optimizes spare parts inventory

✔ Improves worker safety by preventing sudden failures

? Predictive Maintenance in Different Industries

? Automotive: Detects engine & transmission faults early.

? Manufacturing: Prevents failures in CNC machines & robotic arms.

? Food Industry: Monitors refrigeration & food processing equipment.

? Education: Ensures uptime for lab equipment & technical training tools.

? Shipping: Predicts failures in cargo handling & logistics machinery.

? Customized Predictive Maintenance Strategy for the Automotive Industry

Predictive Maintenance (PdM) in the automotive industry uses IoT sensors, AI, and data analytics to prevent equipment failures in vehicle manufacturing plants, fleet operations, and aftermarket services. This strategy reduces downtime, extends machine life, and optimizes maintenance schedules.

? Key Components of Predictive Maintenance in the Automotive Industry

1. IoT-Enabled Equipment Monitoring ??

? Sensors track vibration, temperature, pressure, and wear in critical machines.

? Real-time monitoring helps detect early signs of failure.

? Cloud-based dashboards provide remote diagnostics and alerts.

? Example: Ford uses IoT sensors to monitor robotic arms in assembly lines.

2. AI & Machine Learning for Failure Prediction ??

? AI analyzes machine data to identify failure patterns.

? Machine learning models improve prediction accuracy over time.

? AI-powered diagnostics help reduce unnecessary maintenance costs.

? Example: BMW uses AI to predict failures in manufacturing robots before they occur.

3. Digital Twin for Virtual Simulation ???

? Creates real-time digital replicas of machines and production lines.

? Simulates different maintenance scenarios to optimize strategies.

? Reduces downtime by testing repairs before applying them in real production.

? Example: Daimler uses digital twins to improve predictive maintenance in its plants.

4. Fleet Predictive Maintenance for Automotive Logistics ???

? Monitors engine health, brake wear, and tire conditions for fleet vehicles.

? GPS & telematics track driving behavior and fuel efficiency.

? Reduces unplanned breakdowns, optimizing vehicle uptime.

? Example: Tesla uses telematics to perform over-the-air predictive maintenance updates.

5. Augmented Reality (AR) for Smart Maintenance ???

? AR-powered maintenance guides help technicians perform repairs faster.

? Remote experts assist with troubleshooting using AR overlays.

? Reduces repair time and labor costs.

? Example: Volkswagen uses AR to assist mechanics in complex vehicle repairs.

? Implementation Roadmap for Automotive Predictive Maintenance

? Phase 1: IoT & Data Collection (0-6 months)

? Install IoT sensors on critical equipment and fleet vehicles.

? Collect historical failure data to train AI models.

? Deploy cloud-based dashboards for real-time monitoring.

? Phase 2: AI & Predictive Models (6-12 months)

? Train AI-driven predictive maintenance models.

? Implement machine learning algorithms for failure detection.

? Automate maintenance scheduling based on data-driven insights.

? Phase 3: Digital Twin & AR Integration (12-24 months)

? Develop digital twins of production lines for maintenance simulations.

? Introduce AR-based maintenance solutions for technicians.

? Scale predictive maintenance across multiple plants and fleet operations.

? Benefits of Predictive Maintenance for the Automotive Industry

✔ Reduces unplanned downtime by up to 50%

✔ Lowers maintenance costs by 20-40%

✔ Increases equipment lifespan and efficiency

✔ Enhances worker safety and operational reliability

✔ Optimizes spare parts inventory, reducing waste

?? Predictive Maintenance Strategy for the Food Industry

Predictive Maintenance (PdM) in the food industry prevents equipment failures in food processing plants, cold storage, packaging lines, and supply chain logistics. Using IoT sensors, AI, and real-time analytics, PdM ensures continuous food production, reduces waste, and meets strict food safety regulations.

? Key Components of Predictive Maintenance in the Food Industry

1. IoT Sensors for Equipment Monitoring ??

? Temperature sensors track cold storage and cooking equipment conditions.

? Vibration and pressure sensors monitor mixers, conveyors, and production lines.

? Humidity sensors maintain optimal conditions for food processing.

? Real-time dashboards provide alerts to prevent sudden breakdowns.

? Example: A dairy processing plant uses IoT sensors to detect refrigeration failures before milk spoils.

2. AI & Machine Learning for Failure Prediction ??

? AI analyzes historical maintenance data to predict potential equipment failures.

? Machine learning improves prediction accuracy over time.

? Reduces unplanned downtime by ensuring timely repairs and part replacements.

? Example: A bakery chain uses AI to predict oven malfunctions, preventing production losses.

3. Digital Twin for Virtual Food Plant Maintenance ???

? A digital twin is a virtual replica of a food production facility.

? Simulates different maintenance strategies before applying them.

? Reduces downtime by testing optimal machine configurations.

? Example: A beverage company creates a digital twin of its bottling plant to optimize predictive maintenance.

4. Smart Cold Chain Management for Food Safety ❄??

? IoT-enabled real-time temperature tracking in cold storage and transport.

? AI analyzes data to prevent refrigeration failures.

? Blockchain ensures transparent food traceability and compliance.

? Example: A seafood exporter uses predictive analytics to prevent freezer breakdowns during shipments.

5. Augmented Reality (AR) for Smart Repairs ???

? AR guides technicians with real-time maintenance instructions.

? Reduces repair time and labor costs.

? Enables remote expert assistance for troubleshooting.

? Example: A chocolate factory uses AR to assist workers in fixing conveyor belt issues.

? Implementation Roadmap for Food Industry Predictive Maintenance

? Phase 1: IoT & Data Collection (0-6 months)

? Install IoT sensors on key equipment like ovens, mixers, chillers, and packaging lines.

? Gather historical failure data to train AI models.

? Deploy cloud dashboards for real-time equipment monitoring.

? Phase 2: AI-Driven Predictive Models (6-12 months)

? Train AI-based predictive maintenance models.

? Automate early failure detection and maintenance scheduling.

? Optimize spare parts inventory using data-driven insights.

? Phase 3: Digital Twin & AR Integration (12-24 months)

? Develop digital twins of food processing plants.

? Implement AR-based maintenance assistance for workers.

? Scale predictive maintenance across multiple food production sites.

? Benefits of Predictive Maintenance for the Food Industry

✔ Prevents food spoilage and contamination risks

✔ Reduces unplanned downtime by up to 50%

✔ Lowers maintenance costs by 20-40%

✔ Optimizes energy consumption in food processing plants

✔ Ensures compliance with food safety regulations

? Predictive Maintenance Strategy for the Education Industry

Predictive Maintenance (PdM) in the education sector ensures the reliability of school infrastructure, laboratory equipment, IT systems, and campus facilities. By using IoT sensors, AI, and data analytics, PdM reduces operational costs, minimizes disruptions, and enhances safety in educational institutions.

? Key Components of Predictive Maintenance in Education

1. IoT Sensors for Campus Infrastructure Monitoring ??

? HVAC systems: Sensors monitor temperature, humidity, and air quality in classrooms.

? Lighting & electrical systems: Detects faulty wiring and energy inefficiencies.

? Plumbing & water supply: Monitors leaks and pipe pressure for early detection.

? Example: A university uses IoT sensors to predict HVAC failures, ensuring comfortable classrooms.

2. AI & Machine Learning for Asset Maintenance ??

? AI analyzes historical maintenance records to predict failures.

? Machine learning optimizes maintenance schedules for cost reduction.

? AI-powered diagnostics prevent downtime of critical learning infrastructure.

? Example: A technical institute uses AI to predict electrical failures in lab equipment.

3. Predictive Maintenance for IT & Smart Classrooms ??

? Monitors projectors, smart boards, and computer labs for technical faults.

? Prevents Wi-Fi and server outages with AI-driven network monitoring.

? Ensures 24/7 operational IT systems for uninterrupted learning.

? Example: A digital campus uses predictive analytics to prevent server crashes during exams.

4. Lab & Technical Equipment Maintenance ???

? Monitors engineering, science, and medical lab equipment for wear and tear.

? Reduces costly breakdowns and ensures calibration accuracy.

? Supports STEM education by keeping research labs fully functional.

? Example: A medical college predicts failure in MRI machines, preventing disruption in student training.

5. Smart Security & Safety Systems ??

? Uses AI to monitor fire alarms, CCTV cameras, and access control systems.

? Predicts security hardware malfunctions before they fail.

? Ensures a safe learning environment for students and staff.

? Example: A smart school tracks surveillance cameras to prevent system failures.

? Implementation Roadmap for Predictive Maintenance in Education

? Phase 1: IoT Sensor Deployment (0-6 months)

? Install IoT sensors in buildings, classrooms, labs, and IT systems.

? Collect historical maintenance data for AI model training.

? Set up a real-time monitoring dashboard.

? Phase 2: AI & Data Analytics (6-12 months)

? Develop predictive models for different campus systems.

? Automate maintenance alerts and service scheduling.

? Optimize energy usage and infrastructure efficiency.

? Phase 3: Digital Twin & Smart Automation (12-24 months)

? Implement digital twins of campus facilities to simulate maintenance needs.

? Integrate AI-driven automation for self-healing IT networks.

? Scale the predictive maintenance model to multiple institutions.

? Benefits of Predictive Maintenance for Education

✓ Reduces maintenance costs by 20-40%

✓ Ensures uninterrupted learning experiences

✓ Extends the lifespan of expensive lab & IT equipment

✓ Improves campus energy efficiency

✓ Enhances student and faculty safety

? Predictive Maintenance Strategy for the Shipping Industry

Predictive Maintenance (PdM) in the shipping industry leverages IoT, AI, and real-time analytics to prevent mechanical failures in ships, port infrastructure, and cargo handling equipment. By monitoring engines, hulls, fuel systems, and navigation equipment, PdM reduces downtime, optimizes operational efficiency, and ensures regulatory compliance.

? Key Components of Predictive Maintenance in Shipping

1. IoT Sensors for Ship Equipment Monitoring ??

? Engine & propulsion systems: Sensors track temperature, pressure, and vibration.

? Fuel systems: Monitors fuel efficiency and detects potential leaks.

? Hull & structure monitoring: Uses ultrasound sensors to detect corrosion and cracks.

? Cargo handling equipment: Tracks wear and tear in cranes, conveyors, and storage units.

? Example: Maersk uses IoT sensors to monitor ship engines, reducing fuel costs and improving efficiency.

2. AI & Machine Learning for Failure Prediction ??

? AI analyzes historical data to detect maintenance patterns.

? Predicts engine failures, pump breakdowns, and electrical issues before they occur.

? Reduces unplanned downtime by enabling proactive maintenance scheduling.

? Example: Rolls-Royce's AI-powered system predicts marine engine failures, ensuring smooth voyages.

3. Digital Twin for Ship & Port Maintenance ???

? Creates a virtual replica of a ship or port facility for real-time monitoring.

? Simulates maintenance scenarios to optimize repair strategies.

? Reduces dry-dock downtime by testing solutions before applying them.

? Example: Port of Rotterdam uses digital twins to enhance maintenance and reduce port congestion.

4. Smart Fleet Management for Cargo & Passenger Ships ??

? Uses telematics and IoT to track engine performance and hull integrity.

? Ensures compliance with IMO (International Maritime Organization) safety standards.

? AI-driven fuel optimization reduces carbon footprint and operational costs.

? Example: Carnival Cruise Line uses predictive analytics to optimize ship performance and fuel efficiency.

5. AR & Remote Maintenance Assistance ???

? AR-enabled maintenance guides help crew members repair ship components quickly.

? Remote experts provide real-time support using augmented reality interfaces.

? Reduces the need for onboard specialized technicians.

? Example: A shipyard uses AR-assisted maintenance to reduce repair time by 40%.

? Implementation Roadmap for Predictive Maintenance in Shipping

? Phase 1: IoT & Sensor Deployment (0-6 months)

? Install IoT sensors on engines, fuel systems, and cargo handling equipment.

? Gather historical maintenance data for AI model training.

? Deploy real-time monitoring dashboards for ship operators.

? Phase 2: AI & Predictive Models (6-12 months)

? Train AI-driven predictive maintenance models.

? Automate alerts for potential equipment failures.

? Optimize spare parts inventory based on predictive insights.

? Phase 3: Digital Twin & Remote AR Assistance (12-24 months)

? Develop digital twins for key ships and port facilities.

? Implement AR-based remote maintenance support.

? Scale predictive maintenance solutions across multiple vessels and ports.

? Benefits of Predictive Maintenance for Shipping

✔ Reduces unplanned downtime by up to 50%

✔ Lowers fuel consumption and operational costs

✔ Extends equipment lifespan and prevents critical failures

✔ Improves regulatory compliance and safety standards

✔ Enhances fleet reliability and cargo delivery efficiency

? Supply Chain Visibility (SCV): A Complete Overview

Supply Chain Visibility (SCV) refers to the real-time tracking, monitoring, and transparency of products, inventory, and logistics across the entire supply chain. It enables companies to gain insights into the movement of goods, detect potential disruptions, and optimize operations for efficiency, cost savings, and customer satisfaction.

? Key Components of Supply Chain Visibility

1. Real-Time Data Tracking & Monitoring ??

? Uses IoT sensors, RFID tags, and GPS to track shipments and inventory.

? Provides live updates on production, transportation, and warehouse stock levels.

? Enhances decision-making by detecting potential delays or supply chain disruptions.

? Example: An automotive company tracks components in transit to avoid production halts.

2. End-to-End Transparency for All Stakeholders ??

? Improves communication among suppliers, manufacturers, distributors, and retailers.

? Helps companies track supplier performance and quality compliance.

? Reduces risks by identifying bottlenecks in production and logistics.

? Example: A food company ensures ingredient traceability from farm to fork.

3. AI & Predictive Analytics for Demand Forecasting ??

? Uses AI to analyze historical data, market trends, and customer demand patterns.

? Reduces stockouts and overstocking by optimizing inventory levels.

? Prevents supply chain disruptions by identifying risk factors early.

? Example: A retailer predicts holiday season demand spikes and stocks inventory accordingly.

4. Blockchain for Secure & Transparent Transactions ??

? Ensures data integrity and prevents fraud by using blockchain-ledger technology.

? Tracks product authenticity and ethical sourcing in industries like pharmaceuticals and luxury goods.

? Enhances supply chain traceability by providing an immutable record of transactions.

? Example: A pharmaceutical company verifies drug authenticity to prevent counterfeits.

5. Cloud-Based Supply Chain Management Platforms ☁??

? Centralized platforms provide real-time dashboards and analytics.

? Enables multi-location tracking for warehouses, shipments, and suppliers.

? Enhances collaboration across global supply chain networks.

? Example: An e-commerce giant manages global inventory and logistics from a single cloud-based dashboard.

? Benefits of Supply Chain Visibility

✓ Reduces delays and supply chain disruptions

✓ Improves inventory management and reduces carrying costs

✓ Enhances customer satisfaction with accurate delivery tracking

✓ Minimizes fraud, counterfeiting, and compliance risks

✓ Optimizes logistics and lowers transportation costs

? Smart Warehousing in Smart Manufacturing

A smart warehouse in smart manufacturing integrates IoT, AI, robotics, and automation to improve inventory management, order fulfillment, and logistics operations. It enables real-time tracking, predictive analytics, and seamless coordination between production, storage, and distribution.

? Key Components of Smart Warehousing in Smart Manufacturing

1. IoT & Real-Time Inventory Tracking ??

? RFID & barcode scanners: Automate stock tracking and reduce human error.

? IoT sensors: Monitor inventory levels, temperature, and humidity for sensitive goods.

? GPS & cloud integration: Provide live updates on warehouse stock movement.

? Example: An automotive manufacturer tracks spare parts in real time, reducing stockouts.

2. AI-Powered Predictive Analytics ??

? Uses AI to analyze demand trends and optimize inventory levels.

? Predicts stock shortages or overstock issues based on production needs.

? Reduces carrying costs by forecasting product demand and reorder schedules.

? Example: A food company uses AI to predict ingredient usage and prevent spoilage.

3. Robotics & Automation for Order Fulfillment ??

? Autonomous Mobile Robots (AMRs): Transport goods within the warehouse.

? Automated Storage & Retrieval Systems (AS/RS): Speed up picking and packing.

? Collaborative Robots (Cobots): Assist human workers in sorting and packing.

? Example: An electronics manufacturer uses robotic pickers to speed up assembly line supply.

4. Digital Twin & Warehouse Simulation ???

? Creates a virtual replica of the warehouse to simulate logistics operations.

? Optimizes warehouse layout for space efficiency and faster order processing.

? Detects bottlenecks in inventory movement before they impact production.

? Example: A smart factory uses a digital twin to optimize forklift routes and storage zones.

5. Blockchain for Supply Chain Transparency ??

? Ensures secure and tamper-proof inventory records.

? Tracks raw material sourcing and product movement to prevent fraud.

? Improves traceability for compliance and regulatory audits.

? Example: A pharmaceutical company uses blockchain to track medicine batches from production to delivery.

? Benefits of Smart Warehousing in Manufacturing

✓ Increases efficiency and reduces manual labor costs

✓ Enhances inventory accuracy with real-time tracking

✓ Speeds up order fulfillment and reduces lead times

✓ Minimizes errors, waste, and stock discrepancies

✓ Improves warehouse space utilization and workflow

? Cost Reduction in Smart Manufacturing

Smart Manufacturing reduces costs by leveraging automation, IoT, AI, robotics, and data analytics to improve efficiency, minimize waste, and optimize resources. By integrating real-time monitoring, predictive maintenance, and digital twins, companies can cut operational costs while enhancing productivity and quality.

? Key Strategies for Cost Reduction in Smart Manufacturing

1. Predictive Maintenance to Reduce Downtime ???

? IoT sensors monitor machinery health and detect failures before breakdowns.

? AI-driven analytics optimize maintenance schedules, reducing repair costs.

? Prevents unplanned downtime, which can be costly in industries like automotive and electronics.

? Example: An automotive plant reduced maintenance costs by 30% using predictive maintenance.

2. Energy Optimization with Smart Sensors ??

? AI-based energy management systems adjust power usage based on demand.

? IoT sensors track electricity consumption across production lines.

? Reduces energy waste by shutting down idle equipment automatically.

? Example: A food processing plant reduced electricity bills by 20% using AI-powered energy monitoring.

3. Robotics & Automation for Labor Efficiency ??

? Cobots (Collaborative Robots) assist workers in repetitive tasks, reducing labor costs.

? Automated Assembly Lines improve speed and precision, lowering rework expenses.

? Warehouse Automation reduces errors in inventory management.

? Example: An electronics factory cut labor costs by 40% using robotic assembly arms.

4. Digital Twin & Simulation for Process Optimization ???

? Creates a virtual replica of the factory to simulate production scenarios.

? Identifies bottlenecks, reducing production inefficiencies.

? Optimizes raw material usage to minimize waste and costs.

? Example: A dairy manufacturer reduced waste by 15% using digital twin simulations.

5. Supply Chain Optimization with AI & Blockchain ??

? AI-driven demand forecasting reduces excess inventory and storage costs.

? Blockchain enhances supply chain transparency, reducing fraud and inefficiencies.

? Automated supplier management optimizes procurement costs.

? Example: A retail company cut logistics costs by 25% using AI-driven supply chain visibility.

6. Smart Manufacturing Quality Control ???

? AI-powered defect detection reduces faulty product production.

? IoT-enabled real-time quality monitoring minimizes recalls and rework.

? Automated data analysis ensures consistent production standards.

? Example: A pharmaceutical company reduced product defects by 35% using AI-based quality control.

? Benefits of Cost Reduction in Smart Manufacturing

✓ Lower operational and maintenance costs

✓ Reduced labor costs through automation

✓ Minimized waste and raw material usage

✓ Optimized supply chain and logistics costs

✓ Improved energy efficiency for lower utility expenses

? Cost Reduction Strategy for Smart Manufacturing in the Automotive Industry

In the automotive industry, cost reduction in smart manufacturing involves automation, predictive analytics, digital twins, and AI-driven supply chain optimization to minimize expenses while improving efficiency, quality, and sustainability.

? Key Strategies for Cost Reduction in Automotive Smart Manufacturing

1. Predictive Maintenance for Equipment & Robotics ???

? IoT sensors monitor vehicle assembly machines to prevent costly breakdowns.

? AI-based predictive maintenance reduces downtime and unnecessary repairs.

? Automated alerts ensure timely part replacements, avoiding emergency shutdowns.

? Example: Ford saved millions annually by implementing predictive maintenance in robotic welding systems.

2. Robotics & Automation to Reduce Labor Costs ??

? Automated guided vehicles (AGVs) transport parts, reducing manual labor.

? Robotic arms improve assembly line speed and precision, minimizing errors.

? AI-powered collaborative robots (Cobots) assist workers in repetitive tasks, reducing fatigue and errors.

? Example: Tesla's Gigafactories use high levels of robotic automation, reducing production costs per vehicle.

3. Energy Efficiency & Smart Grid Integration ??

? AI-driven energy management optimizes lighting, HVAC, and machine operations.

? Smart grids and renewable energy integration lower electricity costs.

? Waste heat recovery systems repurpose excess heat from manufacturing.

? Example: BMW's plant in Leipzig reduced energy consumption by 50% with smart energy management.

4. Digital Twin for Process & Production Optimization ???

? Creates a virtual replica of automotive plants to simulate and test production changes.

? Identifies bottlenecks and optimizes workflows before physical implementation.

? Reduces material waste and production errors by testing layouts and processes digitally.

? Example: Mercedes-Benz optimized its EV production lines using digital twin technology.

5. AI-Driven Supply Chain Optimization ??

? AI-based demand forecasting minimizes overproduction and inventory costs.

? Blockchain enhances supply chain transparency, preventing counterfeiting and fraud.

? Automated supplier selection and contract management optimize procurement expenses.

? Example: Toyota reduced logistics costs by 25% using AI-powered supply chain analytics.

6. Smart Manufacturing for Quality Control ???

? AI-based defect detection reduces waste from faulty parts.

? Machine vision technology automates inspection for quality consistency.

? IoT-enabled real-time monitoring ensures compliance with automotive safety standards.

? Example: Volkswagen uses AI-driven defect detection, reducing vehicle recalls.

? Benefits of Cost Reduction in Automotive Smart Manufacturing

✓ Lower operational and labor costs with automation

✓ Reduced downtime and maintenance expenses

✓ Improved energy efficiency, reducing utility costs

✓ Optimized supply chain, lowering logistics expenses

✓ Higher production efficiency and minimized material waste

?? Cost Reduction Strategy for Smart Manufacturing in the Food Industry

In the food industry, cost reduction in smart manufacturing focuses on automation, energy efficiency, AI-driven supply chain management, and waste minimization to lower operational expenses while maintaining quality and safety.

? Key Strategies for Cost Reduction in Food Smart Manufacturing

1. Predictive Maintenance for Food Processing Equipment ???

? IoT sensors track machine performance to prevent unexpected breakdowns.

? AI-driven predictive maintenance schedules repairs efficiently, reducing downtime.

? Automated cleaning systems (CIP – Clean in Place) optimize water and chemical usage.

? Example: A dairy plant reduced maintenance costs by 30% by using IoT for early fault detection in pasteurization machines.

2. Energy Efficiency & Smart Utility Management ??

? AI-based energy monitoring optimizes refrigeration, heating, and processing units.

? Heat recovery systems repurpose excess heat from food processing.

? Smart lighting & automation reduce unnecessary power consumption in warehouses.

? Example: A bakery reduced energy costs by 20% by integrating AI-powered temperature control in ovens.

3. Robotics & Automation to Reduce Labor Costs ??

? Automated sorting, packaging, and palletizing speed up production and reduce manual errors.

? Collaborative robots (Cobots) assist workers in repetitive tasks like quality checks.

? AI-powered vision systems ensure packaging accuracy and consistency.

? Example: A frozen food company reduced packaging costs by 25% using robotic arms for sorting and boxing.

4. AI & Blockchain for Supply Chain Optimization ??

? AI-powered demand forecasting prevents overproduction and food waste.

? Blockchain-based inventory tracking ensures food safety and regulatory compliance.

? Automated warehouse systems reduce storage costs and optimize logistics.

? Example: A beverage company reduced logistics costs by 15% using AI for real-time delivery route optimization.

5. Smart Manufacturing for Waste Reduction ???

? AI-driven quality control minimizes raw material wastage.

? Food waste analytics track spoilage trends, improving production efficiency.

? Automated portioning and ingredient dispensing optimize recipe consistency and reduce waste.

? Example: A meat processing plant reduced ingredient waste by 10% by using smart portioning systems.

? Benefits of Cost Reduction in Food Smart Manufacturing

✔ Lower operational and labor costs with automation

✔ Reduced downtime and maintenance expenses

✔ Optimized energy efficiency, lowering utility bills

✔ Minimized food waste and improved raw material usage

✔ Streamlined supply chain, reducing storage and logistics costs

? Cost Reduction Strategy for Smart Manufacturing in the Education Industry

In the education industry, cost reduction in smart manufacturing applies to the production of learning materials, lab equipment, smart devices, and educational infrastructure. By leveraging automation, AI-driven resource management, and energy efficiency, institutions and manufacturers can cut costs while improving quality and accessibility.

? Key Strategies for Cost Reduction in Smart Manufacturing for Education

1. Automation & Robotics for Educational Equipment Production ??

? Automated assembly lines reduce labor costs in making lab tools, furniture, and smartboards.

? AI-driven quality control minimizes defects in educational products.

? 3D printing for rapid prototyping lowers material waste and production costs.

? Example: A manufacturer of STEM kits reduced production costs by 30% using robotic assembly.

2. Energy Efficiency in Educational Manufacturing ??

? Smart energy management systems optimize electricity usage in production plants.

? IoT-powered HVAC and lighting controls reduce utility costs in educational buildings.

? Solar-powered systems cut long-term energy expenses.

? Example: A textbook printing facility reduced power bills by 25% using AI-controlled energy monitoring.

3. AI & Blockchain for Supply Chain Optimization ??

? AI-based inventory tracking prevents overproduction of books and learning materials.

? Blockchain ensures transparency in educational product supply chains.

? Automated warehouse solutions lower storage costs.

? Example: A university supply chain cut costs by 20% using AI to forecast student demand for learning materials.

4. Digital Twins for Process Optimization ???

? Simulates production of educational tools to reduce waste before full-scale manufacturing.

? Predicts bottlenecks in supply chain operations to optimize production schedules.

? Improves layout and process efficiency in educational material production plants.

? Example: A school furniture manufacturer reduced material waste by 15% using digital twin simulations.

5. Smart Manufacturing for Cost-Effective Lab Equipment Production ??

? AI-driven predictive maintenance minimizes downtime in lab equipment factories.

? Robotic precision manufacturing ensures cost-efficient lab tools.

? 3D-printed models for science and engineering courses reduce production expenses.

? Example: A medical university reduced lab equipment procurement costs by 20% using locally 3D-printed tools.

? Benefits of Cost Reduction in Smart Manufacturing for Education

✓ Lower labor and operational costs with automation

✓ Reduced waste and optimized material usage

✓ Energy efficiency, lowering long-term expenses

✓ More affordable educational products and tools

✓ Improved supply chain efficiency for cost-effective learning resources

? Cost Reduction Strategy for Smart Manufacturing in the Pharmaceutical Industry

In the pharmaceutical industry, cost reduction in smart manufacturing focuses on automation, AI-driven quality control, supply chain optimization, and energy efficiency to cut expenses while maintaining compliance, safety, and production efficiency.

? Key Strategies for Cost Reduction in Pharmaceutical Smart Manufacturing

1. AI-Powered Predictive Maintenance for Equipment ???

? IoT sensors monitor drug manufacturing machinery to prevent breakdowns.

? AI-driven predictive maintenance reduces unplanned downtime and costly repairs.

? Automated alerts ensure timely maintenance, avoiding equipment failures.

? Example: A biotech firm reduced equipment maintenance costs by 25% using AI-driven failure detection.

2. Robotics & Automation for Drug Manufacturing ??

? Automated robotic arms improve precision in drug formulation and packaging.

? Collaborative robots (Cobots) assist in quality inspection and sterile handling.

? AI-powered robotic dispensing systems minimize human error in pharmaceutical compounding.

? Example: A pharmaceutical company cut labor costs by 30% by implementing robotic filling and labeling systems.

3. AI & Blockchain for Supply Chain Optimization ??

? AI-based demand forecasting prevents overproduction and excess inventory costs.

? Blockchain enhances supply chain transparency, reducing counterfeit risks.

? Automated supplier selection and tracking optimize procurement expenses.

? Example: Pfizer reduced logistics costs by 20% using AI-driven supply chain analytics.

4. Digital Twin for Process & Drug Development Optimization ???

? Creates a virtual replica of manufacturing plants to optimize production efficiency.

? Simulates drug formulation processes to reduce material waste and testing costs.

? Predicts production bottlenecks before implementing real-world changes.

? Example: A vaccine manufacturer reduced raw material waste by 15% using digital twin simulations.

5. Energy Efficiency & Sustainable Manufacturing ??

? Smart energy management systems optimize HVAC, refrigeration, and clean rooms.

? AI-driven environmental monitoring ensures minimal energy waste.

? Heat recovery systems repurpose excess heat from production processes.

? Example: A pharma plant cut energy costs by 30% using AI-based energy optimization.

6. Smart Manufacturing for Quality Control & Waste Reduction ???

? AI-based defect detection minimizes production waste.

? Real-time monitoring systems ensure compliance with pharmaceutical safety regulations.

? Automated data analytics improve batch consistency and regulatory reporting.

? Example: A drug manufacturing facility reduced recall rates by 40% using AI-powered quality inspection.

? Benefits of Cost Reduction in Pharmaceutical Smart Manufacturing

✔ Lower operational and labor costs with automation

✔ Reduced waste and optimized raw material usage

✔ Energy efficiency, lowering utility costs

✔ Enhanced quality control, reducing recalls and compliance risks

✔ Streamlined supply chain, lowering logistics and inventory costs

?? Waste Management in Smart Manufacturing

Smart manufacturing leverages automation, AI, IoT, and data analytics to optimize waste management, reducing material loss, energy consumption, and environmental impact while improving efficiency and cost savings.

? Key Strategies for Waste Management in Smart Manufacturing

1. Predictive Waste Analytics with AI & IoT ??

? AI-powered data analysis predicts waste patterns and identifies inefficiencies.

? IoT sensors track waste production in real-time across production lines.

? Machine learning algorithms optimize resource usage, reducing raw material waste.

? Example: An automotive plant reduced material waste by 20% using AI-driven waste tracking.

2. Lean Manufacturing & Process Optimization ???

? Just-in-Time (JIT) production minimizes excess inventory and raw material waste.

? Value Stream Mapping (VSM) identifies waste reduction opportunities in the production process.

? Continuous improvement (Kaizen) principles refine workflows to prevent inefficiencies.

? Example: A food processing plant cut raw ingredient waste by 15% through lean manufacturing.

3. Smart Recycling & Circular Economy Integration ???

? Automated sorting systems separate reusable materials from waste.

? AI-powered quality control ensures defective products are repurposed instead of discarded.

? Closed-loop manufacturing reuses production scraps, reducing reliance on new materials.

? Example: A smartphone manufacturer recycles 98% of its production waste using AI-powered recycling.

4. Energy & Resource Efficiency Optimization ??

? Smart energy monitoring systems optimize power and water usage.

? Heat recovery systems capture and repurpose excess heat from production processes.

? AI-driven water recycling minimizes wastewater in industries like textiles and food processing.

? Example: A textile factory reduced water waste by 30% using AI-driven water recycling.

5. Blockchain for Waste Tracking & Compliance ??

? Blockchain-based waste tracking ensures compliance with environmental regulations.

? Smart contracts automate waste disposal processes, preventing delays and inefficiencies.

? Supply chain transparency helps reduce waste at every stage, from sourcing to distribution.

? Example: A pharmaceutical company reduced expired product waste by 25% using blockchain-based inventory tracking.

? Benefits of Smart Waste Management in Manufacturing

✔ Lower material and production costs

✔ Reduced environmental impact and regulatory risks

✔ Optimized energy and resource consumption

✔ Improved recycling and circular economy integration

✔ Higher operational efficiency and sustainable manufacturing practices

? Customized Waste Management Strategy for Smart Manufacturing in the Pharmaceutical Industry

In pharmaceutical manufacturing, waste management is critical for cost reduction, regulatory compliance, environmental sustainability, and operational efficiency. Smart manufacturing technologies such as AI, IoT, blockchain, and automation can significantly reduce pharmaceutical waste in drug production, packaging, and distribution.

? Key Strategies for Smart Waste Management in Pharmaceuticals

1. AI-Driven Predictive Waste Analytics ??

? AI-powered analytics predict potential waste sources and optimize production.

? IoT sensors track waste in real-time, identifying inefficiencies in drug formulation.

? AI algorithms suggest process improvements to minimize material loss.

? Example: A biotech firm reduced active ingredient waste by 20% using AI-based production analytics.

2. Lean & Continuous Manufacturing for Waste Reduction ??

? Continuous manufacturing techniques replace batch processes, reducing material waste.

? Lean Six Sigma methodologies optimize drug formulation and minimize variability.

? Real-time monitoring adjusts ingredient usage dynamically to prevent overproduction.

? Example: A vaccine manufacturer cut excipient waste by 30% using real-time process monitoring.

3. Smart Inventory & Expiry Tracking with Blockchain ??

? Blockchain-based supply chain management prevents expired drug accumulation.

? AI-driven demand forecasting optimizes inventory, reducing overproduction.

? Automated alerts ensure first-expiry-first-out (FEFO) inventory rotation.

? Example: A pharmaceutical distributor reduced expired product waste by 25% using blockchain-based inventory tracking.

4. Sustainable & Smart Packaging Optimization ???

? Biodegradable and recyclable materials minimize packaging waste.

? AI-powered packaging optimization reduces excess material usage.

? 3D printing for custom packaging lowers waste in small-batch production.

? Example: A pharmaceutical company cut packaging waste by 40% using AI-based package design.

5. Energy & Water Waste Optimization in Drug Production ??

? AI-driven energy monitoring optimizes power usage in manufacturing plants.

? Smart water recycling systems reduce waste in drug formulation and purification.

? Heat recovery systems repurpose excess heat from production processes.

? Example: A pharma plant reduced water waste by 30% using AI-driven wastewater recycling.

6. Reverse Logistics & Drug Take-Back Programs ??

? Smart collection systems enable efficient return and disposal of expired drugs.

? AI-powered reverse logistics optimizes drug take-back programs.

? Blockchain ensures secure disposal tracking, preventing counterfeit drug risks.

? Example: A global pharma company reduced landfill waste by 50% through AI-driven reverse logistics.

? Benefits of Smart Waste Management in Pharmaceuticals

✔ Lower material and operational costs

✔ Regulatory compliance and risk reduction

✔ Energy-efficient and sustainable drug production

✔ Minimized expired product losses through smart inventory management

✔ Improved public safety with optimized drug disposal methods

?? Customized Waste Management Strategy for Smart Manufacturing in the Food Industry

In food manufacturing, waste comes from raw material loss, packaging waste, energy consumption, and expired products. Smart manufacturing techniques, including AI, IoT, blockchain, and automation, can optimize waste reduction, improve sustainability, and cut costs.

? Key Strategies for Smart Waste Management in the Food Industry

1. AI-Driven Food Waste Analytics & IoT Sensors ??

? AI-powered data analysis predicts spoilage and reduces ingredient waste.

? IoT sensors track food quality in real time, preventing unnecessary disposal.

? Smart inventory management ensures optimal stock rotation (FIFO & FEFO methods).

? Example: A bakery reduced ingredient waste by 25% using AI-driven demand forecasting.

2. Lean Manufacturing & Process Optimization ???

? Just-in-Time (JIT) production minimizes overproduction and food waste.

? Lean Six Sigma techniques optimize portion control and reduce raw material losses.

? Automated portioning and precision cutting minimize trimming waste.

? Example: A meat processing plant cut raw material waste by 30% using automated portioning.

3. Smart Inventory & Expiry Tracking with Blockchain ??

? Blockchain-based tracking prevents expired and spoiled food in warehouses.

? AI-driven demand forecasting ensures precise supply chain management.

? Automated alerts notify suppliers of approaching expiration dates.

? Example: A dairy manufacturer reduced expired product waste by 40% with blockchain-based inventory tracking.

4. Sustainable Packaging & Recycling Initiatives ???

? Edible and biodegradable packaging reduces plastic waste.

? AI-powered package optimization lowers excess material use.

? Automated sorting systems streamline waste recycling processes.

? Example: A beverage company cut packaging waste by 35% using AI-optimized design.

5. Energy & Water Efficiency in Food Processing ??

? AI-driven energy monitoring optimizes refrigeration and processing equipment.

? Smart water recycling systems reduce wastewater in food production.

? Heat recovery systems repurpose excess heat for cooking and drying processes.

? Example: A dairy plant reduced energy costs by 20% using smart energy monitoring.

6. Circular Economy & Food Waste Repurposing ???

? Upcycling food waste into animal feed, biofuel, or compost.

? AI-driven sorting systems separate edible vs. non-edible food waste.

? Reverse logistics programs recover unsold food for redistribution.

? Example: A supermarket chain repurposed 50% of food waste into bioenergy using AI-driven waste classification.

? Benefits of Smart Waste Management in Food Manufacturing

✔ Lower ingredient and operational costs

✔ Sustainable food production with minimal waste

✔ Optimized energy and water usage for efficiency

✔ Improved food safety and regulatory compliance

✔ Stronger supply chain visibility with blockchain tracking

? Customized Waste Management Strategy for Smart Manufacturing in the Automotive Industry

In the automotive industry, waste comes from scrap metal, defective parts, excess materials, energy consumption, and hazardous waste. Smart manufacturing techniques, including AI, IoT, blockchain, and automation, can significantly reduce waste, improve sustainability, and cut costs.

? Key Strategies for Smart Waste Management in the Automotive Industry

1. AI-Driven Waste Analytics & IoT Sensors ??

? AI-powered analytics predict waste generation and optimize resource usage.

? IoT sensors track material consumption in real time to reduce scrap and defects.

? Automated alerts prevent excess raw material ordering and stockpiling.

? Example: A car manufacturer reduced metal waste by 25% using AI-powered waste tracking.

2. Lean Manufacturing & Process Optimization ???

? Just-in-Time (JIT) production minimizes excess inventory and material waste.

? Lean Six Sigma techniques reduce defects and rework in assembly lines.

? Automated precision cutting and welding optimize material utilization.

? Example: An EV manufacturer cut raw material waste by 30% with AI-driven lean manufacturing.

3. Smart Inventory & Defect Tracking with Blockchain ??

? Blockchain-based tracking ensures transparency in material usage and defect handling.

? AI-driven demand forecasting prevents excess parts production and inventory waste.

? Automated quality control detects defects early, reducing scrapped components.

? Example: A tier-1 auto supplier reduced defective part disposal by 40% with blockchain-based quality tracking.

4. Sustainable Materials & Circular Economy Integration ???

? Recycled and eco-friendly materials reduce waste in vehicle production.

? End-of-life vehicle (ELV) recycling maximizes component recovery.

? AI-powered disassembly lines optimize part reuse and remanufacturing.

? Example: A car brand increased recyclable content in its vehicles by 50% using smart material tracking.

5. Energy & Water Efficiency in Auto Manufacturing ??

? AI-driven energy monitoring optimizes power consumption in factories.

? Smart water recycling systems reduce wastewater in painting and cooling processes.

? Heat recovery systems repurpose excess heat from welding and casting.

? Example: An automotive plant reduced energy waste by 20% using AI-driven energy monitoring.

6. Hazardous Waste & Emission Reduction Strategies ??

? IoT-based emissions monitoring ensures compliance with environmental regulations.

? AI-optimized solvent recovery minimizes hazardous chemical disposal.

? Automated waste treatment systems improve recycling and reduce landfill waste.

? Example: A paint shop cut hazardous waste by 35% with AI-driven solvent recovery.

? Benefits of Smart Waste Management in Automotive Manufacturing

✓ Lower material and operational costs

✓ Increased sustainability with reduced waste and emissions

✓ Optimized energy and water consumption

✓ Higher production efficiency and quality

✓ Enhanced compliance with environmental regulations

? Automated Systems in Smart Manufacturing

Automated systems in smart manufacturing integrate AI, robotics, IoT, and data analytics to enhance efficiency, reduce waste, and improve product quality. These systems allow factories to operate with minimal human intervention, making real-time decisions based on data from sensors, machines, and digital models.

? Key Automated Systems in Smart Manufacturing

1. Robotics & Cobots (Collaborative Robots) ???

? Industrial robots perform repetitive tasks like welding, assembly, and packaging.

? Cobots work alongside humans to enhance productivity and safety.

? AI-powered robots adapt to changing production requirements.

? Example: An automotive plant uses robotic arms for precision welding, reducing defects by 30%.

2. AI-Driven Predictive Maintenance ???

? Machine learning algorithms analyze equipment health in real-time.

? Predictive analytics prevent unexpected breakdowns and downtime.

? IoT sensors monitor vibrations, temperature, and wear-and-tear.

? Example: A food manufacturing plant reduced machine failures by 40% using AI-driven maintenance.

3. Autonomous Guided Vehicles (AGVs) & Drones ??

? AGVs transport materials and components within factories without human drivers.

? Drones monitor inventory levels in warehouses and large production sites.

? AI optimizes routes to minimize energy consumption and improve efficiency.

? Example: An electronics factory uses AGVs to move components, cutting labor costs by 50%.

4. Smart Quality Control & AI Vision Systems ??

? AI-powered cameras inspect products for defects in real-time.

? Computer vision systems detect surface imperfections and assembly errors.

? Automated feedback loops improve quality by adjusting processes dynamically.

? Example: A pharmaceutical company reduced defect rates by 25% with AI-based visual inspection.

5. Digital Twins & Virtual Simulations ??

? Digital twins create virtual models of manufacturing systems for real-time monitoring.

? AI-driven simulations predict outcomes before making physical changes.

? IoT integration allows continuous updates for performance optimization.

? Example: An automotive manufacturer optimized production efficiency by 20% using digital twins.

6. Smart Supply Chain & Automated Inventory Management ??

? Blockchain and AI track and optimize supply chain operations.

? Automated inventory management systems prevent overstocking and shortages.

? Real-time data sharing improves supplier collaboration and reduces waste.

? Example: A retail company reduced inventory costs by 30% with AI-powered supply chain automation.

? Benefits of Automated Systems in Smart Manufacturing

✔ Increased production speed and efficiency

✔ Reduced operational costs and material waste

✔ Enhanced quality control and product consistency

✔ Lower maintenance costs with predictive analytics

✔ Greater workplace safety with robotic assistance

? Applications of Smart Manufacturing Across Industries

Smart Manufacturing integrates AI, IoT, automation, robotics, and data analytics to enhance efficiency, flexibility, and sustainability in production processes. These advanced technologies optimize operations, reduce costs, and improve product quality across various industries.

? Key Applications of Smart Manufacturing

1. Automotive Industry ??

? Predictive maintenance prevents unexpected machine failures.

? AI-powered quality control detects defects in car components.

? Robotics and cobots automate assembly, welding, and painting.

? Digital twins simulate production lines to optimize efficiency.

? 3D printing enables rapid prototyping and on-demand parts manufacturing.

? Example: Tesla uses AI and robotics in vehicle assembly and battery production, reducing defects and increasing efficiency.

2. Food Industry ???

? AI-driven demand forecasting minimizes overproduction and food waste.

? IoT-based refrigeration monitoring ensures food safety and freshness.

? Automated sorting and packaging enhances speed and accuracy.

? Blockchain traceability tracks food from farm to consumer.

? Smart inventory management prevents expired products from reaching consumers.

    ? Example: Nestlé uses blockchain technology to track ingredient sources and ensure food safety.

3. Pharmaceutical Industry ??

    ? AI-driven drug discovery speeds up new medicine development.

? Automated production lines ensure precision in medicine manufacturing.

? IoT sensors monitor storage conditions to maintain drug quality.

? Blockchain-based inventory tracking prevents counterfeit drugs.

? Predictive maintenance reduces downtime in pharmaceutical plants.

    ? Example: Pfizer uses AI-powered robotic automation to improve vaccine production efficiency.

4. Electronics & Consumer Goods ??

    ? AI-powered defect detection enhances product quality.

? Robotic assembly lines speed up smartphone and semiconductor production.

? IoT-enabled smart factories improve real-time monitoring and efficiency.

? Automated supply chains reduce waste and improve delivery times.

? 3D printing enables rapid prototyping and small-batch production.

    ? Example: Apple's smart factories use robotic automation and AI-driven quality control for iPhone production.

5. Education & Training ??

    ? Smart manufacturing labs provide real-time industry training.

? Digital twins and VR simulations train students in factory operations.

? AI-driven learning systems customize training based on student performance.

? IoT-connected equipment allows remote monitoring of student projects.

? Blockchain certification secures academic records and training credentials.

    ? Example: Universities collaborate with Industry 4.0 factories to create smart learning environments for engineers.

6. Shipping & Logistics ??

    ? AI-driven route optimization reduces delivery time and fuel costs.

? Automated warehouses use robotics to speed up order fulfillment.

? Blockchain-based inventory tracking prevents loss and theft.

? IoT-enabled fleet monitoring improves logistics efficiency.

? Predictive maintenance reduces downtime of delivery trucks and ships.

    ? Example: Amazon uses AI-powered robotics in warehouses to automate order processing.

7. Textile & Apparel Industry ??

    ? AI-driven demand forecasting optimizes raw material use.

? Automated sewing machines increase production speed.

? IoT-based quality monitoring detects defects in fabric production.

? 3D knitting technology produces customized apparel with minimal waste.

? Blockchain tracking ensures ethical sourcing of materials.

    ? Example: Nike uses automated laser-cutting and smart knitting to reduce fabric waste.

? Benefits of Smart Manufacturing Applications

    ✓ Higher production efficiency and lower costs

✓ Improved product quality with AI-driven quality control

✓ Reduced waste and better sustainability

✓ Enhanced supply chain visibility with IoT and blockchain

✔ Greater flexibility to adapt to market demands

Question Bank

Unit I - Lean Manufacturing
2 marks

Objectives of Lean Manufacturing

1. What are the primary objectives of lean manufacturing?
2. How does lean manufacturing aim to reduce waste?

Key Principles and Implications of Lean Manufacturing

1. List any two key principles of lean manufacturing.
2. What is meant by 'value' in the context of lean manufacturing?

Traditional Vs Lean Manufacturing

1. Mention two differences between traditional manufacturing and lean manufacturing.
2. How does inventory management differ between traditional and lean manufacturing systems?

Flow

1. What is meant by 'flow' in lean manufacturing?
2. Why is continuous flow important in lean manufacturing?

Continuous Improvement/Kaizen

1. Define the term 'Kaizen'.
2. How does Kaizen contribute to continuous improvement?

Worker Involvement

1. Why is worker involvement important in lean manufacturing?
2. Mention two ways workers can contribute to lean manufacturing.

5S Principles

1. List any two of the 5S principles.
2. What is the purpose of implementing 5S in a workplace?

Elements of JIT

1. What are the key elements of Just-In-Time (JIT) manufacturing?
2. Mention two benefits of implementing JIT.

Uniform Production Rate

1. What is meant by 'uniform production rate'?
2. Why is achieving a uniform production rate essential in lean manufacturing?

Kanban System

1. What is a Kanban system?
2. How does a Kanban system help in inventory management?

Lean Implementation

1. Mention any two steps involved in implementing lean manufacturing.
2. What is the significance of value stream mapping in lean implementation?

Reconciling Lean with Other Systems

1. What challenges are faced when reconciling lean with traditional systems?
2. Why is it necessary to reconcile lean manufacturing with other systems?

Lean Six Sigma

1. What is Lean Six Sigma?
2. How does Lean Six Sigma differ from standard lean manufacturing?

Lean and ERP

1. How can ERP systems support lean manufacturing?
2. What are the challenges of integrating ERP with lean manufacturing?

Lean with ISO 9001:2000

1. How can lean principles be integrated with ISO 9001:2000 standards?
2. Why is it important to align lean manufacturing with ISO 9001:2000?

13 marks

Objectives of Lean Manufacturing

- Explain the primary objectives of lean manufacturing and discuss how these objectives contribute to overall operational efficiency and cost reduction.

Key Principles and Implications of Lean Manufacturing

- Discuss the key principles of lean manufacturing. How do these principles influence decision-making and process improvement within an organization?

Traditional Vs Lean Manufacturing

- Compare and contrast traditional manufacturing with lean manufacturing, focusing on aspects such as inventory management, production flow, quality control, and workforce involvement. Provide examples to support your answer.

Flow and Continuous Improvement/Kaizen

- Explain the concept of 'flow' in lean manufacturing. How does continuous improvement (Kaizen) contribute to achieving and maintaining efficient flow in manufacturing processes?

Worker Involvement and 5S Principles

- Discuss the role of worker involvement in lean manufacturing. How does the implementation of the 5S principles contribute to enhancing productivity and workplace organization?

Just-In-Time (JIT) and Uniform Production Rate

- Explain the elements of Just-In-Time (JIT) manufacturing and how it supports achieving a uniform production rate. Discuss the benefits and challenges associated with implementing JIT in manufacturing.

Kanban System and Lean Implementation

- Describe the Kanban system and its application in lean manufacturing. Explain the steps involved in implementing lean manufacturing within an organization and how Kanban supports this process.

Reconciling Lean with Other Systems

- Discuss the challenges and strategies involved in reconciling lean manufacturing with other systems such as Six Sigma, ERP, and ISO 9001:2000. Provide examples of successful integrations.

Lean Six Sigma and ERP Integration

- Explain Lean Six Sigma and its relevance to modern manufacturing. How can ERP systems be integrated with lean manufacturing principles to enhance operational efficiency?

Lean and ISO 9001:2000

- Discuss how lean manufacturing principles can be aligned with ISO 9001:2000 standards to achieve quality management objectives. Provide examples of best practices and common challenges.

Unit II - Agile Manufacturing
2 marks

Agile Manufacturing Vs Mass Manufacturing

1. Define Agile Manufacturing.
2. State two key differences between Agile Manufacturing and Mass Manufacturing.
3. List two benefits of Agile Manufacturing over Mass Manufacturing.

4. Mention any two challenges of implementing Agile Manufacturing compared to Mass Manufacturing.

Agile Practice for Product Development

1. What is the purpose of Agile practices in product development?
2. Name any two agile practices commonly used in product development.
3. How does Agile product development enhance customer satisfaction?
4. Mention two tools or frameworks used in Agile product development.

Manufacturing Agile Practices

1. Define Manufacturing Agile Practices.
2. State two characteristics of Manufacturing Agile Practices.
3. List two advantages of implementing Manufacturing Agile Practices.
4. What is the role of flexibility in Manufacturing Agile Practices?

Implementing New Technology

1. Mention two factors to consider when implementing new technology in manufacturing.
2. What is the significance of technology adoption in Agile Manufacturing?
3. List two barriers to implementing new technology in manufacturing.
4. How does technology integration improve manufacturing agility?

A Checklist for Implementing New Technology

1. Mention any two points included in a checklist for implementing new technology.
2. Why is a checklist important for implementing new technology?
3. List two steps to ensure successful implementation of new technology.
4. What is the purpose of evaluating readiness in a technology implementation checklist?

Technology Applications that Enhance Agility

1. Name two technology applications that enhance manufacturing agility.
2. How does IoT enhance agility in manufacturing?
3. Mention two benefits of using AI in Agile Manufacturing.
4. Explain the role of automation in enhancing agility.

Agile Technology Make or Buy Decisions

1. Define 'Make or Buy' decisions in Agile Manufacturing.
2. List two factors influencing make or buy decisions in Agile Manufacturing.
3. What is the importance of make or buy decisions in Agile Manufacturing?
4. Give two examples of technology components that may be bought rather than made.

Costing for Agile Manufacturing Practices

1. What is the purpose of costing in Agile Manufacturing?
2. Mention two costing techniques suitable for Agile Manufacturing.

3. How does Agile Manufacturing impact cost management?
4. List two factors that influence costing in Agile Manufacturing.

13 marks

Agile Manufacturing Vs Mass Manufacturing

1. Compare and contrast Agile Manufacturing and Mass Manufacturing with respect to flexibility, cost, product variety, and lead time. Provide suitable examples.
2. Discuss the advantages and disadvantages of Agile Manufacturing compared to Mass Manufacturing in a highly competitive market environment.

Agile Practice for Product Development

1. Explain various Agile practices used in product development. How do these practices contribute to faster and more efficient product development cycles?
2. Describe the Agile product development process with a suitable case study. Discuss the benefits and challenges faced during the implementation of Agile practices.

Manufacturing Agile Practices

1. Discuss the key principles of Manufacturing Agile Practices. Explain how these principles help in responding to changing market demands.
2. Evaluate the importance of agility in manufacturing. Describe various strategies employed to achieve agility in manufacturing processes.

Implementing New Technology

1. Explain the process of implementing new technology in Agile Manufacturing. Discuss the challenges encountered during implementation and suggest possible solutions.
2. Analyze the role of technological advancements in enhancing manufacturing agility. Illustrate with examples of successful implementation of new technology.

A Checklist for Implementing New Technology

1. Design a comprehensive checklist for implementing new technology in an Agile Manufacturing setup. Justify the importance of each point included in the checklist.
2. Discuss the steps involved in developing and using a checklist for implementing new technology. How can such a checklist contribute to minimizing implementation risks?

Technology Applications that Enhance Agility

1. Discuss various technology applications that enhance agility in manufacturing. Highlight their benefits, limitations, and potential impact on productivity.
2. Evaluate the role of technologies such as IoT, AI, and Robotics in enhancing manufacturing agility. Provide relevant examples from the industry.

Agile Technology Make or Buy Decisions

1. Discuss the concept of 'Make or Buy' decisions in Agile Manufacturing. What factors should be considered while making such decisions? Illustrate with examples.
2. Critically analyze the implications of make or buy decisions on Agile Manufacturing. Discuss how these decisions influence cost, quality, and flexibility.

Costing for Agile Manufacturing Practices

1. Explain various costing methods applicable to Agile Manufacturing. How do these methods help in maintaining cost-effectiveness while ensuring agility?
2. Discuss the challenges associated with costing in Agile Manufacturing. Suggest strategies to overcome these challenges and maintain profitability.

Unit III - Sustainable Manufacturing
2 marks

Concepts of Competitive Strategy and Manufacturing Strategies

1. Define competitive strategy.
2. What is a manufacturing strategy?
3. List two differences between competitive strategy and manufacturing strategy.
4. Mention two objectives of a competitive strategy in manufacturing.

Development of a Strategic Improvement Programme

1. What is a strategic improvement programme?
2. List two benefits of developing a strategic improvement programme.
3. Mention any two steps involved in developing a strategic improvement programme.
4. What is the importance of monitoring in a strategic improvement programme?

Manufacturing Strategy in Business Success

1. How does manufacturing strategy contribute to business success?
2. List two characteristics of a successful manufacturing strategy.
3. Mention two ways in which manufacturing strategy aligns with business objectives.
4. What is the role of manufacturing strategy in gaining a competitive advantage?

Strategy Formation and Formulation

1. Define strategy formulation.
2. Mention two key elements of strategy formation.
3. List two differences between strategy formation and strategy formulation.
4. What is the significance of structured strategy formulation?

Structured Strategy Formulation

1. What is meant by structured strategy formulation?
2. List two steps involved in structured strategy formulation.
3. Mention two benefits of structured strategy formulation.
4. How does structured strategy formulation enhance decision-making?

Sustainable Manufacturing System Design Options

1. Define sustainable manufacturing.
2. List two options for designing sustainable manufacturing systems.
3. Mention two benefits of sustainable manufacturing system design.
4. What is the importance of sustainability in manufacturing system design?

Approaches to Strategy Formulation

1. Mention two approaches to strategy formulation.
2. Define the top-down approach to strategy formulation.
3. List two characteristics of the bottom-up approach to strategy formulation.
4. How does collaborative strategy formulation differ from traditional approaches?

Realization of New Strategies/System Designs

1. What is meant by realization of new strategies?
2. Mention two steps involved in the realization of new system designs.
3. List two challenges in realizing new strategies.
4. What is the role of evaluation in realizing new strategies?

13 marks

Concepts of Competitive Strategy and Manufacturing Strategies

1. Discuss the relationship between competitive strategy and manufacturing strategy. How do these concepts contribute to achieving long-term business success?
2. Analyze various types of manufacturing strategies and their impact on competitiveness. Provide suitable examples to illustrate your points.

Development of a Strategic Improvement Programme

1. Explain the process of developing a strategic improvement programme. Discuss the challenges and benefits associated with implementing such programmes.
2. Discuss the key components of a strategic improvement programme. How can it be used to enhance manufacturing efficiency and competitiveness?

Manufacturing Strategy in Business Success

1. Explain the role of manufacturing strategy in achieving business success. Discuss how alignment between manufacturing strategy and business objectives leads to a sustainable competitive advantage.
2. Critically analyze how manufacturing strategy influences product development, cost management, and market responsiveness. Provide relevant examples.

Strategy Formation and Formulation

1. Explain the process of strategy formation and formulation. Discuss the differences between the two processes and their importance in achieving business objectives.

2. Discuss the various stages involved in strategy formulation. Explain how structured strategy formulation contributes to effective decision-making.

Structured Strategy Formulation

1. Discuss the concept of structured strategy formulation. Explain the steps involved and how this approach helps in achieving consistency and coherence in strategic planning.
2. Explain the benefits of structured strategy formulation in manufacturing. Provide examples of how this approach has been successfully implemented in various industries.

Sustainable Manufacturing System Design Options

1. Explain different options for designing sustainable manufacturing systems. Discuss the benefits and challenges associated with each option.
2. Discuss the importance of sustainability in manufacturing system design. Explain how companies can integrate sustainable practices into their manufacturing strategies.

Approaches to Strategy Formulation

1. Compare and contrast top-down, bottom-up, and collaborative approaches to strategy formulation. Discuss the advantages and disadvantages of each approach.
2. Discuss various approaches to strategy formulation. Provide examples of how different approaches are applied in manufacturing to achieve competitive advantage.

Realization of New Strategies/System Designs

1. Explain the process of realizing new strategies and system designs. Discuss the challenges encountered during implementation and how they can be overcome.
2. Discuss the importance of monitoring, evaluation, and continuous improvement in the realization of new strategies. Provide relevant case studies to support your answer.

Unit IV - Intelligent Manufacturing
2 marks

Concepts of Competitive Strategy and Manufacturing Strategies

1. What is competitive strategy?
2. Define manufacturing strategy.
3. List two objectives of a competitive strategy in manufacturing.
4. Mention any two differences between competitive strategy and manufacturing strategy.

Development of a Strategic Improvement Programme

1. What is a strategic improvement programme?
2. List two benefits of developing a strategic improvement programme.
3. Mention two key steps in developing a strategic improvement programme.
4. Why is monitoring important in a strategic improvement programme?

Manufacturing Strategy in Business Success

1. How does manufacturing strategy contribute to business success?
2. List two characteristics of an effective manufacturing strategy.
3. Mention two ways in which manufacturing strategy aligns with business objectives.
4. What is the role of manufacturing strategy in achieving competitive advantage?

Strategy Formation and Formulation

1. Define strategy formation.
2. What is strategy formulation?
3. List two differences between strategy formation and strategy formulation.
4. Mention any two steps involved in strategy formulation.

Structured Strategy Formulation

1. What is structured strategy formulation?
2. List two benefits of structured strategy formulation.
3. Mention two components of a structured strategy formulation process.
4. How does structured strategy formulation improve decision-making?

Sustainable Manufacturing System Design Options

1. Define sustainable manufacturing.
2. List two benefits of sustainable manufacturing system design.
3. Mention two design options for achieving sustainable manufacturing.
4. Why is sustainability important in manufacturing system design?

Approaches to Strategy Formulation

1. List two approaches to strategy formulation.
2. What is the top-down approach in strategy formulation?
3. Mention two characteristics of the bottom-up approach in strategy formulation.
4. How does collaborative strategy formulation differ from traditional approaches?

Realization of New Strategies/System Designs

1. What is meant by the realization of new strategies?
2. List two steps involved in the realization of new system designs.
3. Mention two challenges faced during the realization of new strategies.
4. Why is evaluation important in realizing new strategies?

13 marks

Concepts of Competitive Strategy and Manufacturing Strategies

1. Discuss the relationship between competitive strategy and manufacturing strategy. How do these concepts contribute to achieving long-term business success?
2. Analyze different types of manufacturing strategies and explain how they align with competitive strategies to achieve business objectives. Provide suitable examples.

Development of a Strategic Improvement Programme

1. Explain the process of developing a strategic improvement programme. Discuss its importance and the key challenges faced during its implementation.
2. Discuss the components of a strategic improvement programme. How can such a programme enhance manufacturing performance and competitiveness? Provide relevant examples.

Manufacturing Strategy in Business Success

1. Explain the role of manufacturing strategy in achieving business success. Discuss how alignment between manufacturing strategy and business objectives leads to competitive advantage.
2. Critically analyze how a well-defined manufacturing strategy influences product development, cost management, quality, and market responsiveness. Support your answer with examples.

Strategy Formation and Formulation

1. Discuss the differences between strategy formation and strategy formulation. Explain the importance of each process in achieving organizational goals.
2. Describe the process of strategy formulation. Explain how structured strategy formulation contributes to effective decision-making and improved manufacturing performance.

Structured Strategy Formulation

1. Explain the concept of structured strategy formulation. Discuss its benefits, challenges, and relevance to achieving strategic manufacturing goals.
2. Discuss the steps involved in structured strategy formulation. Provide examples of how structured strategy formulation has been successfully implemented in various industries.

Sustainable Manufacturing System Design Options

1. Explain different options for designing sustainable manufacturing systems. Discuss the benefits, challenges, and implications of adopting sustainable practices in manufacturing.
2. Discuss the importance of sustainability in manufacturing system design. How can companies integrate sustainable practices into their manufacturing strategies? Provide relevant case studies.

Approaches to Strategy Formulation

1. Compare and contrast top-down, bottom-up, and collaborative approaches to strategy formulation. Discuss the advantages and disadvantages of each approach.
2. Discuss various approaches to strategy formulation. Provide examples of how different approaches are applied in manufacturing to achieve strategic objectives.

Realization of New Strategies/System Designs

1. Explain the process of realizing new strategies and system designs. Discuss the challenges encountered during implementation and how they can be effectively addressed.
2. Discuss the importance of monitoring, evaluation, and continuous improvement in the realization of new strategies. Provide relevant case studies to support your answer.

Unit V - Smart Manufacturing
2 marks
Introduction to Various Smart Manufacturing Techniques

1. Define Smart Manufacturing.
2. List any two benefits of Smart Manufacturing.
3. Mention two technologies commonly used in Smart Manufacturing.
4. What is the role of automation in Smart Manufacturing?

Supply Chain Management

1. What is Supply Chain Management?
2. List two objectives of Supply Chain Management.
3. Mention any two challenges in Supply Chain Management.
4. How does digitalization improve Supply Chain Management?

Blockchain of Inventory Management

1. Define Blockchain in the context of Inventory Management.
2. List two benefits of using Blockchain for Inventory Management.
3. What is the purpose of a decentralized ledger in Blockchain?
4. Mention two industries that benefit from Blockchain-based Inventory Management.

Plant Digitization

1. What is Plant Digitization?
2. List two advantages of Plant Digitization.
3. Mention two technologies used in Plant Digitization.
4. How does Plant Digitization enhance productivity?

Predictive Maintenance

1. What is Predictive Maintenance?
2. List two benefits of Predictive Maintenance.
3. Mention two techniques used in Predictive Maintenance.
4. How does Predictive Maintenance reduce downtime?

Supply Chain Visibility

1. What is meant by Supply Chain Visibility?
2. List two benefits of improving Supply Chain Visibility.
3. Mention two tools used for achieving Supply Chain Visibility.
4. Why is real-time data important for Supply Chain Visibility?

Warehouse

1. Define Warehouse Management.
2. List two functions of a Warehouse.

3. Mention two technologies used in Smart Warehousing.
4. What is the role of automation in Warehouse Management?

Cost Reduction

1. What is Cost Reduction in manufacturing?
2. List two strategies for achieving Cost Reduction.
3. How does automation contribute to Cost Reduction?
4. Mention two challenges faced in Cost Reduction efforts.

Waste Management

1. Define Waste Management in manufacturing.
2. List two benefits of effective Waste Management.
3. Mention two techniques for Waste Management.
4. How does Smart Manufacturing contribute to Waste Management?

Automated Systems

1. What are Automated Systems in manufacturing?
2. List two advantages of using Automated Systems.
3. Mention two types of Automated Systems used in manufacturing.
4. How do Automated Systems improve efficiency?

Applications

1. List two applications of Smart Manufacturing in the automotive industry.
2. Mention two applications of Predictive Maintenance.
3. How is Blockchain applied in Inventory Management?
4. Give two examples of Plant Digitization in manufacturing.

13 marks

Introduction to Various Smart Manufacturing Techniques

1. Discuss various Smart Manufacturing techniques and their impact on productivity, quality, and flexibility in manufacturing. Provide relevant examples.
2. Explain how Smart Manufacturing techniques are transforming traditional manufacturing systems. Discuss the benefits and challenges associated with their implementation.

Supply Chain Management

1. Discuss the role of Supply Chain Management in Smart Manufacturing. Explain how digitalization enhances efficiency, transparency, and responsiveness in the supply chain.
2. Explain the key components of Supply Chain Management. Discuss how smart manufacturing technologies can optimize supply chain performance.

Blockchain of Inventory Management

1. Explain the application of Blockchain technology in Inventory Management. Discuss its benefits, challenges, and implications for improving transparency and security.
2. Discuss how Blockchain-based Inventory Management can enhance traceability, accountability, and efficiency in the manufacturing sector. Provide relevant examples.

Plant Digitization

1. Explain the concept of Plant Digitization. Discuss its role in enhancing productivity, operational efficiency, and decision-making in manufacturing.
2. Discuss various technologies used in Plant Digitization. Explain how these technologies contribute to achieving Industry 4.0 standards.

Predictive Maintenance

1. Discuss the concept of Predictive Maintenance. Explain its advantages over traditional maintenance approaches, with relevant examples.
2. Explain the technologies and techniques used in Predictive Maintenance. Discuss how these techniques help in improving equipment reliability and reducing downtime.

Supply Chain Visibility

1. Explain the importance of Supply Chain Visibility in Smart Manufacturing. Discuss how technologies such as IoT and Blockchain contribute to achieving visibility.
2. Discuss the challenges faced in achieving Supply Chain Visibility and suggest strategies to overcome these challenges.

Warehouse

1. Discuss the role of Smart Warehousing in manufacturing. Explain how automation, IoT, and data analytics contribute to efficient Warehouse Management.
2. Explain the impact of automated systems on Warehouse Management. Discuss the benefits and challenges of implementing automation in warehouses.

Cost Reduction

1. Discuss various strategies for Cost Reduction in Smart Manufacturing. Explain how automation, digitization, and predictive maintenance contribute to cost efficiency.
2. Explain the challenges associated with implementing cost reduction strategies in manufacturing. Discuss how smart technologies can help overcome these challenges.

Waste Management

1. Discuss the role of Smart Manufacturing in improving Waste Management. Explain how digital tools and automation contribute to reducing manufacturing waste.
2. Explain various techniques for effective Waste Management in Smart Manufacturing. Discuss how they contribute to sustainability and profitability.

Automated Systems

1. Discuss the application of Automated Systems in Smart Manufacturing. Explain their impact on productivity, efficiency, and quality.
2. Explain various types of Automated Systems used in manufacturing. Discuss their benefits, challenges, and future potential.

Applications

1. Discuss the applications of Smart Manufacturing techniques across various industries, such as automotive, food, pharmaceutical, and education. Provide relevant examples.
2. Explain the role of Smart Manufacturing techniques in enhancing supply chain visibility, predictive maintenance, and cost reduction. Discuss with suitable case studies.

www.ingramcontent.com/pod-product-compliance
Lightning Source LLC
Chambersburg PA
CBHW040206110726
48005CB00019B/2916